THOMAS TOUGHILL has laboured in
Intelligence Officer in Hong Kong, and
singer and Richard Nixon. A graduate of (
and German and a former Infantry Offic.. ... .
now lives in the Mediterranean with his wife and family.

His first book, *Oscar Slater, The Mystery Solved*, was published in 1993.
It is an exposé of how a German Jew, often referred to as the Scottish
equivalent of the Frenchman, Alfred Dreyfus, was framed by the
British authorities for murder. The book forms part of the Law Course
at Edinburgh University.

A WORLD TO GAIN

THE BATTLE FOR GLOBAL DOMINATION AND WHY AMERICA ENTERED WWII

THOMAS TOUGHILL

CLAIRVIEW

With malice towards none, this book is dedicated to the continent of Europe and all her children.

Clairview Books
An imprint of Temple Lodge Publishing
Hillside House, The Square
Forest Row, RH18 5ES

www.clairviewbooks.com

Published by Clairview 2004

First published in an earlier version by Cal Cal LLC, Gibraltar, 1999

Cover by Andrew Morgan Design
Typeset by DP Photosetting, Aylesbury, Bucks.
Printed and bound by Cromwell Press Limited, Trowbridge, Wilts.

Contents

... And if Mr Willkie, this man of honour, declares that there are only two possibilities: Either Berlin will be the capital of the world, or Washington, then I can only say that Berlin does not even want to be the world's capital and Washington will never be the world's capital ...

Hitler in a speech to his Party Old Guard in Munich, 8 November 1941

... There is no use for us to consider a stalemate or a regulated peace ... This leaves us two alternative settlements for a future world – a German settlement or an American settlement ...

Douglas Miller, former Commercial Attaché to the US Embassy in Berlin, in his bestselling book *You Can't Do Business with Hitler* (1941)

It's another Carthage.

Harry Hopkins, President Roosevelt's adviser, as he flew over the ruins of Berlin in late May 1945

Acknowledgements

I would like to acknowledge the help I received from the following while I researched and wrote this book: the Rt. Hon. Michael Foot; Christopher Hunt, Deputy Keeper, Department of Printed Books, Imperial War Museum; the staff of the *Chicago Tribune*; Ellen Jones of the Bibliographic & Interlibrary Loan Center, Chicago Public Library; Emily Clark, Associate Librarian, Chicago Historical Society; Patricia Solley, Unit Chief, Office of Public and Congressional Affairs, Federal Bureau of Investigation, Washington; Matthias Frank, Head of Information Centre, German Embassy, London; the staff of the Public Record Office, Kew; the staff of the Institute of Historical Research, London; the staff of the German Historical Institute, London; the staff of the Mitchell Library, Glasgow; the staff of the Library, University of Glasgow; and the staff of the National Library of Scotland, Edinburgh.

At a more personal level, I would like to express my gratitude to Mr Searle for providing me with access to that remaining treasure of the British Empire, the Garrison Library in Gibraltar.

I would like to thank Drs Georg and Brigitte Heuser of Rothenburg, Bavaria, as well as their daughter, Beatrice, and her husband, Cyril Buffet, for their kindness and guidance.

I owe a special thanks to Arthur Cooper for posing some penetrating questions, and to Robin Odell for bolstering my morale at a crucial moment. My thanks also to my late friend Jack Quar TD, LL B for keeping me informed about developments.

My thanks go to the Bertrand Russell Peace Foundation for permission to quote from Bertrand Russell's 1923 book, *Prospects of Industrial Civilisation*, to Cassell PLC for allowing me to quote extracts from Basil Liddell Hart's *Memoirs* and *The Other Side of the Hill*, and to

Weidenfield & Nicholson (Orion Publishing Group) for permission to quote from *Hitler's Table Talk*.

I wish to state that I have made every effort to obtain contact details of copyright holders. If, however, I have failed to acknowledge anyone who thinks that he or she should be acknowledged, I offer my apologies.

Once again, I find myself unable to express in words the debt I owe my wife and sons for putting up with me while I wrote this book (or, for that matter, at any other time).

It remains only for me to say that the views expressed in this book are mine and mine alone.

T.T.

Introduction

How did things ever go so far?

Don Vito Corleone, surveying the ruinous Five Families War
in Mario Puzo's *The Godfather*

This project has its origin in a number of questions which formed in
my mind as I walked through Berlin during a trip I made there in the
spring of 1992.

On my first day, I walked through the Brandenburg Gate from the
Unter den Linden, leaving behind what until recently had been the
beginning of the Soviet Empire which once stretched all the way to the
Pacific Ocean. Just beyond the gate was a military show put on by units
of the occupying powers. The kilted pipes and drum band of a Scottish
regiment played some traditional martial tunes and was followed by a
song and dance troupe from the Russian Army. In the background,
through the trees, could be seen the rejuvenated Bundestag building,
formerly the Reichstag, and watching the show was a small, but
appreciative, group of Berliners who applauded with as much enthusiasm as the beer and sausages they were consuming would allow.

When the show was finished, I entered the Tiergarten Park and
inspected the nearby Soviet Memorial, the monument to the units of
the Red Army which stormed Berlin in the spring of 1945. Afterwards,
I crossed through the Park towards the Potsdamer Platz, the area
which was to pre-war Berlin what Piccadilly Circus is to London, or
Times Square to New York, but which was obliterated during the war
and left a virtual wasteland. Somewhere between there and the then
barren area to the north which led back to the Brandenburg Gate was
the site of Hitler's bunker, where he, the Führer of the Third Reich,
chose to spend the last few months of his life and of the regime he had
created.

The following day, I visited nearby Potsdam, the suburban residence of the Hohenzollern kings and the home of Prussian militararism. The town had been part of East Germany, the Communist German Democratic Republic, and looked it. Grey, dusty, and dismal, its buildings still pitted with bullet holes from the fighting of 1945, the town had obviously undergone no redevelopment since the war. But it was the palaces of the Prussian kings that I had come to see and these were not disappointing, in particular Sanssouci, which Frederick the Great, 'Old Fritz', (1712–1786) had built as a place in which to spend his leisure time, well away from the business of state. From here he went hunting with his beloved dogs, next to which (in his third grave) he is now buried, and here too he entertained the great minds of his time, including of course Voltaire, with whom he discussed philosophy and other matters of mutual interest.

On the hill behind Sanssouci is an old windmill, which was already old when Frederick began building his palace. The then owner of the windmill protested to Frederick's officials that the new palace would block the wind, thereby depriving his family of the livelihood they had enjoyed since the Middle Ages, and he threatened to take the King to court over the issue. Frederick's officials laughed this matter off, saying that the King was not answerable to the courts. However, Frederick himself took a different view. He pointed out that he must be seen to obey the law himself, otherwise his power would come to rest on fear and cynicism and not genuine respect. And when that happened, Frederick insisted, his authority would start to crumble. Frederick resolved the dispute by having the windmill raised, at his own expense, to a point where the wind was unrestricted by the palace building.

It is difficult to imagine Adolf Hitler behaving in this manner. Nevertheless, Frederick the Great was Hitler's greatest hero. Hitler, although a rich man from the royalties of his notorious book, *Mein Kampf*, which outsold the Bible during the Third Reich, and from the use of his profile on Germany's stamps, eschewed material wealth. One of the very few possessions he brought with him to his bunker in early 1945 was a painting of the Prussian King. Shortly before committing suicide there, Hitler took the painting off the wall and gave it to an aide.

Such affection would surely have been totally unrequited, for to compare Hitler with Frederick the Great would be akin to likening Al Capone to Thomas Jefferson. 'Old Fritz' was a despot to be sure, but he was a highly cultured man, and an icon of the Enlightenment. Hitler, by contrast, had the mentality of a thug, albeit a very clever one. Frederick's designation is not in vain: he was a great general and ruler. Hitler was neither.

Why, then, I asked myself as I continued my visit to Berlin, did the Germans stand by Hitler to the very end? From mid-1943, Berlin had been subjected to very heavy bombing by the British and American airforces and then, in early 1945, it was assaulted by the Red Army, by which time hope of victory had vanished from the thoughts of all but the most fanatical of Hitler's followers. The Italians shot Mussolini, Hitler's ally, and hung his body (with that of his mistress, who died alongside him) from the roof of a petrol station for a crowd to abuse. But the Germans carried on obeying the will of their Führer until the whole nation was bludgeoned to the point of extinction. The Berliners fought until they were simply overwhelmed, by which time their once imposing city was almost totally obliterated. How had this come about? Fear of the Russians was an obvious factor, but it was clearly not the full answer, as a comparison with Napoleon shows.

In 1814, Napoleon — beset by almost every country in Europe including, of course, Russia — was allowed to abdicate and settle in an island in the Mediterranean. Even after his attempt to regain power was thwarted at Waterloo in June 1815, the British Government, which took him prisoner, merely removed him to an island in the South Atlantic. Hitler, who in personal terms can hardly be compared with Napoleon, could have expected no mercy if he had been taken prisoner by his enemies; he would have been hanged alongside the other Nazis in Nuremberg. However, what is important here is that Napoleon's enemies drew a clear distinction between Napoleon and France. Indeed, Napoleon was overthrown not only by external force, but also by internal opposition in which the Emperor's own Foreign Minister, Talleyrand, played a leading role. Moreover, once Napoleon was out of the way, and a 'safe' regime installed in Paris, in the form of the restored Bourbons, France's neighbours were content and the

European family of nations returned to its peaceful business. Hitler's enemies refused to draw such a distinction. Germany herself became their target, not just the Nazi regime. Why?

Why did Hitler allow this situation to arise in the first place? Why did he *choose* to fight three powerful opponents simultaneously? It is true that Britain and France declared war on him. He defeated France in one swift campaign, but he chose to attack the Soviet Union before conquering, or at least making peace with, Britain. And then, when still engaged in a titanic struggle with the Soviet Union, came the strangest decision of all, the step which virtually ensured the defeat of Germany. On 11 December 1941, Hitler, in support of his Japanese allies, declared war on America, a move which has baffled historians to this day and which is generally seen as his fatal blunder. Why then did he take such a step?

After my return from Berlin, I tried to answer these, and other, questions about the Second World War, still the most dramatic episode in human history. Naturally, I read what there was available on the war itself. The bibliography on this subject is certainly huge, but despite this I was at the end of the day none the wiser. I was still unable to answer satisfactorily the questions which my trip to Berlin had produced. I soon realized that, in order to find such solutions, I would have to carry out my own research. I also realized that I would have to adopt a different approach from that of conventional, academic historians, albeit while maintaining at all times the same standards of accuracy and objectivity. This suited me, for in addition to being a history graduate of a medieval Scottish university, I have also been a colonial police detective. It was only natural therefore that I looked upon this subject as a case to be solved and as another opportunity to ask, 'Who benefits?' To answer this question, and the others which grew from it, I turned not to the 'hearsay' of historians but as far as possible to the primary material – the testimony of the participants and eyewitnesses themselves. Only in this way could I hope to show what happened and why.

Certainly, this approach – to get 'back to basics', as it were – is one which writers on the war have strangely neglected, especially in more recent years. As a young man, I studied avidly the works of Basil

Liddell Hart, J.F.C. Fuller and Chester Wilmot, men who had lived through the war and who produced books on it which, quite apart from their many other attractions, provided clear guidance as to where further research should be carried out. Unfortunately, this guidance does not seem to have sufficiently inspired subsequent students of the war. Consequently, the historiography of the conflict has suffered. Errors have crept in; assumptions have become accepted as fact; and obvious lines of inquiry have been ignored. Perhaps the most striking example of all involves the attitude of President Roosevelt towards Nazi Germany, a subject which in fact forms the core of this book.

Many writers have stated baldly that Roosevelt wanted to stay out of the war. The late A.J.P. Taylor, in his controversial *The Origins of the Second World War*, even goes so far as to say that, before entering the war in December 1941 as a result of the Japanese attack on Pearl Harbor, America had 'asked only to be left alone'. Some historians have also expressed surprise that, once in the war, Roosevelt should have chosen to make Germany his prime target and not Japan. Sir Max Hastings begins his classic book on the Normandy invasion, *Overlord*, by describing Roosevelt's decision to defeat Germany first as 'Not the least remarkable aspect of the Second World War...' Max Hastings goes on immediately to draw attention to the fact that 'from December 1941 until June 1944, it was the Americans who were passionately impatient to confront the German army on the continent, while the British, right up to the eve of D-Day, were haunted by the deepest misgivings about doing so.'

A close study of what actually went on in Roosevelt's administration in 1941 reveals a very different picture. The memoirs of Roosevelt's advisers, and of Winston Churchill, show that Roosevelt saw very clearly that, as the head of the world's foremost trading nation, he simply could not stand by and let Hitler conquer the whole of Europe. This basic strategic fact was emphasized in a top-secret paper submitted to Roosevelt in September 1941 by General Marshall, the US Chief of Staff, who recommended that America should enter the European war at once and bring about 'the complete military defeat of Germany'. This confidential cry for war was then being publicly echoed by Douglas Miller, the former Commercial Attaché to the

American Embassy in Berlin, whose bestselling book *You Can't Do Business with Hitler*, published in the summer of 1941, claimed that Hitler's socialist policies posed such an economic threat to the United States that Germany should be *attacked* at once 'with every resource of our vast, free, and vigorous American nation'.[1] Victory for Hitler in Europe, Miller asserted, would be a disaster for America, whereas Germany's defeat, coupled with the adoption of the policies outlined in the last chapter of his book, entitled 'Our Post-War Policy', meant that America would have 'a world to gain'.

Roosevelt's attitude to this belligerence cannot be doubted. Not only did he praise Miller's book and criticize those Americans who thought that they could 'do business' with Hitler, he gave Miller an important job in his Government. A few months before America eventually entered the war, Douglas Miller became assistant to William Donovan, Roosevelt's spymaster, which meant that he was well placed to advise his President on how Germany should be defeated and America's world hegemony established. In short, Roosevelt's decision to fight Germany first was not as remarkable as Max Hastings, and others, have supposed. Amazing as it may seem, *this was a policy advocated in a book which guided Roosevelt into and through the Second World War.*

If Winston Churchill ever read *You Can't Do Business with Hitler*, he certainly did not appreciate the significance of the last chapter in the book, where Miller stated that there must be no compromise peace with Germany and that Britain's position was so weak that the Americans 'could undoubtedly secure British assent to any and all peace proposals that we had in mind'. As will be shown in due course, what all of this meant in practice came as a very rude shock to Churchill and led to a crude attempt to conceal what actually took place. That attempt has succeeded until now, when, for the first time, the astonishing truth about the adoption of 'Unconditional Surrender' as Allied policy is revealed.

My research in the Public Record Office and elsewhere shows that the official version of how this policy came to be accepted is based *on*

---

[1] Page 121 of *You Can't Do Business with Hitler* in the chapter entitled 'America's Decisive Opportunity'.

forged documents. Any standard work on the war will state that the British War Cabinet discussed President Roosevelt's policy of 'Unconditional Surrender' on the afternoon of 20 January 1943, and that the Cabinet agreed in principle to its adoption as Allied policy. I shall show that *this is not true* and that Churchill and his Cabinet were in fact tricked by Roosevelt into accepting this policy, which Roosevelt announced at the end of the Casablanca Conference in January 1943 in front of the world's press and without prior consultation with his allies. In accordance with Douglas Miller's book, this policy effectively ruled out a compromise peace with Germany and ensured that the Germans would fight to the very last against enormous odds. That struggle continued until Berlin itself was reduced to rubble.

The volume which follows is an attempt by a historical detective to explain in some detail how Berlin came to suffer this fate. Other than to state that Hitler's evil (and incredibly stupid) regime had to be destroyed, there is no attempt here to criticize, condemn or moralize. After all, great powers will try to become even greater powers and politician are ... well, politicians. There is, though, an important lesson to be learned here. The reunification of Germany and her burgeoning strength − the so-called 'German problem' of how to accommodate Germany within Europe − has returned, as it did before the Second World War. With the new, futuristic Berlin seemingly set to become the unofficial centre of Europe, it is surely essential to understand exactly what happened between 1939 and 1945 in order to ensure that the continent never again suffers such a disaster. Roosevelt, it must be remembered, justified his wartime policies on the grounds that they offered a reasonable guarantee of world peace for 50 years.

Those 50 years are now up and the division of post-war Europe created by Roosevelt and his main wartime ally, the Soviet dictator Joseph Stalin, disappeared with the collapse of the Soviet Union in the early 1990s. A new and harmonious Europe is now being formed, one that is moving slowly but clearly towards some sort of unity. France and Germany are now almost one country and a modernizing Russia is shifting ever closer towards them. People have tended, however, to enthuse about all of this without stopping to reflect on the deeper implications of these changes and without considering whether the end of the so-called Cold War has in fact made the world less, and not more, secure.

In this regard, it is instructive to quote the former US Secretary of State Henry Kissinger who, on page 813 of his book *Diplomacy*, says more about American foreign policy in one paragraph than many writers do in a whole book:

> Geopolitically, America is an island off the shores of the large landmass of Eurasia, whose resources and population far exceed those the United States. The domination by a single power of either of Eurasia's two principal spheres — Europe or Asia — remains a good definition of strategic danger for America, Cold War or no Cold War. For such a grouping would have the capacity to outstrip America economically and, in the end, militarily. That danger would have to be resisted even were the dominant power apparently benevolent, for if the intentions ever changed, America would find itself with a grossly diminished capacity for effective resistance and a growing inability to shape events.

This is a sharp reminder of the old diplomatic adage that countries do not have permanent friends, only permanent interests. And one of America's permanent interests is to ensure that Europe does not become its rival. In fulfilling this aim, America has naturally inherited Britain's traditional policy of opposing the strongest country in Europe — *whichever one that may be* — in order to maintain a balance of power on the continent.

By the end of the 1930s, Germany had become — as it was before the First World War — the most powerful and, in many respects, the most advanced country in Europe. Hitler's naked aggression transformed this potential threat to the United States into a real and present danger. Roosevelt had to enter the European war that broke out in 1939 in order to stop Hitler from uniting Europe, just as in the seventeenth century, Cardinal Richelieu of France intervened in the Thiry Years War in order to prevent the unification of the German-speaking peoples. This is not at all a criticism of the American President, merely a statement of fact. Roosevelt would not have been doing his job if he had acted otherwise.

Now, however, the collapse of the European 'balance of power' which Roosevelt (and his successor, Truman) established with Stalin at the end of the war and the subsequent drift of the continent towards some sort of political union are withering the fruits of America's victory in the Second World War. America's role in Europe is being openly questioned and, with it, the continued relevance — and true purpose — of the NATO Alliance. Modern Europe is peaceful and democratic, but, as Henry Kissinger writes, this characteristic merely modifies the strategic danger to America. *It does not remove that danger.*

In this context, it is relevant to note that Cardinal Richelieu did not *prevent* the unification of Germany; he merely *delayed* it for some two centuries. As long as the Germans remained divided, France was *la Grande Nation*, at once universally copied, envied, admired and hated, in much the same way as America is now. The arrival of Bismarck's united Germany after the Franco–Prussian War of 1870 changed that. Here was a virile, new country which eclipsed France as the major power in Europe and proved itself a match for the rest of the continent put together. The strategic lesson is clear: European union *per se* is a danger to America, *la Grande Nation* of our age.

There is an additional factor to consider: America's geopolitical position, as Kissinger points out, is Janus-like. The United States must look not just *east* to Europe, but also *west* to Asia. The main Asian threat to Roosevelt's America was of course Japan. The main current threat to America from Asia is perceived to be China, whose economy, many say, will become more powerful than that of the United States within the next few decades. Modern China is not a democracy, but a totalitarian state practising a form of state-controlled capitalism with considerable success. On the other hand, it is a traditionally peaceful country with, at the time of writing, no expansionist tendencies.

Here, though, Kissinger's caveat must be noted. The academic historian turned diplomat states unequivocally that the possibility of Europe or Asia falling under the effective control of *any dominant power*, even one which appeared to be friendly, would have to be resisted by the United States. He does not elaborate on what form that resistance would take, but his comments must surely be considered by anyone interested in the future of mankind.

I hope that the following work will provide much food for thought on the Second World War and its aftermath. I understand that not everyone will find this food palatable, but I can only say that a historian must be dispassionate and objective to the extent that human nature will permit. Anyone who seriously attempts to reconstruct the past — *to find out what happened and why* — must strive to put aside all personal feelings and all nationalistic pride. Indeed, a historian, it has been wisely said, should have no nationality. Propaganda and mythology doubtless have their place, but if the truth about the past is to be found, a historian must treat his material in the same way as a doctor his patient, a lawyer his case, and a mechanic his car.

After all, human progress is achieved by asking the right questions and finding the correct answers. To fail to follow this dialectic, the careful process of cause and effect, is to do insult to the unique feature of our species and by extension to all that we have accomplished. Hamlet, who is himself tormented by a question central to his very existence, addresses this same subject:

> What is a man,
> If his chief good and market of his time
> Be but to sleep and feed? a beast, no more.
> Sure he that made us with such large discourse,
> Looking before and after, gave us not
> That capability and god-like reason
> To fust in us unus'd.

THE RIVALRY

Stand less between me and the sun.

Diogenes to Alexander the Great

1

Collision Course

The lights were burning late in the *Wolfsschanze*, Hitler's headquarters in the swampy forests near Rastenburg, East Prussia, 400 miles north-east of Berlin. It was around midnight, but Hitler's senior military advisers – the contemptibly obsequious Field Marshal Wilhelm Keitel and his dour Bavarian deputy, Colonel General Alfred Jodl – were still at work in the map room, poring over the latest dire reports from the Russian front.

In the five months since the onset of *Operation Barbarossa* – the German invasion of the Soviet Union – on 22 June 1941, the *Wehrmacht*, in an awesome display of martial skill, had overcome all that nature, geography and the Red Army could set against it. Vast wheat-growing areas of the Ukraine had been seized. The way to the oil-rich Caucasus mountains had been opened. Over three million prisoners had been taken. Leningrad, the city renamed after the founder of the Bolshevik movement, was under siege. The defences of Moscow itself had been breached, allowing a German unit to get within sight of the Kremlin. It seemed that all that was required was one further push through the horrendous winter weather and the regime of the Soviet dictator, Joseph Stalin, would collapse, paving the way for the German colonization of the Russian heartland.

But now suddenly all such hopes had been shattered in a strategist's nightmare. The previous day, the Red Army had launched out of the tundra-like conditions a totally unexpected counter-offensive along a 200-mile front around Moscow. Using fresh troops drawn from the far-eastern parts of the Soviet Union, Stalin smashed through the exhausted and overstretched German units around his capital. The German front line caved in, leaving the *Wehrmacht* in danger of disintegration in the near-arctic wasteland west of Moscow. The ghost of Napoleon now hovered over the scene.

The door to the map room suddenly opened and, to the generals' surprise, there entered from the freezing night the Führer himself – that extraordinary man who had risen from the dosshouses of Vienna to bewitch a country and then conquer a continent. But Hitler's face did not reflect the sombre news from Russia. On the contrary, he was excited and he was waving a communiqué which had just been handed to him in his bunker, where he had been entertaining friends. This, Hitler exclaimed, was 'der Wendepunkt' (the turning point). 'Now,' he said in his grating, guttural voice, 'it is impossible for us to lose the war. Now we have an ally who has never been vanquished in 3,000 years...'

Several hundred miles to the west on that fateful day, Sunday 7 December 1941, Hitler's implacable opponent, Winston Churchill, Prime Minister of Great Britain, was also entertaining. Churchill was at Chequers, his official country home in the south of England, where he dined alone but for two distinguished American guests – Averell Harriman, a wealthy businessman who was in Britain as the representative of President Roosevelt, and John G. Winant, the US Ambassador. After dinner, Churchill turned on his small radio to hear the nine o'clock news, which contained reports on the Russian front and the war in North Africa. There then followed a few sentences on a subject which so shocked Churchill and his guests that they wondered if they had heard correctly. At that moment, Sawyers, Churchill's butler, came into the room and confirmed that he, too, had heard the news.

With the Ambassador close behind, Churchill hurried to his office and put a call through to the White House in Washington. On hearing the familiar, patrician tones of his American counterpart on the line, Churchill asked, 'Mr President, what's this about Japan?' 'It's quite true,' Roosevelt replied. 'They have attacked us at Pearl Harbor. We are all in the same boat now.'

Roosevelt put down the telephone and returned to his interrupted meeting. He had gathered around him his closest advisers – Secretary of War Henry Stimson, Secretary of State Cordell Hull, Secretary of the Navy Frank Knox, Chief of Staff General George C. Marshall, and his naval counterpart, Admiral Stark – and with them was trying to analyse the worst American military debacle since the war of 1812, when the British army captured Washington and set fire to the very building in which he and his compatriots were sitting.

Harry Hopkins, Roosevelt's lanky *alter ego*, who lived in the White House (and who, incidentally, had presented Churchill with the radio with which the Prime Minister heard the news of Pearl Harbor), was also there. In his private papers, Hopkins noted that the atmosphere in which the conference was held was quite calm, and explained why:

> . . . I think that all of us believed that in the last analysis the enemy was Hitler and that he could never be defeated without force of arms; that sooner or later we were bound to be in the war and that Japan had given us an opportunity.

This comment speaks volumes about the Second World War. Even while the American battleships were still burning in Pearl Harbor, and even before the first flush of anger against Japan had worn off, Roosevelt and his advisers were viewing the Japanese strike as the chance to wage war on Japan's ally, Germany, which had known nothing in advance about the surprise attack. Indeed, *that very day*, Roosevelt authorized General Marshall to put into effect the war plans that had been drawn up in the preceding months and which gave priority to the defeat of Germany. This was not an aim the President concealed from the American people. In his first 'fireside chat' after Pearl Harbor, on 9 December when the United States and Germany were still officially at peace, Roosevelt told his listeners that 'it would serve us ill if we [defeated Japan] and found that the rest of the world was dominated by Hitler and Mussolini.'

Hitler, needless to say, had a different opinion. Pierre Huss, a journalist with the International News Service, recorded a conversation he had with Hitler some months before Pearl Harbor about the pos-sibility of America's entry into the war. While the two men were pre-paring to set off on a walk through the woods surrounding the *Wolfsschanze*, Hitler drew his greatcoat tightly around him as protection against the chill air and said to Huss, 'Roosevelt wants to run the world and rob us all of a place in the sun. He says he wants to save England but he means he wants to be ruler and heir of the British Empire.'

The Second *World* War cannot be properly understood unless it is seen for what it was — a struggle for world hegemony between the United States and Germany. By the early years of the twentieth century, the rise of America to the point where she would come to dominate the world had already been predicted. In his *Prospects of Industrial Civilization*, the English philosopher, Bertrand Russell, wrote that America was better placed to secure this position than any previous challenger, and gave the following reasons:

> First of all, America is self supporting in all the necessaries of war; both industry and agriculture could be preserved in almost complete efficiency without commerce with any other continent. Secondly, America has the largest white population of any state except Russia, and its population is superlatively skilled, energetic and physically courageous. Thirdly ... the whole of North America must be counted as belonging to the United States in considering the possibilities of a world war. Fourthly, America could, after the outbreak of the war, build a sufficiently powerful navy to defeat any possible hostile naval combination. Fifthly, all Europe is in America's debt and we in England are dependent upon America for our very existence, owing to our need of raw cotton and Canadian wheat. Lastly, the Americans surpass even the British in sagacity, apparent moderation and the skilful use of hypocrisy by which even themselves are deceived. Against such a combination no existing state could hope to prove victorious.

Russell wrote this in 1923. However, by the late 1930s such a state had arisen in the restless, aggressive form of Nazi Germany, which, driven by Hitler's insistence that time was not on his side, sought to create quickly and violently a German-dominated 'New Order' in Europe, from Portugal to the Urals, a monolith which could surpass America to become the primary economic and military power on the planet. The scene was thus set for a showdown between the United States and Nazi Germany – and a deadly battle of wits between their respective leaders.

Franklin Delano Roosevelt, or FDR as he was known, the polio-stricken 32nd President of the United States, was an almost exact political contemporary of Hitler. Adolf Hitler became Chancellor of

Germany on 30 January 1933 (ironically FDR's birthday), while Roosevelt moved into the White House on 4 March that year, and resided there until his death from a brain haemorrhage on 12 April 1945, 18 days before Hitler, in the ruins of Berlin, blew his brains out rather than be taken alive by the advancing Russians.

In 1933, the two men inherited countries still suffering from the effects of the Wall Street Crash of 1929 and the consequent worldwide depression, disasters for which America herself had been largely responsible. Roosevelt introduced his controversial 'New Deal' and told Americans that they had 'nothing to fear but fear itself'. Hitler, who knew a great deal about the use of fear, ruthlessly set about rearming Germany and rebuilding her economy in accordance with the tenets of National Socialism, a dynamic philosophy which unleashed the power of a nation in a manner and to an extent not seen since the days of Revolutionary France.

Roosevelt's New Deal policies met with great Congressional opposition and effectively ran out of steam in the late 1930s. Moreover, in 1937 a sudden new depression, which was more or less confined to America, sent unemployment rocketing once more to over 10 million, with the result that by the time the European war broke out in September 1939, America's economy, though easily the most powerful in the world, was underused and undercapitalized, and her share of world trade was at its lowest point since before the First World War. On the other hand, Germany's greatly reduced unemployment rate and her performance in the first year of the war showed that Hitler had built something special, albeit deeply sinister, in his Third Reich. An unholy pact with the Soviet dictator, Joseph Stalin, gave the Führer the peace in eastern Europe which allowed him to attack in the west, where in an astonishing six-week campaign he achieved what Imperial Germany had failed to do in the entire four years of the First World War – defeat France and expel the British army from the Continent.

Describing Hitler's successes as an impending crisis for America, Roosevelt declared a 'limited emergency' and began a massive rearmament programme. In effect he was saying that he could not allow Hitler to do what the Americans themselves had done – create a nation out of a continent. A united Europe under Hitler, Roosevelt argued, would constitute an immense threat to the United States, for both military and economic reasons. It was not just the German armed forces that Roosevelt feared, but the Reich's centrally controlled economy with its bartering system of *autarky* (self-sufficiency) which Hitler, determined to free his country from the control of international financing, sought to make the basis of his rule, first in Germany herself and then in the New Order he was establishing in Europe. As early as April 1934, Douglas Miller, then the Commercial Attaché to the American Embassy in Berlin, informed his government:

> Germany is to be made the economic center of a self-sustaining territorial bloc whose dependent nations in Central and Eastern Europe will look to Berlin for leadership. This bloc is to be so constituted that it can defy wartime blockade and be large enough to give the peoples in it the benefit of free trade now enjoyed by the forty-eight American states.

Hitler's policies, Roosevelt told his countrymen, would result not in 'an American wall to keep Nazi goods out' but in 'a Nazi wall to keep us in'. Indeed, so seriously did Roosevelt take this threat to America that he publicly praised Douglas Miller's book *You Can't Do Business with Hitler*, which appeared in the summer of 1941 and which claimed that trading with a Hitler-dominated Europe would result in the appearance of state socialism in the United States. The only effective way for America way to deal with this danger, Miller stated openly, was to *attack* Germany at once 'from the West'.

As the renowned military historian J.F.C. Fuller wrote in his seminal work *The Decisive Battles of the Western World*, Hitler's economic strategy constituted a 'financial pistol' aimed primarily at America because that country held most of the world's gold and because its system of mass production required it to export about 10 per cent of its produce in order to avoid unemployment.

Hitler touched on this very subject in a speech on 10 December 1940, when he gave full vent to his anti-capitalist sentiments. It was true, Hitler declared, that 'two worlds are face to face with one another' and that his opponents were right to say that they could not reconcile themselves to the National Socialist world. So great was the divide,

Hitler stated, that it was not possible for 'a narrow minded capitalist' to agree to his principles. 'It would be easier for the devil to go to church and cross himself with holy water,' Hitler announced, 'than for these people to comprehend the ideas which are accepted facts to us today.' As for his enemies' claim that they were fighting for the maintenance of the gold standard, Hitler commented:

> That I can well believe, for the gold is in their hands. We too once had gold, but it was stolen and extorted from us. When I came to power, it was not malice which made me abandon the gold standard. Germany simply had no gold left... But, my *Volksgenossen*, I did not regret it, for we have constructed our economic system on a wholly different basis. In our eyes, gold is not of value to us. It is only an agent by which nations can be suppressed and dominated.

The differences, though, between Nazi Germany and the other powers of the time went far beyond economics. Nazi ideology sought to control all aspects of life in order to 'protect' Germany against what was seen as the corrupting influence of the outside world. Douglas Miller summed this up chillingly well in a dispatch to his government on 18 December 1933:

> To the Nazi mind a Russian communist and a New York or London banker are both members of the same movement which is striving to sap the foundations of society, weaken the Nordic race, destroy the aristocratic principle, undermine the Christian religion, the obedience of children to their parents, of wives to their husbands, and replace in its stead a mechanised, materialistic, godless world, filled with peoples of mixed and inferior races, devoted to international trade and the pursuit of wealth and luxury.

Despite Roosevelt's public statements and accusations, there is no evidence that Hitler ever actually *planned* to wage war on the United States or to make any military move into the western hemisphere. Indeed, Hitler's aim, as already indicated, was to make a German-dominated Europe economically self-sufficient through eastward expansion and then cut it off from the rest of the world by a series of trade and cultural barriers. This was something which Roosevelt simply could not allow to happen, not just for the immediate economic harm that would be done to America, but because, as already mentioned, such a European monolith with its larger population and direct access to the vast mineral resources of Siberia and Central Asia would have become more powerful than America. Here was a clash which William L. Shirer, author of the famed *The Rise and Fall of the Third Reich*, said in December 1940 was 'as inevitable as that of two planets hurtling inexorably through the heavens towards each other'.

Shirer's friend, Douglas Miller, wrote in his May 1941 book, *You Can't Do Business with Hitler*, that, according to the Nazis, 'there are two opposite poles in the world: Germany, the pole of order, discipline, and scientific progress; and the United States, the pole of democratic anarchy, decadent Christianity, and the degeneration and loss of efficiency which accompanies a system of free enterprise.' Miller added a warning to his American readers: 'Hitler's conquest is only partial and incomplete until we are brought into his world system.'

Hitler certainly recognized the global rivalry with the United States and the open hostility displayed towards his country by many influential Americans. Speaking to his party faithful in Munich in November 1941, Hitler commented contemptuously on remarks made by Wendell Willkie, the Republican politician who had stood unsuccessfully against FDR in 1940:

> I am of the conviction that this continent will not be the second continent of the world, but that it will remain hereafter as before, the first continent of the world. And if Mr Willkie, this man of honour, declares that there are only two possibilities: either Berlin will be the capital of the world, or Washington, then I can only say that Berlin does not want to be the world's capital and Washington will never become the world's capital. There would even be half a hundred middle-sized cities in Europe, so I believe, that would protest against such a cultural affliction of humanity.

Brigadier Raymond E. Lee, a US Army intelligence officer who served as Military Attaché at the American Embassy in London from 1940 to 1941, sheds in his diary a great deal of light on official US government thinking at that time. Before leaving for London in June 1940, he was told by his superiors that for the past two years Roosevelt had been 'hugely alarmed' at the prospect of a Nazi victory in Europe. In May 1941, Lee was informed by Brigadier Joseph T. McNarney, who was then involved in drawing up secret plans for America's entry into the war, that he thought Roosevelt was determined to join the war *at the earliest opportunity*. Lee did not know how that could be done, but he did reflect upon Roosevelt's tactics: 'I wonder if it ever occurs to the people in Washington that they have no God-given right to declare war. They may wake up one day to find that war has suddenly been declared upon the United States. That is the way Germany and Japan do business. Or can this be that this is what Roosevelt's manoeuvring for?'

What Roosevelt was manoeuvring for remains one of the great controversies of the war. Indeed, Roosevelt himself remains controversial, a polemical figure who attracted both adulation and hatred. Even those close to him admitted that they did not really know him. Frances Perkins, his Secretary of Labor and long-time associate, called Roosevelt the 'most complicated human being I ever knew'. Robert Sherwood, the playwright who was also one of FDR's speechwriters, found him 'contradictory to a bewildering degree' – ruthless and vindictive but also forgiving, cynical and worldly but also religious, outspokenly progressive but also deeply conservative. His most famous biographer, James MacGregor Burns, called him the 'Lion and the Fox', a reference to Machiavelli who writes in *The Prince* that a successful ruler must combine the attributes of both animals – the lion to frighten off wolves and the fox to recognize traps. It is interesting here to note Machiavelli's elaboration of this metaphor:

> Everyone realises how praiseworthy it is for a prince to honour his word and to be straightforward rather than crafty in his dealings; nonetheless contemporary experience shows that princes who achieved great things have been those who have given their word lightly, who have known how to trick men with their cunning, and who, in the end, have overcome those abiding by honest principles.

No one can doubt that Roosevelt achieved 'great things'. If there is one undisputed fact about the Second World War, it is that America won it. By the end of hostilities, Britain was bankrupt, Russia was dead on her feet, and the defeated nations a pile of rubble. America on the other hand had boomed during the war, making her not just the richest country in the world but, as John Keegan points out in his book *The Second World War,* 'the richest there had ever been, with an economy almost equal in productivity to that of the rest of the world put together.' A.J.P. Taylor attributes this to FDR: 'Of the great men at the top, Roosevelt was the only one who knew what he was doing; he made the United States the greatest country in the world at virtually no cost.'

Obviously, Roosevelt did not achieve all of this on his own. Even before America entered the war, FDR surrounded himself with people who shared his views on Hitler and on America's destiny. A memorable example of this is Henry Morgenthau, Roosevelt's Secretary of the Treasury, who when interviewing a person for a Government post always asked the candidate if he 'hated Hitler's guts'. There is, though, one man amongst Roosevelt's advisers who deserves special mention.

This man, although a general, never became a household name like Eisenhower, Patton, or MacArthur. Nor does he feature prominently in the historiography of the Second World War. One would look in vain for any reference to him in such standard works on the war as William Shirer's *The Rise and Fall of the Third Reich*, Chester Wilmot's *The Struggle for Europe*, Basil Liddell Hart's *History of the Second War*, or Alan Bullock's classic biography of Hitler. At first, this may seem strange in view of the fact that this man probably did more to bring about the defeat of Germany than any American except Roosevelt and the US Chief of Staff, George Marshall. The reason is, of course, that he was, in common parlance, a spy – a man who worked mostly in the shadows (perhaps a hall of mirrors would be a better metaphor). As a result, it has proved difficult to identify, let alone appreciate, his real contribution to the war effort. The man was William ('Wild Bill') Donovan, the founder of the Office of Strategic Services – the forerunner of the Central Intelligence Agency.

According to Hitler, Donovan was 'an utterly worthless creature'. To begin to understand how Hitler came to this conclusion it is necessary to return to the dramatic summer of 1940, when the German army — having overrun France, Belgium, Holland, Norway, Denmark and Luxemburg in a matter of weeks — seemed about to add Britain to its list of conquests.

2

Donovan Visits London

The waiters in Claridge's, one of the finest hotels London has to offer, are of necessity discreet. Their hotel attracts important, influential persons from all over the world who naturally see the splendour of their surroundings as conducive to the proper conduct of business or the furthering of relationships. Such people would expect to be waited on in the proper manner, with the correct balance struck between attention and privacy.

It might be argued, though, that an exception could be made in the case of a conversation which took place between two Americans over breakfast on 2 August 1940, and that the waiters on duty that day would have been justified in allowing their personal feelings to overcome their professional restrictions. After all, what the two Americans were discussing, quite clinically and objectively, was whether Britain had the ability and the will to withstand Hitler's threatened invasion. What were the chances that the waiters around them would soon be doing what had already become routine for their counterparts in the top Paris hotels – serving German generals?

The younger man, who bore an enviable resemblance to the then King of Hollywood, Clark Gable, was Brigadier Raymond Lee, the Military Attaché to the American Embassy in London. He thought the British had a two-to-one chance of survival. The other American, a bulky man in his late 50s who did not look like a matinée idol, estimated the chances at 60–40 in Britain's favour. Lee, an ardent anglophile, was relieved. After all, 'Wild Bill' Donovan's view mattered where it counted – in the White House.

Donovan was in London at the request of President Roosevelt, whom he had known since the two men studied together at Columbia Law School. This is not to suggest that they came from the same background. FDR, of course, was a member of one of the great established families of the United States. Donovan, on the other hand, was a striking example of the American meritocrat, a man who rose from a humble background to the very top of his profession through ability and energy. If he had been born in England, in all probability he would have been denied a proper education and condemned to a life of drudgery in the mines or in a factory. In America, he flourished to the point where, but for his Roman Catholic religion, he would have been considered a serious candidate for Roosevelt's job, albeit as a representative of the Republican Party.

Donovan was born into a poor Irish family with Fenian connections in Buffalo, New York, in 1883, although such antecedents did not stop him from marrying a wealthy Protestant. He graduated from Columbia in 1907 and served with great distinction in the First World War as the commander of the famous 'Fighting 69th', earning for himself the Congressional Medal of Honour and his nickname, 'Wild Bill', a handle which was to some extent misleading in that he was, in fact, a modest man and (like Hitler) a teetotaller. After the war, he became one of the most successful lawyers in America, and from 1925 to 1929 he was Assistant Attorney-General under President Coolidge. He was denied the post of Attorney-General by the incoming President, Herbert Hoover, for whom he had campaigned, and in 1932 he failed in his attempt to become Governor of New York. These were possibly the only major set-backs in his professional life. He returned to his highly successful law practice, although he spent a lot of time touring trouble spots such as the Italian campaign in Abyssinia and the Spanish Civil War. During these trips, he formed very strong opinions about the danger the European dictators posed to America.

This was a view that was shared by his old student friend, President Roosevelt. In fact, as war in Europe loomed, Roosevelt made it known that he would like to have Donovan in his Cabinet, but found it politically difficult to do so in view of the fact that he already had two Republicans in mind — Henry Stimson as Secretary for War and the newspaper owner Frank Knox as Secretary of the Navy. (Knox had stood as the Republican Vice-Presidential candidate in the 1936 election.) However, Donovan was far too valuable a man to be left redundant in a time of national crisis. A job would be found for him.

The German victories in the early summer of 1940 forced Roosevelt to make a choice: give Britain the war equipment for which Churchill, the British Prime Minister, was pleading almost daily or abandon her as lost and concentrate instead on arming America in preparation for what seemed to the President and his advisers the inevitable showdown with Hitler. Roosevelt believed that Britain was worth saving and that she was in effect America's first line of defence. As he saw it, the loss of Britain and her fleet, then the world's largest, to Hitler would be a disaster for America. However, there was little point in sending supplies to Britain if she was going to be overrun by Hitler in the next few weeks. Roosevelt's solution, first suggested by William Stephenson, the Canadian businessman who headed the New York-based British Security Co-ordination (BSC), the British intelligence network in North America, was to send an unofficial envoy to Britain to see the situation for himself. The man Roosevelt chose was Donovan.

The trip was to be kept a closely guarded secret, and not just from the Germans. Roosevelt was then the leader of a country which was deeply divided over the war. Most Americans sympathized with the British, but were still hostile to any notion that America should get involved in another European war. These isolationists believed that America's destiny lay in containing herself to the western hemisphere. If, in Shakespeare's words, the English channel served England 'in the office of a wall,/Or as a moat defensive to a house', then surely, these people argued, the Atlantic and Pacific oceans were insuperable obstacles to any country which meant America harm. Roosevelt and the interventionist lobby disagreed. However, FDR, faced with such opposition and handicapped by the considerable restrictions of the American Constitution, had to tread very carefully, or 'educate the people' as he termed it. If isolationist leaders such as the aviator Charles Lindbergh or Senator Burton Wheeler, a major opponent of FDR, learned of the extent to which Roosevelt was secretly prepared to help Britain, the President would find himself in serious political trouble – facing possible impeachment or, more likely, defeat in the forthcoming election.

Another person who was kept in the dark about the trip was Senator Wheeler's one-time supporter Joseph Kennedy, the United States

Ambassador to Great Britain, and a man whom Roosevelt called 'a pain in the neck'. To FDR's great embarrassment (and Churchill's fury) Kennedy – who had strong German connections, including apparently Hitler's deputy, Hermann Göring – was in the habit of expressing defeatist, anti-British sentiments to anyone prepared to listen. Donovan, although of Irish extraction himself, had no time for Kennedy. He made scathing comments about the Ambassador to Brigadier Lee, saying that Kennedy's pessimism was affecting Wall Street and doing great harm at home.[1]

Carrying credentials issued by the United States Government and a letter of credit for $10,000, but travelling officially under the guise of a special correspondent attached to the *Chicago Daily News* (owned by Frank Knox, Secretary of the Navy), Donovan flew to London on a Pan-American Clipper on 14 July. William Stephenson, who had already struck up a good relationship with Donovan, urged the British Government to 'bare their breast' to their American visitor. This the British did. During his hectic time in Britain, practically no door was left closed to Donovan as he carried out his inspection of the country's defences and the will of her people to fight.

According to William Stephenson, in *A Man Called Intrepid*, the first person to whom Donovan was taken was the King himself, who, with the Queen, had met Roosevelt on a state visit to America the previous year. The King, according to Stephenson, handed Donovan a copy of Hitler's War Directive No. 16 which Ultra had provided through a successful deciphering of a message sent by the German Enigma signal machine. This directive, dated 16 July, began, 'Since England, in spite of her hopeless military situation, shows no sign of being ready to come to an understanding, I have decided to prepare a landing operation against England, and if necessary, to carry it out.' Hitler wanted a landing to be made 'on a wide front from about Ramsgate to the area west of the Isle of Wight'. However, Hitler insisted that, before this was done, the Royal Air Force 'must be so reduced morally and physically that it is unable to deliver any

---

[1] Aware of Roosevelt's lack of confidence in him, Kennedy resigned after FDR's re-election to the White House in November 1940.

significant attack against the German crossing.' The Battle of Britain was about to begin.

Needless to say, Donovan met Churchill and the British military leaders. But he sought also the advice of United States armed services representatives attached to the American Embassy in London. The airman Lt.-Col. Spaatz thought Britain would survive because the German *Luftwaffe* could not defeat the Royal Air Force. Donovan first met Brigadier Lee on 20 July. Lee took an immediate liking to him and came to consider him 'a very astute and clever, well balanced man, with enough military training to make his opinion valuable.' On 31 July, they had a meeting with General Alan Brooke, the Commander of British Home Forces, who in December 1941 would become the Chief of the Imperial General Staff, the professional head of Britain's armed forces. Lee considered him highly strung, but more intelligent than his predecessor, Ironside. Presumably under instructions from Churchill, Brooke gave a straight answer to all of the questions put to him by his American visitors, and struck Lee as being 'cheerful about the prospects'.

Privately, Donovan told Lee that he was also in London to study the British conscription laws and to learn 'what sort of legislation is required to operate a counter-espionage organisation'. Donovan expected to be heard by Congress on these subjects on his return. Conscription would come to America soon, Donovan felt, and he thought that 'our attitude towards it would be a test of our soul'.

His immediate purpose, though, was to assess Britain's chances of survival and he disclosed his view to Lee in positive terms over breakfast in Claridge's. Two days later, he flew back to America and reported to Secretary Knox that British morale was high and that Britain would beat off a German attack. He conveyed this personally to Roosevelt (who was already campaigning for his third term in the White House) while spending two days travelling with the President through New England. Donovan then passed his message to congressmen and businessmen and, via a radio broadcast, to the American people.

Donovan had answered Roosevelt's strategic question: Britain was still America's first line of defence and had to be supported. But in the event the expected invasion never came. The RAF beat off Göring's *Luftwaffe* and Hitler turned his interest away from Britain to what he considered his life's work — the annihilation of the Soviet Union and the use of its territory as living space for the German people. Yet that did not mean that Britain was safe. To live, Britain needed to keep her Atlantic sea lanes open against the ever-increasing threat from German submarines, the dreaded U-boats which had almost forced the British to surrender in the First World War and which under the command of Hitler's favourite, and chosen successor as Führer, Admiral Dönitz, were now showing themselves capable of repeating, and surpassing, that achievement.

To meet this threat, the Royal Navy needed more protection for her convoys. Donovan brought back with him to America a list of equipment and supplies which Britain needed. At the top of the list was a request for 50 destroyers. So pressing was this need that Churchill mentioned it in the first communication he made with Roosevelt after becoming Prime Minister on 10 May. On 31 July, he told Roosevelt that, with the Germans in control of the entire French coastline, it had 'become most urgent for you to let us have the destroyers, motor-boats and flying boats for which we have asked'. Churchill was optimistic about the war if Britain could only get through the next few months. This should not be taken for granted, Churchill warned in his letter, for 'the loss of destroyers by air attack may well be so serious as to break down our defence of the food and trade routes across the Atlantic'.

Before Donovan's visit, and before the Democratic Convention in July where the destroyers could have become a damaging political issue, Roosevelt was not keen to commit himself. However, by early August, Roosevelt felt able to respond to Churchill's pleading. Roosevelt was concerned not just with the possibility that a defeated Britain would hand over its fleet to Hitler but that a puppet British government would allow the Germans to use British bases in the western hemisphere, strongholds which, as Churchill pointed out, were 'in the old days, the stepping stones by which America could be attacked from Europe or from England'. This very subject had in fact featured prominently in the pan-American Havana Conference of July 1940, where the United States expressed concern that European colonies captured by the Axis could be turned into 'strategic centres of aggression'. It was agreed by delegates that any such territories should be held in 'collective trusteeship' and eventually given the right of self-determination.

Delicate negotiations began between the British and American governments over the transfer of the British bases to America in return for 50 old American destroyers. There were constitutional problems here for Roosevelt, but Donovan, the lawyer, helped by pointing out that Roosevelt would not have to place such a deal before Congress as it was a clear exercise of the executive power that the President traditionally enjoyed in foreign affairs. In this view Donovan was supported by Henry Stimson, the Secretary for War, Robert Jackson, the Attorney-General, and Dean Acheson, the Assistant Secretary of State. On 21 August, William Stephenson, the head of the British Security Co-ordination in New York, told Menzies in London that, according to Donovan, the British Government could expect 'very favourable news' in the next few days.

The final arrangement was a diplomatic one. In return for the destroyers, Churchill assured Roosevelt that he would not surrender or scuttle the British fleet and that, 'in friendship and goodwill', he was prepared to lease for 99 years the naval and air bases in Newfoundland, Bermuda, Bahamas, Jamaica, Antigua, St. Lucia, Trinidad, and British Guyana. In the House of Commons on 5 September, Churchill said that Hitler would be displeased by the deal struck and would 'pay the United States out, if he ever gets the chance'.

Roosevelt, for his part, was able to say that the bases were essential for the defence of the United States and that he had secured them at a bargain price. Nobody could argue with this point, for the destroyers involved were, in many cases, barely seaworthy and had been fetching about $4–5,000 each as scrap.

The reason why Churchill agreed to such a disadvantageous transaction would soon become apparent, and in such a manner as to spark off the battle for America's soul which Donovan had foreseen.

3

Safe on Third

On 5 November 1940, Roosevelt made history by becoming the first man to win three terms in the White House. His victory, against Republican Wendell Willkie, was a convincing one, though not overwhelming. Roosevelt won over 27 million votes and 449 electoral votes, overshadowing the 22 million votes and 82 electoral votes obtained by Willkie.

Although Willkie also had promised aid to Britain, Churchill was delighted with the result of the election and immediately sent to Roosevelt a congratulatory telegram in which he expressed his 'comfort' that the American people had once again chosen to put their trust in their sitting President. As the campaign slogan had predicted, Roosevelt was 'Safe on Third'. He could now prepare the American people and himself for what he saw as their 'date with destiny'. In doing so, however, he had to abide with the position on the war adopted at the Chicago Conference where he had accepted the nomination of the Democratic Party. This read: 'We will not participate in foreign wars, and we will not send our Army, naval or air forces to fight in foreign lands outside of the Americas, except in case of attack.' On 3 December, Roosevelt suddenly left Washington and travelled south to Miami, where he boarded the cruiser *Tuscaloosa* and sailed off into the Atlantic. The President, it was officially announced, would inspect some of the new bases which had recently been acquired in the West Indies and would be away for about two weeks. Unofficially the impression was given to the three pressmen allowed on the trip that the President was simply on vacation. Certainly he had with him only his closest adviser, Harry Hopkins, and his doctor, Navy Surgeon Ross T. McIntyre.

During his tour of the Caribbean, the President was visited off Eleuthra Island by the Duke of Windsor, the once but not future King of Britain, whose renunciation of the throne for an American divorcée and his subsequent closeness to the Nazis so embarrassed the wartime British Government that Churchill appointed him Governor of the suitably distant and peaceful Bahamas. Near the French island of Martinique, Roosevelt met the US Consul for a briefing on the political situation in the French colony. A major point of interest was the French aircraft carrier *Béarn* in the harbour, a vessel which, the Americans feared, could one day end up in Hitler's hands. As far as relaxation was concerned, the President spent his evenings playing poker or watching movies such as *Northwest Mounted Police* starring Gary Cooper. The days were devoted to fishing. The President received expert advice from the writer Ernest 'Papa' Hemingway, who told Roosevelt by radio to try a stretch of water between Dominica and Puerto Rico where many large fish had recently been spotted, and to use a feathered hook with a piece of pork attached. Despite Hemingway's help, Roosevelt caught nothing.

Since moving into the White House as Roosevelt's aide on 10 May 1940 (the day on which Churchill moved into 10 Downing Street as Prime Minister), Harry Hopkins had grown to know the President well. The ungainly and sickly Hopkins, a one-time social worker who had shot from obscurity to become the second most powerful man in America, felt that his boss, for all his enthusiastic holiday-making, had something on his mind and that he was in fact 'refuelling' – a process others who knew Roosevelt well have commented upon. Hopkins's suspicions were justified, for on 9 December a navy seaplane landed beside the *Tuscaloosa* and delivered a mail pouch containing a long letter from Churchill. Roosevelt took the letter and retired alone to his chair on the deck of the warship. Hopkins later told Churchill that Roosevelt 'read and re-read this letter' and that 'for two days he did not seem to have reached any conclusions. He was plunged in intense thought, and brooded silently.'

Roosevelt had already been alerted to the impending crisis by Lord Lothian, the highly respected British Ambassador to Washington, whose sudden and, but for his adherence to Christian Science, avoidable death only three days later meant a temporary set-back for the growing Anglo-Saxon alliance. Now Churchill confirmed the situation in a letter which he called one of the most important he ever wrote, and which he drafted three times and only sent following approval by the Chiefs of Staff, the Treasury and the War Cabinet.

The letter was a long one, some 4,000 words, and contained Churchill's views on 'the outlook for 1941'. Here, and at length, Churchill stated his belief that, as the 'danger of Great Britain being destroyed by a swift, overwhelming blow has for the time being very greatly receded', it would be 'in shipping and in the power to transport across the oceans, particularly the Atlantic Ocean, that in 1941 the crunch of the whole war will be found.' Important as this was, Churchill kept the vital and pressing business for the final paragraphs (the emphases are in the original):

> 17. Last of all I come to the question of finance. The more rapid and abundant the flow of munitions and ships which you are able to send us, the sooner will our dollar credits be exhausted. *They are already as you know very heavily drawn upon by payments we have made to date. Indeed as you know orders already placed or under negotiation, including expenditure settled or pending for creating munition factories in the United States, many times exceed the total exchange resources remaining at the disposal of Great Britain. The moment approaches* when we shall no longer be able to pay cash for shipping and other supplies. While we will do our utmost and shrink from no proper sacrifice to make payments across the exchange, I *believe that you would agree that it would be wrong in principle and mutually disadvantageous in effect if, at the height of this struggle, Great Britain were to be divested of all saleable assets* so that after victory was won with our blood, civilisation saved and time gained for the United States to be fully armed against all eventualities, we should stand stripped to the bone...

In short, Britain was almost broke. Since the beginning of the war, she had paid out over $4,500 million in cash, leaving her with little more than investments totalling some $2,000 million. If she were to continue the struggle against Hitler, Britain needed American credit of some sort. This was a stark and unpleasant fact at which even Churchill baulked. In one of the unsent drafts of the letter, he had written, 'I should not be willing even in the height of the struggle to divest Great Britain of every conceivable asset.' He had, however, changed his mind.

Roosevelt eventually reached a firm conclusion. On his return to Washington on 16 December, he called a press conference for the next day. Beginning in a low-key manner, Roosevelt said he did not think there was any particular news, except perhaps one subject. He then went on to say few Americans doubted that America's defence was best served by enabling Britain to defend herself. To help Britain, Roosevelt declared, it was now necessary to get away from traditional thinking, such as loaning money to her from the American Government or private banks or making an outright gift of supplies to her.

Roosevelt suggested that British orders for war material could be turned into American orders and then delivered to Britain, who would put them to much better use than if they had been kept in storage in America. Essentially, Roosevelt maintained, what he was trying to do was to 'get rid of that silly, foolish old dollar sign'. His idea was to lend supplies and equipment to Britain on condition that they were returned, or replaced, at the end of the war. To illustrate his point, Roosevelt used the analogy of a man lending his hose to a neighbour to put out a fire in the neighbour's house, on condition that, once the fire was extinguished, he got his hose back or a new one in its place.

Robert Sherwood, in his book on Harry Hopkins, maintains that through this homely comparison FDR won the support of the broad mass of Americans in securing for Britain (and other countries) what was to become known as 'Lend-Lease'. Certainly, shortly after the Washington press conference, Roosevelt spoke directly to the American people on this subject during a 'fireside chat', which he stated at the outset was not about war, but about national security. The President did not mince his words in expressing his view of America's position:

> If Great Britain goes down, the Axis powers will control the continents of Europe, Asia, Africa, Australasia, and the high seas — and they will be in a position to bring enormous military and naval resources against this hemisphere. It is no exaggeration to say that

all of us, in all the Americas, would be living at the point of a gun – a gun loaded with explosive bullets, economic as well as military.

Roosevelt repeated that America's best defence was to equip and supply Britain in her fight against Hitler. 'We must be the great arsenal of democracy,' he declared in one of his most memorable phrases, although it had already been used in a newspaper editorial. He declared that there was no thought of sending an American army to Europe and that his policy was directed not towards war, but towards keeping 'war away from our country and our people'. 'You can,' Roosevelt told his listeners, 'therefore nail any talk about sending armies to Europe as deliberate untruth.' (It should be noted here that a few weeks earlier, Admiral Stark, the professional head of the US Navy, had written a memorandum to Frank Knox, Secretary of the Navy, in which he stated his belief that to defeat Germany it would probably be necessary for America 'to send large air and land forces to Europe or Africa, or both, and to participate strongly in this land offensive.')

Roosevelt also hit out in his speech at the enemy within – American citizens, 'many of them in high places' who, wittingly or otherwise, were helping Nazi agents at work in America. (In accordance with his usual practice, he named no names.) These American 'appeasers', Roosevelt maintained, were calling for a 'negotiated peace', which, he claimed, would be no peace at all, but 'only another armistice, leading to the most gigantic armament race and the most devastating trade wars in all history.' By 'appeasers' Roosevelt meant the isolationists – those in America who did not share his views on Hitler and Germany and who believed that America's interests would be best served by staying out of Europe's war and looking only to her own hemisphere or even her own frontiers. Roosevelt's Lend-Lease proposals, submitted to Congress as H.R. 1776 on 10 January 1941 under the vague title 'A Bill to Further Promote the Defense of the U.S. and For Other Purposes', brought his simmering dispute with the isolationists and their fellow-travellers to the boil.

America's involvement in the First World War, although militarily decisive in defeating Imperial Germany, had left Americans with the feeling that the enterprise had been a mistake and that what went on in

Europe should be left to the Europeans themselves. This was vividly demonstrated immediately after the war by the US Senate which, in one of the greatest domestic political embarrassments ever inflicted upon an American President, rejected President Wilson's plans for American membership of the newly formed League of Nations, an organization which ironically had been Wilson's brainchild. In 1934, a Congressional Committee concluded that America had been dragged into the war by bankers and industrialists intent on making huge profits. To prevent this happening again, Congress passed legislation, most notably the Neutrality Acts which, in the event of war, imposed a US arms embargo on all belligerents, and banned the use of American ships for the transport of non-contraband goods to a belligerent country. After the war started in Europe in 1939, Roosevelt succeeded in changing the law to allow belligerents, which in practice meant only Britain and France, to buy arms.

The amending of the Neutrality Act, and the sale of destroyers, were important victories for FDR against the isolationists. However, it was small beer compared to the provisions of the Lend-Lease Act, which would provide the President with sweeping powers and unquestionably move America closer to the war. Under this Bill, FDR would be given the power to compel American businesses to manufacture or repair whatever items of war he deemed necessary for the defence of America; to decide which governments (including possibly the USSR!) would be made beneficiaries of Lend-Lease and under what terms of repayment; and to convey to these governments any defence information he considered appropriate.

It is impossible to detach the debate over this Bill from Roosevelt himself. As previously mentioned, Roosevelt is one of the most polemical figures in American history, a man who was a hero to some and a charlatan to others. Although a leading member of the American plutocracy, his 'New Deal' policies, through which he sought to change society, led some to suspect him of being a socialist; while others, including Hitler and many isolationists, alleged that he was simply a man obsessed with power. A self-professed idealist, he was also a secretive and deceitful politician who dominated his faction-ridden administrations through a seemingly deliberate policy of divide and rule. A man who was for ever extolling the virtues of democracy, he once tried to pack the Supreme Court with his own appointees in order to facilitate the adoption and implementation of his legislation. His decision in 1940 to break with a strongly held tradition and run for a third term in the White House confirmed the worst fears of many Americans that here was a man who wanted to be President for life. It is little wonder, then, that the isolationists named Roosevelt's Lend-Lease proposals the 'Dictator's Bill' and that they feared FDR would use it to lead America into war.[1]

The isolationist cause was led by the America First Committee, which had been founded in September 1940 by Robert Douglas Stuart Jnr, a young Princeton graduate, and financed initially by General Robert E. Wood, a First World War hero who became its national chairman. The committee attracted some 800,000 members from all levels of American society, but had its geographical power base in Chicago and the Midwest. Most members were, of course, patriots who genuinely believed that America should stick to her own hemisphere, and that she had nothing to fear from a Nazi-dominated Europe. However, the movement also drew support from people who were political innocents or members of pro-Nazi organizations or, in some cases, paid German agents.

The darling of the movement was the hero Charles Lindbergh, who flew solo across the Atlantic in 1927, earning himself the nickname 'The Lone Eagle'. The son of a man who opposed America's entry into the First World War, Lindbergh had visited Nazi Germany and was clearly impressed by what he had seen, even to the extent of accepting a medal for services to aviation from Hermann Göring, the head of the German *Luftwaffe* and Hitler's Second-in-Command. Lindbergh saw Nazi ideals as representing the future and believed that they should be adopted by other countries. Before the war in Europe started, Roosevelt offered him a place in his Cabinet as Secretary for Air on condition that he remained silent. Lindbergh spurned this blatant bribe and

---

[1] It is worth noting here that in January 1933, Louis Howe, Roosevelt's dishevelled and deeply cynical political mentor, declared in a speech to the Columbia School of Journalism, 'You can't adopt politics as a profession and remain honest. If you're going to make your living out of politics you can't do it honestly.'

carried on with his pro-German and isolationalist radio broadcasts and speeches. It was these that undid him. While addressing the first mass meeting of the America First Committee in April 1941, he effectively said that European countries were wrong to resist Hitler's aggression. In a subsequent press conference, Roosevelt branded him an appeaser and a defeatist, thereby forcing Lindbergh to resign his commission in the US Army Air Corps Reserve. Even more damaging was a speech Lindbergh made in Des Moines on 11 September 1941, when he linked his views with Hitler's by claiming that the Jews in America were using their influence in government and the media to drag the United States into the war. Lindbergh never recovered from this blunder. He was refused employment by the US Government during the war, but found a job with Henry Ford, the car manufacturer, whose anti-British sentiments were vociferous.

The most influential politician in the isolationist camp was probably Senator Burton K. Wheeler from Montana, a one-time supporter of Joseph Kennedy and, indeed, of Roosevelt himself. However, during Roosevelt's Presidency, Wheeler proved to be one of FDR's most persistent critics and opponents. He led the Senatorial fight to stop Roosevelt from packing the Supreme Court. He investigated claims that Roosevelt was guilty of nepotism in respect of his sons. From early on, he made no secret of his isolationist views. He was a member of the Congressional Committee which in 1934 concluded that America had been dragged into the First World War by big business. In 1935, he told William Dodd, the American Ambassador to Berlin, that Germany should dominate Europe, Japan the Far East, and America the western hemisphere. He and his wife became active supporters of the American First Committee. His reaction to Roosevelt's Lend-Lease Bill was typically frank: 'It will plow under every fourth American boy.' This remark infuriated FDR who, at a press conference on 14 January 1941, fired back: 'I regard [Wheeler's comment] as the most untruthful, as the most dastardly, unpatriotic thing that has ever been said. Quote me on that. That really is the rottenest thing that has been said in public life in my generation.'

There was another active interventionist who was on bad terms with Wheeler – William Donovan. The bad blood between the two men dated back to the Teapot Dome scandal of 1923 (the Watergate of its day) and the subsequent accusations of corruption which reverberated throughout American politics. In 1924, Wheeler, a newly elected US Senator, successfully forced through a resolution that the conduct of the Attorney-General, Harry M. Daugherty, be investigated. While this was under way, Wheeler was himself indicted by a Grand Jury in Montana on charges of accepting money from an oil syndicate in return for prospecting leases. Wheeler claimed – and it was widely believed – that Daugherty had framed him. Even so, his trial proceeded, under the direction of William Donovan, who had recently been appointed Assistant US Attorney-General and had nothing to do with the original indictment. Wheeler was acquitted, but he never forgave Donovan for subjecting him to this humiliation and refused to have anything further to do with 'Wild Bill'.

As far as the Congressional hearings on the Lend-Lease Bill were concerned, the first step was to convince the legislators that Britain was indeed broke, a fact which many Americans found hard to believe. This task fell naturally to Henry Morgenthau Jnr, the Secretary of the Treasury, who, in a truly historic moment, displayed to the Congressional Committee the facts and figures provided by the British Government (and corroborated by the US Treasury). These showed not only how dire Britain's financial position was, but also how willing she was to dispose of her few remaining assets in order to continue the fight against Hitler. The last Roman Emperor fell fighting the Turks in the breached walls of his capital, Constantinople. Napoleon's Imperial dreams collapsed with the repulse of his Guard on the slopes of Waterloo. In stark contrast, it was via the prosaic medium of ledgers and account books that notice was served that the British Empire, the largest the world had known, was about to pass into history – not through conquest or military defeat, but simple impoverishment.

The recent appointments to Roosevelt's Cabinet – the Republicans Henry Stimson, Secretary for War, and Frank Knox, Secretary of the Navy – both testified that without Lend-Lease Britain would probably fall to Hitler and that, if she did, America would very quickly find herself in a war for which she was unprepared. (Knox, as previously mentioned, was the owner of the strongly interventionist *Chicago Daily*

News. His rival in that city was the staunchly isolationist *Chicago Daily Tribune* run by Col. Robert McCormick and his family.)

Another prominent Republican to testify was Wendell Willkie, the man who had unsuccessfully tried to oust Roosevelt from the White House a few months before. Willkie had just returned from a visit to London, where he had met Churchill and was thus able to talk with authority and conviction of the British Government's determination and ability to carry on the fight, provided it was properly supplied. 'Give us the tools and we shall finish the job!' Churchill had announced in a radio broadcast.

Roosevelt undoubtedly took a risk with his Lend-Lease Bill. However, with his recent convincing Presidential victory behind him – and the support of the man he had beaten – he was always confident of victory. The Bill was passed with comfortable majorities by both Houses of Congress and signed into law by Roosevelt on 11 March 1941. America had discarded any pretence at being a true neutral in the war. What Robert Sherwood called the sham period, in which America tried to protect itself 'by bootlegging methods', was at an end. This was only to be expected; there was little point in manufacturing munitions and weapons for Britain if these could not be sent safely across the Atlantic.

4

More and More Provocative

It was well after 10 a.m. on the morning of 26 May 1941 and the Catalina flying boat had still not spotted anything of interest. The plane, which had left its base in Northern Ireland shortly after midnight for the watery vastness of the mid-Atlantic Ocean, was on loan to British Coastal Command from the US Government, as was perfectly legal under Lend-Lease. However, American participation in this mission went beyond what US law then permitted. The pilot of the craft, Ensign Leonard B. Smith, was, like half the crew, an American. Moreover, this was no training exercise. The Catalina had been sent to this area by a report from a US Coast Guard ship which just *happened* to be in the area and which stated that it had seen fleetingly on the horizon the unmistakable superstructure of the *Bismarck*, the pride of Hitler's fleet and the most powerful battleship in the world.

Intelligence reports from Sweden that the *Bismarck,* accompanied by the heavy cruiser *Prinz Eugen*, had sailed from their German base on 20 May brought the Royal Navy immediately to a position of red alert. At that time, there were 10 supply convoys and a troop convoy crossing the Atlantic. If the *Bismarck* attacked these, as her commander, Admiral Günther Lütjens, had been ordered to do, the results could be catastrophic, not just for the convoys themselves, but also for Britain's prestige and standing. The *Bismarck* had to be found and sunk.

The British battle cruiser *Hood*, the much revered grand old lady of the Royal Navy, and the spanking new battleship *Prince of Wales* were sent to guard the approaches to the Atlantic from the west of Iceland. There, around 5.30 a.m. on 24 May, Vice-Admiral Holland of the *Hood* spotted the German ships steaming towards him through the heavy sea spray and engaged them at once, even though his angle of approach placed him at a disadvantage. Shortly before 6.00 a.m. and at a closing range of about 25,000 yards (over 14 miles), the ships began an exchange of thunderous salvoes, hurling one-ton shells at each other. Almost at once, the superiority of the *Bismarck* was established. She hit the *Hood* several times amidships, causing her to blow up and sink with such suddenness that only three of the *Hood*'s complement of over 1,500 survived. The *Bismarck* then turned her attention to the *Prince of Wales*, several of whose new 14-inch guns were suffering from teething trouble. Four German shells smashed into the *Prince of Wales*, wrecking her bridge. At 6.13 a.m., the *Prince of Wales* broke off combat and sailed away under a smoke screen. The battle, though, had not gone entirely *Bismarck*'s way. One shell from the *Prince of Wales* had punctured the *Bismarck*'s fuel tanks, reducing her top speed to 28 knots, and effectively ending her hunting expedition. Admiral Lütjens could perhaps have returned safely to Germany, but he decided to press on southwards, towards the protection of the German-controlled French port of Brest, over 1,000 miles away.

The Royal Navy ordered every capital ship in the Atlantic to join in the hunt for the *Bismarck*, but the search did not go well. Even though an air strike from the aircraft carrier *Victorious* hit the *Bismarck* with a torpedo, it did little harm. After that attack, the *Bismarck* threw off her pursuers and vanished, leaving the *Prinz Eugen* to make her own way to Brest, which she reached safely. For almost all of 25 May – Lütjens's birthday, on which he received a congratulatory telegram from Hitler – the Royal Navy lost contact with their quarry and suspected that she was heading for the North Sea. Then came the sighting by the American Coast Guard ship, which in turn brought Ensign Smith's Catalina into the search about 700 miles north-west of Brest.

Around 10.30 a.m., Smith thought he saw something through the thick clouds and took his craft down for a closer look. The look he got was far too close for comfort. As the Catalina broke through the heavy clouds into clear air, the enormous grey steel bulk of the *Bismarck* appeared right in front of him, her gunners reacting with frightening speed to this new intrusion. Smith yanked on the controls and turned his plane through 180 degrees as the huge ship spat fire into the air. The plane took hits but managed to reach cloud cover, where it sent off a signal which pinpointed the position of the *Bismarck*, thereby sealing her fate.

Hitler had not authorized the sailing of the *Bismarck* and, when he learned of it on 22 May from Grand Admiral Raeder, the professional head of the German Navy, he asked if the ship could be brought back, expressing fears that surface ships were vulnerable to air attack. Raeder pointed out that a recall would damage morale and Hitler relented, but his instincts were to prove correct.

It was not the British battleships, but the obsolescent Swordfish torpedo planes of the aircraft-carrier *Ark Royal* which caught the *Bismarck*. Their torpedo strikes jammed the *Bismarck*'s rudder, causing her to sail in circles until the Royal Navy battleships arrived and pummelled her into a burning hulk. She eventually sank, probably as the result of scuttling, at around 10.40 a.m. on 27 May, about 24 hours after the sighting by Ensign Smith, whose role in this action, technically illegal under existing American legislation and potentially highly damaging to Roosevelt if leaked to his political opponents, was kept secret for many years.

The battle for control of the Atlantic sea lanes was never far from Roosevelt's mind. He was already allowing British warships to be repaired in American yards. In April, he extended the US Security Zone in the Atlantic to all waters west of longitude 26 degrees, a line roughly equidistant from the continents of America and Europe, and ordered that all German vessels seen in this area were to be reported to the British. Discreet discussions were already under way to enable American forces to occupy Iceland and relieve the British garrison there for service elsewhere, a plan which was executed in July that year. Nevertheless, ever mindful of the power of the isolationists, FDR was still resisting pressure from those advisers who believed that his publicly declared policy of 'all aid short of war' was not enough. *Bismarck*'s foray into the Atlantic gave him the excuse he needed to go one step closer to war.

The disappearance of the *Bismarck* after the sinking of the *Hood* led to wild speculation in Washington that the German battleship was not after the Atlantic convoys, but targets in the western hemisphere. Roosevelt, according to Robert Sherwood, did not think it unlikely that she would turn up in the Caribbean and wondered aloud whether he would be impeached if he ordered American submarines to attack her. (Sherwood recorded that his advisers were of the opinion that Roosevelt would be impeached only if the American submarines missed with their torpedoes!) Although the *Bismarck* was sunk by the British, FDR decided to make use of this episode, and to that end instructed his scriptwriters to add a section to a speech in honour of 'Pan-American Day' which he was scheduled to make on 27 May, the day the *Bismarck* was finally dispatched.

In this speech, which was given in the East Room of the White House before representatives from Canada and 20 Latin-American countries and broadcast worldwide, Roosevelt stated America's national policy as:

> First, we shall actively resist wherever necessary, and with all our resources, every attempt by Hitler to extend his Nazi domination to the Western Hemisphere, or to threaten it. We shall actively resist his every attempt to gain control of the seas. We insist upon the vital importance of keeping Hitlerism away from any point in the world which could be used or would be used as a base of attack against the Americas.
>
> Second, from the point of view of strict naval and military necessity, we shall give every possible assistance to Britain and to all who, with Britain, are resisting Hitlerism or its equivalent with force of arms. Our patrols are helping now to insure delivery of the needed supplies to Britain. All additional measures necessary to deliver the goods will be taken. Any and all further methods or combination of methods, which can or should be utilized, are being devised by our military and naval technicians, who, with me, will work out and put into effect such new and additional safeguards as may be needed.

After reiterating his belief in the 'Four Freedoms' – of speech, of religion, from want, and from terror – FDR announced that he had proclaimed an 'Unlimited National Emergency' which required 'the strengthening of our defense to the extreme limit of our national power and authority'. Under this proclamation, Roosevelt placed all military and civilian defences 'on the basis of readiness to repel any and all acts or threats of aggression directed toward any part of the Western Hemisphere', and called upon all Americans to work together to ensure that 'we may mobilize and have ready for instant defensive use all of the physical powers, all of the moral strength, and all of the material resources of this Nation.'

The telegrams which poured into the White House after the speech were overwhelmingly in favour of what FDR had said, as was the reaction of the press and the public in general. Robert Sherwood, who had helped write the speech, thought that 'Roosevelt's words were taken as a solemn commitment; the entry of the United States into the war against Germany was now considered inevitable and even imminent'. However, to Sherwood's surprise, Roosevelt did not press for war. The reason was easy to identify – the power of the isolationists and their political sympathizers in Congress, which, under the American Constitution, alone has the power to declare war.

Even news that a German submarine had sunk the American freighter *Robin Moor* (albeit with no loss of life) on 21 May in the South Atlantic *en route* to Cape Town with (under US law) a contraband cargo of war material did not prompt Roosevelt to ask Congress to declare war, although he did send a message to Congress on the subject in which he pointed out that the German Government should rest 'assured that the United States will neither be intimidated nor will it acquiesce in the plans for world domination which the present leaders of Germany may have'. The following month, Roosevelt seized all US-based assets belonging to the Axis powers and closed German and Italian consulates in the United States. (The German Embassy in Washington remained open under the Chargé d'Affaires, Hans Thomsen.)

The most striking evidence of the power of the isolationist lobby in Congress during this period was the debate over the extension of the Selective Service Law, America's first peacetime draft, which in September 1940 conscripted young men into the armed services for a period of one year. This had proved very unpopular, not only with the young men themselves, but also with their families, despite Roosevelt's pledge that their sons would not be sent to fight in a foreign war 'except in case of attack'. If the Act was not extended, the conscripts would go home and the army would in effect cease to exist. (The initials O.H.I.O., meaning 'over the hill in October', were found scrawled on walls all over America.) For a while, there was a real danger that this would happen, but following an appeal by the Chief of Staff, George Marshall, the extension was approved, though only by a majority of one in the House of Representatives. 'This vote,' the arch-isolationist Senator Burton K. Wheeler warned the US Government, 'clearly indicates that the Administration could not get a resolution through the Congress for a declaration of war.'

News of this photo-finish reached Roosevelt on 12 August on board the cruiser *Augusta*, which was anchored in Placentia Bay, Newfoundland. This was where, in what is known to history as the 'Atlantic Conference', he and Churchill 'got together', as Roosevelt put it, for the first time during the war. (The two men had met briefly during the First World War. Churchill, already a senior British statesman, did not remember the occasion. Roosevelt, then a relatively junior Under Secretary of the US Navy, did.)

A meeting between Roosevelt and Churchill had been mooted during Harry Hopkins's first visit to Britain in January 1941. (On his arrival, via Lisbon, in a bomb-battered Britain, with its rationing and black-outs, Hopkins felt as if he had landed on the dark side of the moon.) After his first meeting with Churchill, Hopkins wrote to Roosevelt on 14 January:

> *Churchill* [original emphasis] is the gov't in every sense of the word – he controls the grand strategy and often the details – labour trusts him – the army, navy, air force are behind him to a man. The politicians and upper crust pretend to like him. I cannot emphasise too strongly that he is the one and only person over here with whom you have a full meeting of minds.
>
> Churchill wants to see you – the sooner the better – but I have told him of your problem until the [Lend-Lease] Bill is passed. I am convinced this meeting between you and Churchill is essential – and soon – for the battering continues and Hitler does not wait for Congress.

Here Hopkins touched on a point which is often overlooked, but which must be kept in mind if this period of the war is to be understood – namely, the importance to Roosevelt of keeping Churchill in power. In 1941, Britain was visibly weakening, both physically and morally. After the fall of France in the summer of 1940, some very influential people – including Lord Halifax, the new British Ambassador to Washington – had expressed interest in making peace with Hitler. The surprise flight to Britain in May 1941 of Hitler's deputy, Rudolf Hess, on a peace mission is a bizarre and still mysterious episode, but it must strengthen the suspicion that there were people then in Britain actively considering, and perhaps working towards, Churchill's removal. (Churchill himself did not seem overly concerned. On being told of the Deputy-Führer's shock arrival by parachute in Scotland, he said that he was not interested as he was on his way to watch a Marx Brothers film.)

Certainly, there were some who questioned the value of continuing such an unequal struggle at such cost to Britain's finances and long-term strategic position. In June, John Winant, the US Ambassador to London, confided to Roosevelt that the 'Imperial Situation, as a whole, seems to be deteriorating' and that he could not 'see how the British Empire can defeat Germany without the help of God or Uncle Sam.' 'Perhaps,' he added sombrely, 'it will take both.' In September, while possibly under the influence of one of his 'black dog' fits of depression, Churchill warned Harry Hopkins that 'if 1942 opens with Russia knocked out and Britain alone again, all kinds of dangers may arise', a reference to the real possibility that his Government might then fall. There was already cause for concern. British morale had slumped badly since the summer of 1940 and the exciting, defiant days of the Battle of Britain, and a widespread apathy was gripping the people who, with reason, now seemed to fear slow starvation from the U-boat blockade more than invasion.

After reading this message, Hopkins told Roosevelt that all the British people he had spoken to believed that America would enter the war 'on some basis or other', and that if they ever thought that this was not going to happen, 'that would be a very critical moment in the war and the British appeasers might have some influence on Churchill.' Admiral Stark stressed this in a highly revealing letter to Roosevelt in late September 1941. He wrote that *for the past two years* he had assumed that America would not let Britain be overrun by Germany and that, in order to prevent this, America would have to enter the war. Stark's own feelings were that the sooner this happened the better. The point being made was that, if Churchill fell, the new British Government might come to terms with Nazi Germany, which meant that Britain could eventually find itself in the same position as France where, in the summer of 1941, after one year of German occupation, US Ambassador Winant detected no more sense of resistance to Hitler than 'in a wet dish rag'.

The proposed meeting between Roosevelt and Churchill was originally planned for the spring of 1941, but had to be postponed because of the momentous events that took place that year, not least of which was *Operation Barbarossa*, the German invasion of the Soviet Union on 22 June. The two leaders had known about this attack in advance, thanks to the success of the British code-breakers who had unravelled the secrets of *Enigma* (the German cipher machine which was used to pass even the most important messages), and had decided that Stalin had to be supported. Churchill tried to warn Stalin of the impending German attack, but the ever-suspicious Georgian chose to believe that the western democracies were merely trying to embroil Germany and the Soviet Union in a mutually destructive war.

As soon as the invasion began, Churchill promised aid to Stalin. 'If Hitler invaded hell,' he announced, 'I would make at least a favourable reference to the Devil in the House of Commons.' But he also made it clear that he remained, as he had always been, an implacable foe of Communism. Roosevelt released frozen Soviet funds in America and, despite the Neutrality Acts, allowed US ships to transport American goods purchased by Stalin to the Russian port of Vladivostok on the Pacific coast. On 7 November, by which time Russia's dollar reserves had dried up, Roosevelt declared that the defence of the Soviet Union was vital to the security of the United States and authorized the sending of war material to Stalin under the Lend-Lease Act.

The policy of helping Stalin against Hitler was much criticized in both Britain and America, with some people wondering why the two tyrants should not be left to destroy one another. The *Wall Street*

Journal was of the opinion that the main difference between the two dictators was 'the size of their respective moustaches'. Indeed, many Americans considered Stalin a greater threat than Hitler. Communism, as Senator Robert Taft said, 'is a false philosophy which appeals to many. Fascism is a false philosophy which appeals to very few indeed.' On the other hand, the American Communist Party, which had been strongly isolationist, suddenly decided after the German assault on the Soviet Union that it was, after all, interventionist.

One obvious consequence of *Barbarossa* was that Britain was safe from invasion in the immediate future. This was a strategic fact which was brought to Roosevelt's attention almost immediately by the US Secretary of War, Henry Stimson, who, after a meeting with Chief of Staff George Marshall and the War Plans Division of the General Staff, wrote to the President, informing him that his military advisers were unanimously of the opinion that this 'respite should be used to push with the utmost vigour our movements in the Atlantic theatre of operations', and 'that such pressure on our part was the right way to help Britain, to discourage Germany, and to strengthen our own position of defence against our most imminent danger.' It was against this background that Roosevelt and Churchill, who had been corresponding since the war began, finally met.

*   *   *

Still bearing the scars of her encounter with the *Bismarck*, the *Prince of Wales* arrived from her Scottish base in the mist-covered waters of Placentia Bay on Saturday 9 August. She was carrying Churchill, with a prominent military staff, and Harry Hopkins, who was exhausted following an epic trip from Washington to Moscow, via London, to speak to Stalin and then back to Scotland in time for the voyage across the Atlantic. Hopkins was not so tired, though, as to fail to notice Churchill's excitement at the prospect of meeting Roosevelt. 'You'd have thought Winston was being carried up into the heavens to meet God!' he later remarked. Now for Churchill the moment had at last arrived. The outline of the cruiser *Augusta* appeared through the rising mist, and waiting on board was the President of the United States.

The Placentia Bay Conference was, at the personal level, a success in that Roosevelt and Churchill, driven by a common purpose, developed a sound working relationship. This was after all not a foregone conclusion. Although the two leaders came from similar establishment backgrounds, and at FDR's suggestion had been corresponding since the beginning of the war, they had very different personalities and styles of leadership. FDR was by far the more natural politician. Described by Robert Sherwood as an 'artful dodger', he was a complex, secretive man who studied Machiavelli and who kept his mistress, Lucy Mercer, in the White House when his wife was away. Churchill, on the other hand, was essentially a soldier turned statesman, a simple, straightforward patriot who revelled in leading a wartime Britain which he dominated through not just his charisma and seemingly tireless energy but also his awe-inspiring mastery of the English language, which could move even the most hard-headed realist. Roosevelt employed speechwriters, whereas Churchill, a man of both the pen and the sword, wrote his own speeches.

The Conference was certainly of great propaganda value. The film of Roosevelt and Churchill seated side by side at a church service on the deck of the *Prince of Wales*, under the great guns of the battleship with their servicemen paraded around them, was a powerful and unmistakable message to the world which remains to this day one of the great images of the war. (Less than four months later, the *Prince of Wales* was no more. Together with the battleship *Repulse*, she was sunk by Japanese bombers off the Malayan coast on 8 December, with the loss of over 800 of the men who had gathered that day around the two leaders to praise God. Churchill described the news of this disaster as 'the most direct shock' he received in the entire war.)

However, although much was discussed between the American and British delegations (and this will be examined later), little was agreed upon and all that emerged publicly was the 'Atlantic Charter', an eight-point document which laid the groundwork for the establishment of the United Nations. In the Charter, the British and American governments declared, amongst other things, that they sought 'no aggrandisement, territorial or other', they wished 'to see sovereign rights and self-government restored to those who have been forcibly deprived of them', they hoped 'after the final destruction of the Nazi tyranny' to see established 'a peace which will afford to all nations the means of dwelling in safety within their own borders', and they considered the disarmament of those nations who engaged in 'aggression outside of their frontiers' essential.

It was admittedly astonishing that a neutral country should align itself alongside a belligerent in expressing such sentiments. However, the Atlantic Charter proved a let-down to people around the world who had been expecting action, not just more words. Many in Britain, including apparently Churchill himself, had hoped that Roosevelt would use the Conference to announce his intention to ask Congress for a declaration of war. 'I would rather have a declaration of war now and no supplies for six months,' Churchill told Hopkins, 'than double the supplies and no declaration.' But Roosevelt was not willing to countenance this. As he explained to the Prime Minister, 'I may never declare war; I may make war. If I were to ask Congress to declare war they might argue about it for three months.' He would, though, become 'more and more provocative' in the Atlantic in the expectation that this would bring American and German ships into direct confrontation.

Such incidents certainly arose. On 4 September, the USS *Greer*, a destroyer on patrol about 120 miles south-west of Iceland, which was already under the control of American forces, received a signal from a British aircraft flying overhead that there was a German U-boat about 10 miles to the west. The *Greer* located the submarine, *U-652*, and tracked her for several hours, enabling British forces to drop depth charges on her. Although undamaged, the *U-652* turned on the *Greer* and fired one torpedo at her which missed. In a 'fireside chat' a week later, Roosevelt described the U-boat's action as an unprovoked act of piracy and disclosed that he had instructed the US Army and Navy to 'shoot on sight' any German vessels seen in waters protected by American forces. 'When you see a rattlesnake poised to strike,' he proclaimed, 'you do not wait until he has struck before you crush him.'

It was not long until more 'rattlesnakes' were encountered. On the night of 17 October, the USS *Kearny*, a destroyer on convoy escort, dropped depth charges on a German U-boat, which turned and fired a torpedo into her starboard side. The *Kearny* survived, but her 11 dead were the first American casualties of the war. On 31 October, the

Reuben James went down west of Ireland after being torpedoed. She lost 115 of her 160-strong crew, including all her officers.

Roosevelt's speeches consequently became more strident. 'The shooting has started,' he announced with reference to the *Kearny* incident in his Navy and Total Defense Day Address on 27 October. 'And history has recorded who fired the first shot,' he added with a somewhat cavalier attitude towards the truth. 'We Americans have cleared our decks and taken our battle stations,' he declared following the sinking of the *Reuben James*. He also succeeded, albeit by a narrow vote, in persuading Congress to change certain key sections of the Neutrality Laws, which allowed all US merchant ships to be armed and to sail through the war zone to British ports.

But, to the dismay of the British and his closest advisers, Roosevelt did not feel strong enough to go further. Indeed, after the attack on the *Kearny,* General Robert E. Wood of the American First Committee publicly challenged Roosevelt to ask Congress if it was prepared to declare war on Germany. Roosevelt declined because he knew that, despite all he had said and done about Hitler, he would fail to obtain the necessary Congressional support, a fact which was reported to Churchill by Lord Halifax, the British Ambassador to Washington, who explained that Roosevelt was trying to steer a course between the desire of 70 per cent of Americans to do everything to break Hitler even at the cost of war and the determination of 70 per cent of Americans to keep out of the war.

One man who was determined to bring America into the war was Douglas Miller, the former Commercial Attaché to the United States Embassy in Berlin, in which capacity he had, from the inception of the Third Reich in 1933 and often with astonishing accuracy, warned his government of the nature and intentions of Hitler's regime.[1] In mid-1941, Miller, now a Professor of Economics, published *You Can't Do Business with Hitler*, which was publicly endorsed by Roosevelt and recommended as essential reading for every American businessman by William Shirer, the foreign correspondent, who described Miller as the

---

[1] Miller's reports to Washington were published in 1944 under the title *Via Diplomatic Pouch*, with a foreword by William Shirer, the future author of *The Rise and Fall of The Third Reich.*

leading expert in the American Embassy in Berlin on 'all aspects of life under the Nazis'.

In the preface to his book, Miller declared that his long diplomatic service in Berlin qualified him to do 'some plain speaking' on the question of fighting the Nazis.[2] Miller's message, which was directed above all to American businessmen, was certainly blunt: Nazi Germany posed such an economic threat to America that the United States should attack her as soon as possible.

In his book, Miller concerned himself primarily, not with the immoral nature of the Nazi regime or the distant prospect of a Nazi invasion of the western hemisphere, but with the danger posed to America's capitalist system and lifestyle by Hitler's economic policies. A Nazi-controlled Europe, Miller asserted, would be able to subject the United States to great political and economic pressure, via the bartering system which Hitler was using to control international trade, and restrict American access to the lands under his control. To illustrate his point, Miller quoted Hermann Göring as telling him to his face during lunch one day that American firms would come to be regarded as a foreign 'inflammation or irritation' in Germany's economy, and that these businesses should go back home before they got into trouble. Miller also cited a statement by Walther Funk, the Nazi Minister of Economics, to the effect that, after the war, international trade would be carried out only by governments and that private transactions would be abolished.

Simply resisting this pressure from a totalitarian state, Miller warned his businessmen readers, would lead to the amending, or even the suspension, of the American Constitution and to the disappearance of many of the freedoms which Americans had come to take for granted. As for the American economy, that 'would be characterised by easy money, a nervous and depressed stock exchange, rising indebtedness, a high level of employment and wages in the defence industries, and a feeling of dread regarding the future outlook.' Moreover, the loss of America's major trading partners, in particular the British Empire,

---

[2] Miller wrote his preface on 12 May 1941. It is interesting to note that Roosevelt, in his speech on 27 May 1941 in which he declared an 'Unlimited Emergency', attacked those Americans who thought that 'we can "do business" with Hitler'.

would seriously undermine the position of the United States as a trading nation. America would find herself forced to trade with Hitler under terms and conditions highly favourable to Berlin, a situation which would inevitably lead to the appearance in America of Hitler's economic policies and the demise of freewheeling Yankee capitalism. Miller concluded: 'We should be on a fair way to planned economy and a system of State Socialism.'

Miller's answer to this 'picture of the United States left alone in a friendless world' was to call for war against Germany immediately. The existing US policy of 'short of war' was not enough. Only all-out war could defeat Hitler, and the sooner that war was started the better for America, Miller believed. 'Attack is our best defence,' he declared. 'Attack at the heart of the enemy; attack with every resource of our vast, free and vigorous nation.' That America was unprepared for war was not a critical factor, Miller wrote, for such was America's economic strength that she could fight and rearm simultaneously.

What was essential to grasp, Miller emphasized, was that Hitler must not be given time to consolidate his European conquests. To prevent Hitler from establishing his 'New Order' in Europe, he must be struck from the west in a campaign which would first involve destroying the German economy from the air and then culminate 'in a final attack of mechanised land forces upon the Continent'. If this policy were pursued, Miller was confident that Hitler would be defeated. 'The day we declare war will be the day the Nazis know they are beaten,' he announced. It was true that Hitler was in the process of marshalling 'the entire resources of a continent', Miller conceded. 'But,' he reminded his American readers in a reference to what would indeed prove to be the most important strategic fact of the Second World War, 'we too have a continent and a more productive one.'[3]

Miller's work, which was a forceful and timely reminder of the dangers facing America as envisaged by the interventionists, became a nationwide bestseller. Reviewers latched on to such quotes as 'The Nazis believe in 100 per cent or nothing — and 100 per cent for them

---

[3] See in particular pages 115–22 of *You Can't Do Business with Hitler*. It should be noted that Miller wrote his book before Hitler invaded the Soviet Union.

and nothing for us would be the usual arrangement', and 'What the Nazis really would like: to unify Europe and divide America.' Chapter headings such as 'Hitler Is Our Enemy', 'Rebuilding Europe On Nazi Lines' and 'The United States Under Nazi Pressure' could not help but attract newspaper attention. Although Miller's strident tone led the *New York Herald Tribune* to conclude that Miller had himself become 'Nazi minded', there is no doubt that his work was a great success. Indeed, as shall be shown in due course, *You Can't Do Business with Hitler* can seriously be described as the most influential book of the twentieth century.

However, it would take more than a book to convince the American public of the need to wage war on Hitler. Whatever Roosevelt and his advisers believed about the threat posed by Nazi Germany, the American people simply did not want to go to war with her. A Gallup Poll on 22 October 1941 indicated that only 17 per cent of Americans were in favour of fighting Hitler. (In fact, no opinion poll carried out in 1941 showed more than 20 per cent favouring war with Germany.) According to Robert Sherwood, there was more interest shown by the American public in the Army–Notre Dame football game than in the sinking of the *Reuben James*. Sherwood cited two reasons for this attitude. Firstly, the sailors who died were volunteers; the American public would have held a very different attitude if their conscripted sons were being used to protect Atlantic convoys. Secondly, it was the German U-boat campaign of 1917 which had brought America into the First World War and most Americans in 1941 did not see the sinking of ships in the Atlantic as sufficient cause to go to war again.

'Americans want war so little,' Harold Ickes, FDR's Secretary of the Interior, noted in his diary, where he recorded that his countrymen were more interested in enjoying themselves than in 'the fundamental verities of life'. These were sentiments that were not lost on Hitler.

5

This Tremendous Episode

The swastika-strewn Munich beer cellar was heaving with activity and excitement. The Nazi Old Guard (*die Altkämpfer*) had gathered on the evening of 8 November 1941 in the birthplace of their movement for the most important anniversary in their calendar – more special even than 30 January 1933, the date of Hitler's accession to the Chancellorship of Germany. On the morning of 9 November 1923, Hitler – accompanied by Ludendorff, the man who effectively ran Germany in the latter stages of the First World War – led the original Nazi Party faithful out of the Bürgerbräukeller and through the streets of Munich in an attempt to overthrow the Government of Bavaria by force. The attempt failed miserably when the authorities fired on the Nazis and scattered them. Hitler, who dislocated his shoulder in the mêlée, was arrested and briefly imprisoned. Göring was badly wounded and smuggled into Austria by his wife (where the sub-standard medical treatment he received turned him into a drug addict). Yet the legend of the *Beer Hall Putsch* as a heroic moment was founded, and each year Hitler returned to the beer cellar to address his old comrades.[1]

To great cheers and applause, Hitler arrived and marched to the rostrum with his strange, unmanly gait (which Goebbels, the Nazi propaganda chief, tried to ensure never appeared on film). The expectation was perhaps greater than usual. If the Führer intended to respond to Roosevelt's latest 'provocations' in the battle of the Atlantic,

---

[1] The Bürgerbräukeller was destroyed on 9 November 1939 in a still unexplained assassination attempt on Hitler, who had left the hall a few minutes before the bomb exploded. Seven people were killed and sixty injured. It has been suggested that the bomb was planted on Hitler's orders in the hope of blaming the British Government for the attempt on his life. Subsequent anniversary celebrations were held in the more salubrious Löwenbräu beer cellar.

this would be a suitable moment. In a radio broadcast a few weeks before, Churchill had asked why Hitler had not declared war on America. It was not, the Prime Minister pointed out, through any love for American institutions or a lack of pretext. After all, Churchill reflected, Hitler had murdered half a dozen countries for far less. Murderous thoughts seemed to be rarely far from Hitler's mind, but now, he concluded, standing before his raucous Party faithful (the men who, Goebbels once boasted, would jump out of the window if he told them to), was not an appropriate time to express them. Hitler's tone was in fact restrained: 'President Roosevelt has ordered his ships to shoot the moment they sight German ships. I have ordered German ships *not* to shoot when they sight American vessels, but to defend themselves when attacked. I will have any German officer court-martialled who fails to defend himself.'

Since the fall of France the previous summer, when it became clear that Britain was depending for her survival on American goods, Hitler had been under pressure from his naval chiefs to take strong action against the United States. However, Hitler made it clear that he wanted to avoid any incident with America, and in the maintenance of this policy he showed remarkable, and quite uncharacteristic, forbearance. In March 1941, he denied Grand Admiral Raeder permission to attack without warning American warships which were escorting UK-bound convoys as far as Iceland. He also took disciplinary action against German officers who transgressed his instructions, such as the master of the vessel which sank the US merchant ship *Robin Moor*, and the captain of the *U-253* who spotted the American battleship *Texas* within the German-proclaimed blockade zone and attempted to attack her. He ruled that the American occupation of Iceland on 9 July was not an entry into the war by the USA, but 'an act of provocation which should be ignored'. Roosevelt's 'shoot on sight' speech of 17 September, in which he described German warships as 'rattlesnakes', did indeed infuriate Hitler, but he soon recovered his cool, as his address to his *Altkämpfer* showed.

Hitler's determination not to be drawn into war with America is perfectly understandable. He knew from personal experience that it had been America's late entry into the First World War on the Allied side which defeated Imperial Germany. He had taken part (and been gassed) in Ludendorff's massive spring offensive of 1918, which came within an ace of defeating the French and British armies, and which was thwarted only by the arrival of large numbers of fresh American 'doughboys' (one of whom was William Donovan). As a result, Hitler had no intention of fighting America at the same time as the Soviet Union and Britain. Once he had disposed of his European foes, he would deal with America in whatever way was necessary. This was a point he made time and again as he rejected requests from his naval command to answer Roosevelt like with like.

Early in the Soviet campaign, he told Raeder that the German successes in Russia would have 'a favourable effect on the U.S.A. and Japan' and that America would be less inclined 'to enter the war due to the threat from Japan which will then increase'. (Hitler's alliance with Japan, which will be discussed in due course, was designed to keep America out of the war by threatening her with a two-ocean conflict.) Later in the year, Raeder was told by his Führer that a 'victorious campaign on the Eastern front will have a tremendous effect on the whole situation and probably on the attitude of the U.S.A.'

The word 'attitude' should be noted here. Hitler seemed to be saying that, once Stalin had been defeated (and presumably, Britain too), Roosevelt might then conclude that Germany was too powerful to fight and that she should be left alone to establish the 'European New Order'. In fact, in his *Testament*, in an extract dictated on 18 February 1945, Hitler bemoaned the fact that Japan did not help him attack the Soviet Union, adding, 'We should have liquidated Bolshevism by the time winter came [1941-1942], and Roosevelt would have hesitated to take on adversaries as powerful as our two selves.'

In late August 1941, Hitler and Mussolini held a conference of their own in response to the much publicized 'Atlantic Conference' of Roosevelt and Churchill. The meeting, which was held partly at the *Wolfsschanze* and partly at the respective headquarters in the Soviet Union of Field Marshals Hans von Kluge and Gerd von Rundstedt, produced a communiqué on the 'European New Order' in which the two dictators promised to work towards the creation of a Europe freed from both the Bolshevik menace and 'plutocratic exploitation', and able to resist external interference. According to Hitler, this 'New Order' would exist under the direction of a 'New Germany' in which 'all privileges, classes, prejudices and so on' would be removed. Hitler's *Table Talk* during late 1941 sheds a great deal of light on how he saw the future for Europe under German hegemony:

> ...We must no longer allow Germans to emigrate to America. On the contrary, we must attract the Norwegians, the Swedes, the Danes, and the Dutch into our Eastern territories. They'll become members of the German Reich.
>
> ...We shall populate [Russia] and Europeanise it. With this object we have undertaken the construction of roads that will lead to the southernmost part of the Crimea and to the Caucasus. These roads will be studded along their whole length with German towns and around these towns our colonists will settle.
>
> ...There's only one duty: to Germanize this country by the immigration of Germans and to look upon the natives as Redskins.[2]
>
> ...When we are masters of Europe, we will have a dominant position in the world. A hundred and thirty million in the Reich, ninety in the Ukraine. Add to these the other states of the New Europe and we'll be 400 millions as compared with the 130 million Americans.

When Hitler was in this position, he would turn his attention to America, but not before. This, one suspects, was a prospect which Hitler would have enjoyed, for he regarded America with contempt. To Hitler, all democracies were weak, effeminate and corrupt. For example, he saw Britain as 'socially the most backward state in Europe, a state managed solely for the benefit of a relatively small upper class'

---

[2] Morality aside, Hitler's decision to treat the Russians as savages to be slaughtered or herded around was a major blunder. He ignored advice that 'Only Russia can conquer Russia' and that his best strategy was to portray himself as the liberator of the Russian people from their tyrannical ruler, Joseph Stalin, who was indeed hated by large sections of the Soviet population. It is interesting to record that Field Marshal Ewald von Kleist, who ignored Hitler's orders and treated the Russians in a civilized manner, was imprisoned by Stalin after the war for alienating the Soviet people 'through mildness and kindness'. The Field Marshal died in Russia in 1954 and is buried there in an unmarked grave.

which manipulated the democratic process in order to maintain a system that was 'a paradise for the few', but which offered 'the masses only untold misery – miserable food, miserable clothing and, above all, miserable housing...'

The United States, however, struck a particular note of disdain from him. In August 1941, he told Mussolini that he 'could not, for anything in the world, live in a country like the U.S.A., whose conceptions in life are inspired by the most grasping commercialism and which does not love any of the loftiest expressions of the human spirit such as music.' In fact, he saw no future for America, which he regarded as a decayed country, rent with racial problems and social inequalities. According to Albert Speer, Hitler's young architect friend who had been tasked to transform Berlin into the futuristic *Germania*, the Führer thought there was no such thing as an American people, but merely a group of immigrants who came to the United States from all over the world. 'How,' he asked friends, 'could one expect a State like that to hold together – a country where everything is built on the dollar?'

The psychological battle between Roosevelt and Hitler began almost as soon as the two men were in power. Shortly after moving into the White House in March 1933, Roosevelt called upon the major countries of the world to disarm and abolish all offensive weapons. In reply, Hitler told the Reichstag that he was prepared to disband Germany's 'entire military establishment' provided that Germany's neighbours did likewise. This demand for equal treatment sounded reasonable, but it soon became clear not only that Hitler was intent on recovering the territory lost by Germany following her defeat in the First World War, but that he was also prepared to use force to achieve this. Roosevelt, in his famous Chicago speech of 5 October 1937, called for Germany and the other 'aggressor nations', Japan and Italy, to be 'quarantined'.

In the late summer of 1938, Europe hovered on the brink of war as a result of Hitler's demand for the Sudetenland, the German speaking part of Czechoslovakia, to be restored to Germany. (In reality, Hitler wanted the whole of Czechoslovakia.) In late September that year, Roosevelt wrote twice to Hitler, asking him not to break off the diplomatic negotiations which were then under way and resort to violence, as the Führer was threatening to do. The American people wanted peace, FDR told Hitler, but 'in the event of a general war they face the fact that no nation can escape some measure of the consequences of such a world catastrophe'. In his reply, Hitler stated that Germany was not to blame for the existence of the Sudeten German problem and that it was up to the Czech Government as to whether there would be war or not.

War was avoided that autumn, but only because the British and French governments submitted to Hitler's threats and, via an agreement signed in Munich, allowed Hitler to annex the Sudetenland. On his return to England, Neville Chamberlain, the British Prime Minister, declared that he had obtained 'Peace with Honour', but in reality he had obtained only a postponement of hostilities. Within a few months, Hitler took over the whole of Czechoslovakia and turned his attention to Poland, which was created after the First World War in part from territory which had belonged to Imperial Germany. It was this claim which sparked off war between Germany and the Allied democracies, Britain and France, in September 1939.

On 14 April, Roosevelt had made yet another personal appeal to Hitler. In an open letter, FDR listed a number of European and Middle East countries, which included Poland, and asked Hitler if he was willing to give an assurance to these countries that he would not attack them or their possessions in the next 10 years, provided that reciprocal promises were given. Such assurances, Roosevelt went on, would make it possible for nations, including the United States, to discuss peacefully 'two essential problems' – the armament race, which was proving economically ruinous, and 'the most practical manner of opening up avenues of international trade to the end that every Nation of the earth may be enabled to buy and sell on equal terms in the world market as well as to possess assurance of obtaining the materials and products of peaceful economic life.'

On 28 April, Hitler responded to Roosevelt's letter in a speech to the Reichstag which was heard in the United States, where English translations were distributed by the German Embassy. William Shirer, the experienced American journalist, considered the speech the most brilliant he ever heard the Führer give. 'For sheer eloquence, craftiness, irony, sarcasm and hypocrisy,' Shirer wrote, the speech attained an unsurpassed level. The result was a propaganda coup for Hitler where radio listeners actually heard Reichstag members guffawing as Hitler, displaying great timing, disposed of Roosevelt's letter point by point, stopping on each occasion to use the word 'Antwort' (answer) before delivering his response.

'Mr Roosevelt' maintained, Hitler declared, that all international problems could be solved at the council table. Hitler's 'Answer' was to point out that America herself refused to join the League of Nations. Moreover, the 'freedom of North America was not achieved at the conference table any more than the conflict between the North and South was decided there.' Turning to Roosevelt's request for an assurance that Germany would not attack the countries mentioned in his letter, Hitler read out the list (deftly omitting Poland) and then, to howls of laughter from Reichstag members, he gave his 'Answer', saying that he had asked all the countries on the list if they felt themselves threatened by Germany, and that 'The reply was in all cases negative.' Hitler could not speak for certain countries on the list, such as Syria and Palestine, which were then occupied by 'the military agents of democratic states' (i.e. France and Britain).

Hitler did not object to answering Roosevelt's questions about European affairs, although he knew that if he ever asked about US policy in Latin America, he would be referred to the 'Monroe Doctrine', which had been invented by the American Government to prevent outside interference in the affairs of the western hemisphere, and told to mind his own business. Elaborating, Hitler gave an assurance about the western hemisphere: 'I here solemnly declare that all the assertions which have been circulated in any way concerning an intended German attack or invasion on or in American territory are rank frauds and gross untruths, quite apart from the fact that such assertions, as far as the military possibilities are concerned, could have their origin only in a stupid imagination.' As intended, these remarks produced uproarious laughter in the Reichstag. However, Hitler was making a serious point, namely that he had no intention of repeating an enormous blunder committed by Germany during the First World War.

Shortly after Ludendorff's decision in early 1917 to wage unrestricted submarine warfare in the Atlantic, the German Foreign Minister, Arthur Zimmermann, sent a coded telegram to the Mexican Government with the suggestion that, in the event of war with America, Germany should form an alliance with Mexico. Under this pact, Mexico would receive generous financial support from Germany and be helped to retrieve land which she had lost to America in the war of 1846–8. Unfortunately for Germany, this telegram, in one of the greatest espionage coups of all time, was snatched from the ether and deciphered in England by the cryptographers of the Royal Navy's Room 40, which was under the control of the legendary intelligence agent, Rear-Admiral Sir William Reginald ('Blinker') Hall, who ensured that this gross interference by Germany in the affairs of America and her neighbours came to the notice of the US Government and press. The resultant furore virtually guaranteed America's entry into the First World War.

Nevertheless, that Hitler posed a threat to the western hemisphere was, from the outset, a central theme of Roosevelt's anti-Nazi propaganda. In his 'quarantine' speech of 5 October 1937, Roosevelt warned his listeners, 'Let no one imagine that America will escape, that the Western Hemisphere will not be attacked.' In his 'fireside chat' of 29 December 1940, when he declared that America must become 'the great arsenal of democracy', Roosevelt told his listeners that 'the vast resources and wealth of this American hemisphere constitute the most tempting loot in all the round world' for the Nazis, and that 'any South American country in Nazi hands would always constitute a jumping-off place for a German attack on any one of the other Republics of this hemisphere.'

When Rudolf Hess, the Deputy-Führer, flew to Britain in May 1941 in an apparent attempt to bring about peace between Britain and Germany, Roosevelt asked Churchill to provide him with any information supplied by Hess on what 'Germany's plans really are in relation to the United States or to other parts of the Western Hemisphere, including commerce, infiltration, military domination, encirclement of the United States etc.' FDR thought that such information would be 'valuable to public opinion' in America and should be featured separately from anything else provided by Hess. However, Churchill was unable to supply such material, almost certainly because Hess had no information on the western hemisphere to divulge.

This propaganda campaign reached its peak in Roosevelt's 'Navy and Total Defense Day Address' on 27 October 1941, when – in the same speech as the one in which he declared that, following the exchange of fire between the USS *Kearny* and a German U-boat, 'the shooting has started' – FDR produced startling evidence which seemed to bear out all that he had been saying about Hitler's intentions towards the western hemisphere.

> ...I have in my possession a secret map made in Germany by Hitler's Government – by the planners of the new world order. It is a map of South America and a part of Central America, as Hitler proposes to reorganize it. Today in this area there are fourteen separate countries. But the geographical experts of Berlin have ruthlessly obliterated all existing boundary lines; they have divided South America into five vassal states, bringing the whole continent under their domination. And they have also so arranged it that the territory of one of these puppet states includes the Republic of Panama and our great life line – the Panama Canal.
>
> That is his plan. It will never go into effect.
>
> This map, my friends, makes clear that the Nazi design is not only against South America but against the United States as well.
>
> Your Government has in its possession another document, made in Germany by Hitler's Government. It is a detailed plan, which, for obvious reasons, the Nazis did not wish and do not wish to publicize just yet, but which they are ready to impose, a little later, on a dominated world – if Hitler wins. It is a plan to abolish all existing religions – Catholic, Protestant, Mohammedan, Hindu, Buddhist, and Jewish alike. The property of all churches will be seized by the Reich and its puppets. The cross and all other symbols of religion are to be forbidden. The clergy are to be forever liquidated, silenced under penalty of the concentration camps, where even now so many fearless men are being tortured because they have placed God above Hitler.

In the place of the churches of our civilization, there is to be set up an International Nazi Church — a church which will be served by orators sent out by the Nazi Government. And in the place of the Bible, the words of *Mein Kampf* will be imposed and enforced as Holy Writ. And in the place of the cross of Christ will be put two symbols — the swastika and the naked sword.

The god of Blood and Iron will take the place of the God of Love and Mercy. Let us well ponder that statement which I have made tonight.

Hans Thomsen, the German Chargé d'Affaires in Washington, informed his government of the President's allegations. On 1 November, Joachim von Ribbentrop, Hitler's Foreign Minister, issued the following statement:

(1) There does not exist in Germany any map drawn up by the Reich Government regarding a partition of Central and South America, nor any document prepared by the Reich Government concerning abolition of religions of the world. In both instances therefore forgeries of the crudest and most brazen kind must be involved.

(2) The allegations as to a German conquest of South America and to an abolition of religions and churches in the world and their replacement by a National Socialist church are so ludicrous and absurd that the Reich Government sees no need for discussing them.

There were certainly many Americans who thought that (for once) Ribbentrop was telling the truth and that their President, wittingly or otherwise, was using forged documents for propaganda purposes. This was a suspicion strengthened by Roosevelt's refusal to allow the documents in question to be scrutinized by the media on the grounds that to do so would compromise the source which supplied the map and threaten the supply of future material. Senator Burton Wheeler, FDR's leading isolationist opponent in Congress, alleged that these documents had been forged by William Stephenson's British Security

Co-ordination (BSC) intelligence organization and passed to the White House by his old enemy 'Wild Bill' Donovan.[3]

In his biography of Stephenson, *The Quiet Canadian*, the distinguished writer H. Montgomery Hyde, who worked for Stephenson during the war, confirms that Stephenson did pass the map to Donovan who forwarded it to Roosevelt. Montgomery Hyde claims, though, that the map was genuine and that it had been stolen from a German courier in Brazil. On the other hand, the German archives, which were captured after the war, contain no mention of these documents and show that Hitler had no intention of invading South America.

In fact, Adolf Berle, the Chairman of the Interdepartmental Committee on Intelligence and Security at the State Department, told his superior Cordell Hull, the Secretary of State, that the BSC had been passing forged documents to the American authorities in an attempt to influence public opinion in America. There is certainly evidence that Roosevelt's broadcast helped with the passage of the amendments to the Neutrality Acts which FDR had requested and which at one time was seriously in doubt. Moreover, the allegations that Hitler intended to abolish all established faiths would have struck a chord in middle America where religion was a very powerful force. It is worth noting that, when he declared an unlimited emergency in America on 27 May, FDR told his listeners: 'The Nazi world does not recognize any God except Hitler; for the Nazis are as ruthless as the Communists in the denial of God.'

In an interview in 1986 (he died in 1989 at the age of 93), Stephenson repeated the courier story, but conceded that the documents in question might not have reflected the policy of Hitler's Government. Like many people in the espionage business, Stephenson seems to have had difficulty in distinguishing between fact and fiction. As far as can be seen, there is no truth in his once widely publicized and credited claims that Churchill gave him the codename 'Intrepid' and that he acted as a secret intermediary between the Prime Minister

---

[3] In *You Can't Do Business with Hitler*, Douglas Miller likened Hitler to the Prophet Muhammad and claimed that Hitler intended to abolish the existing religions in his New Europe and replace them with a faith reflecting Nazi doctrine (pages 70–2). As will be described, Miller became Donovan's assistant shortly after publishing his book.

and Roosevelt. In all probability, Stephenson never met Churchill and never set foot inside 10 Downing Street.

What is not in doubt is Stephenson's closeness to Donovan, a position which was to help make the Canadian the first non-American to receive the Medal of Merit, the highest civilian decoration the United States has to offer. Stephenson, a slightly built man, was known in intelligence circles as 'Little Bill', whereas the bulky Donovan was 'Big Bill'. In a letter to Roosevelt, Donovan wrote that he knew Stephenson well and that he had 'the greatest confidence in his judgment'. This relationship became of great importance to both Britain and America when FDR made Donovan his spymaster.

In early 1941 Donovan submitted a paper to FDR entitled 'Memorandum of Establishment of Service of Strategic Information', in which he laid the groundwork for the creation of an intelligence organization. This document, which had been compiled with the close co-operation of William Stephenson and his UK colleagues (including Admiral John Godfrey, the Chief of Naval Intelligence and his deputy, Ian Fleming, the creator of James Bond), clearly impressed Roosevelt, for on 11 July 1941, he announced that William Donovan was to become his 'Coordinator of Information' (COI), which would require Donovan to 'collect and assemble information and data bearing on national security from the various departments and agencies of the Government' and to 'analyse and collate such materials for the use of the President and such other officials as the President may designate.'

In plain language, this meant that Donovan was to set up an espionage organization, which would gather intelligence on America's potential enemies and carry out clandestine operations, propaganda, psychological warfare and sabotage against them. Donovan's COI of 1941 grew first into the much larger Office of Strategic Services — which under the direction of 'Wild Bill' carried out 'cloak and dagger' operations against Hitler from 1942 onwards — and then after the war into the Central Intelligence Agency.

Brigadier Lee, the US Military Attaché at the US Embassy in London, was pleased by the news and on 14 July wrote to Donovan to say that he was 'extremely gratified that something is finally going to be done to consolidate or to collate all the information which reaches Washington by way of a dozen different channels', a state of affairs which alarmed Lee, who saw the need in the crisis facing America to put inter-departmental rivalries aside so that vital decisions could be made which were based on the proper analysis of all existing intelligence.

However, Donovan's appointment was not welcomed elsewhere in the US intelligence establishment. On 21 July, Lee recorded in his diary that Donovan was encountering 'tremendous opposition' and that he was engaged in a 'frightful row' with 'Stimson and Knox and Marshall and Stark'. Bitter resentment also came from the Federal Bureau of Investigation (FBI), then run by the legendary (some might say notorious) J. Edgar Hoover, who saw Donovan's appointment as a totally unwarranted encroachment upon his own territory. (The FBI kept Donovan under surveillance during the war and maintained an enormous file on him which was released only in 1980. During the war, Donovan was injured in a hit-and-run incident in Washington by a car thought to have belonged to the FBI.)

Another person who was angry at Donovan's appointment was the arch-isolationist himself, Senator Burton Wheeler. In the *Congressional Record* for August 1941, Wheeler, in a reference to the aftermath of the Teapot Dome scandal mentioned earlier, described 'Wild Bill' as the 'man who conducted my prosecution' and, along with 'all the sleuths in the Department of Justice', carried out investigations into other senior American politicians. This experience, Wheeler believed, made Donovan 'a fitting man to head the Gestapo of the United States'.

Needless to say, 'Little Bill' Stephenson held a very different view. It was with relief that he told his superior, Sir Stewart Menzies, the head of British intelligence in London, that his friend had been placed 'in a position of such importance to our efforts'. The very fact that Donovan could expect little help from existing American intelligence organiza-tions made the relationship between Stephenson's network and Donovan's COI all the closer. Indeed, Donovan later stated that he had learned all he knew about espionage from the British. Stephenson, according to H. Montgomery Hyde, considered Donovan's COI to be the American counterpart 'in fact if not in name' of his own BSC.

Co-operation, which started at once, covered all aspects of the espionage business. Stephenson's own deputy, Colonel Charles

Howard Ellis, acted as adviser to Donovan who took up occupancy in the Executive Office Building, conveniently and appropriately located next door to the White House. The COI received much of its early intelligence from BSC sources. The people recruited into the intelligence world by Donovan — some of them by public advertising, a practice only recently adopted by the British Government — were trained initially in BSC schools in Canada (where the forgeries mentioned by Roosevelt in his speech were almost certainly made). Selected officers studied in Britain at the Special Operations Executive, the organization which Churchill had tasked to 'set Europe ablaze' through subversive warfare. The BSC helped Donovan to establish a world-wide clandestine communication network, and let it be known that, in the event of America's entry into the war, the two short-wave radio services under its control (covering Europe, Africa and the Far East) would be made available to the CIO for propaganda purposes. Such was this assistance that in September 1941, Major Desmond Morton, Churchill's liaison officer with the Secret Service, told the Prime Minister's military secretary that 'to all intents and purposes U.S. Security is being run for them at the President's request', and warned that this should be kept secret 'in view of the furious uproar it would cause if known to the isolationists'.

Morton had no need to remind Churchill of this last point, for espionage was not the only area of Anglo-American co-operation which was then being kept concealed from Senator Wheeler and his cronies.

Since late 1940, British and American military staffs had been engaged in discussions designed to formulate a joint strategy in the event of America's entry into war. A US delegation, under Admiral Ghormley, travelled discreetly to London in August 1940. More formal talks, involving Canada as well as the US and Britain, took place in great secrecy in Washington between January and March. The British delegates wore civilian clothes and carried documentation which showed them to be advisers to the 'British Publishing Commission'. All of this was necessary to conceal the discussions not from the Germans but the isolationists, who, it was said, worried Roosevelt and Marshall far more. As Robert Sherwood pointed out, it would have been no disaster if the decisions reached during these talks were revealed to the

Germans or the Japanese. However, if the isolationists in Congress or the press had learned about these plans, then America's preparations for war and Lend-Lease could have been wrecked.

The plans agreed upon were not binding and took into consideration a variety of possibilities. The principle was accepted, however, that Germany was a much greater threat than Japan and that, in the event of America's entry into the war, the main thrust of the Allies would be directed against Hitler. A land offensive was not then considered, but it was agreed that the initial measures to be taken against Germany would be blockade and aerial bombing, together with subversive activities and propaganda.

All of this reflected the views of General George C. Marshall, the sphinx-like and ruthlessly efficient officer whom Roosevelt had personally selected for the crucial post of Chief of Staff over the head of more senior soldiers in the summer of 1939. In a paper entitled the 'Joint Board Estimate of United States Over-all Production Requirements', Marshall and his naval subordinate, Admiral Harold Stark, drew up their own detailed appraisal of America's strategic position and submitted it to President Roosevelt on 11 September 1941. Robert Sherwood, who reproduces this paper almost verbatim in his book on Harry Hopkins,[4] calls it 'one of the most remarkable documents of American history'. It is certainly essential to a proper understanding of America's role in the Second World War and beyond.

After naming Germany, Japan, Italy and Vichy France as 'assumed potential enemies', the Estimate listed the major national objectives of the United States as:

> ... preservation of the territorial, economic and ideological integrity of the United States and the remainder of the Western Hemisphere; prevention of the disruption of the British Empire; prevention of the further extension of Japanese territorial dominion; eventual establishment in Europe and Asia of balances of power which will most nearly ensure political stability in those regions and the future security of the United States; and, so far as practicable, the

---

[4] See Sherwood, *The White House Papers of Harry Hopkins*, pages 413–23.

establishment of regimes favourable to economic freedom and individual liberty.

The Estimate made it clear that these aims could not be obtained if military action were restricted to the western hemisphere: 'These national policies can be effectuated in their entirety only through military victories outside this hemisphere, either by the armed forces of the United States, by the armed forces of friendly Powers, or by both.'

The Estimate stated that, if Germany succeeded in conquering Europe, she might 'wish to establish peace with the United States for several years, for the purpose of organizing her gains, restoring her economic situation, and increasing her military establishment, with a view to the eventual conquest of South America and the military defeat of the United States.' During this period, according to the Estimate, Germany might try to destabilize South America as a precursor to military involvement. On the other hand, it was conceivable that Germany would try to gain a foothold in South America immediately. Likewise, if Japan defeated China and Russia, she would probably seek peace in order to establish her 'East Asia Co-Prosperity Sphere'.

The Estimate went on to outline what should be America's Major Military Policy.

10. It is believed that the overthrow of the Nazi regime by action of the people of Germany is unlikely in the near future, and will not occur until Germany is upon the point of military defeat. Even were a new regime to be established, it is not at all certain that such a regime would agree to peace terms acceptable to the United States.

11. Assuming the truth of the views expressed in the preceding paragraphs, it is the opinion of the Joint Board that Germany and her European satellites can not be defeated by the European Powers now fighting against her. Therefore, if our European enemies are to be defeated, it will be necessary for the United States to enter the war, and to employ a part of its armed forces offensively in the Eastern Atlantic and in Europe or Africa.

12. The Joint Board also holds the view that, if, under present circumstances, Japan should advance against the British in Malaya and against the Dutch in the Netherlands East Indies, British and

Dutch forces probably could not successfully withstand such an advance in the absence of active military assistance by the United States...

After extensively reviewing Germany's probable strategy — which is summarized as 'the complete military and political domination of Europe, and probably of North and West Africa' — as well as Japan's aim to create its 'East Asia Co-Prosperity Sphere', the Estimate discussed the 'Major Strategy of the United States and its Associates'.

21. The Joint Board is convinced that the first major objective of the United States and its Associates ought to be the complete military defeat of Germany. If Germany were defeated, her entire European system would collapse, and it is probable that Japan could be forced to give up much of her territorial gains, unless she had already firmly established herself in such strength that the United States and its Associates could not afford the energy to continue the war against her.

22. An inconclusive peace between Germany and her present active military enemies would be likely to give Germany an opportunity to reorganize continental Europe and to replenish her strength. Even though the British Commonwealth and Russia were completely defeated, there would be important reasons for the United States to continue the war against Germany, in spite of the greatly increased difficulty of attaining final victory. From this it follows that *the principal strategic method employed by the United States in the immediate future should be the material support of present military operations against Germany, and their reinforcement by active participation in the war by the United States while holding Japan in check pending future developments* [original italics].

This was indeed an extraordinary document for an extraordinary time. Here, in September 1941, Roosevelt was being advised by his top military men to enter the war at once in order to bring about the 'complete military defeat of Germany' and the eventual establishment of a 'balance of power' in Europe and Asia designed to ensure political stability and the security of the United States.

The destruction of the Nazi regime, it must be noted here, was not enough for Marshall and Stark, who surely ventured into the realm of politics when they told their President that a new German Government might not agree to America's peace terms (which were not mentioned). In short, even before America entered the war, Roosevelt's Government sought to ensure that there would be no German equivalent of Talleyrand, Napoleon's Foreign Minister who, convinced that his master was out to destroy France and possibly the whole of European civilization, helped bring down the Bonapartist regime and then played a leading role in the creation of the peace which followed the battle of Waterloo. Marshall's aim in this Estimate, it should be stressed, was to replace an overmighty Germany with a European balance of power. Marshall did not elaborate on what form this balance of power should take, but his stated aim seems to be the origin of the division of the continent which Roosevelt and his successor, Harry Truman, reached in due course with Joseph Stalin.

The Estimate seemed to be in vain, though. If FDR and his advisers wanted the war for which Douglas Miller, the author of *You Can't Do Business with Hitler*, was publicly calling, the great majority of Americans did not. Roosevelt could not declare war and could not easily obtain such a declaration from Congress. He was also hampered by his election promise, of which he was often reminded, that he would not engage in a foreign war 'except in case of attack'. Any further provocations by Roosevelt in the Atlantic could have resulted in his impeachment. In any case, Hitler, as already shown, was clearly intent on ignoring US provocations, a fact stressed by Admiral Stark in a letter to Roosevelt in late September. He wrote that Germany would not declare war on America until she is 'good and ready' and that such a move 'will be a cold-blooded decision on Hitler's part if and when he thinks it will pay, and not until then'. After all, Stark pointed out, Hitler 'had every excuse in the world to declare war on us now, if he were of a mind to'.

It seemed that Roosevelt, in Sherwood's words, 'had no more tricks left' and that he and his advisers were destined to remain frustrated spectators as the epic events of 1941 reached their epoch-making climax. Hitler might destroy the Soviet Union and repopulate the conquered land with German settlers. Churchill might fall and with him British resistance to Nazi Germany. Hitler's 'European New Order' of 400 million people might soon be founded, a colossus which would in time outmatch America economically and militarily. Berlin, and not Washington, would then become the capital of the world.

But it was not to be. Early one December morning, there appeared – literally out of the blue – what Churchill termed 'this tremendous episode in American history'. Around 7.30 a.m. on Sunday 7 December 1941, dozens of carrier-borne Japanese planes swooped out of the clear Hawaii sky over Pearl Harbor, America's so-called 'billion dollar fist' in the Pacific, and bombed and strafed all that they found there. By pure chance, the precious aircraft-carriers were at sea, together with the heavy cruisers. However, the battleships, all neatly tied up in 'battleship row', suffered heavily, with six being sunk and two others damaged. The American aircraft, all tightly parked together as protection against saboteurs, were easy targets: 169 were destroyed and 128 damaged. After launching two waves of attacks, the Japanese carriers withdrew, leaving behind enormous destruction and around 3,500 American dead and wounded.

The following day, Roosevelt appeared before Congress and obtained, with the sole exception of a pacifist member, an uncontested declaration of war against Japan to avenge 'the date that will live in infamy'. There were no isolationists now, at least as far as Japan was concerned. Senator Wheeler spoke for them all when he announced that America had to lick hell out of Japan. Germany, though, was still a different matter.

Roosevelt did not ask Congress for a declaration of war against Germany because he knew he would not get one, as Senator Wheeler had already warned. He also knew, through intercepted and deciphered diplomatic messages, that the Japanese Government was pressuring Hitler to declare war on America. After learning of Pearl Harbor, Ribbentrop, the German Foreign Minister, went to his Führer and told him that the Pact between Germany and Japan was of a defensive nature, which meant that Germany was not obliged to support Japan in an aggressive war and could therefore reject her appeals. Hitler thought this over for a while and then replied: 'The Americans have already opened fire on us, so that a state of war exists even now. Japan will never forget it if we do not take the consequences. Besides, soon, and probably at once, we shall be at war with America, for that has been Roosevelt's aim all along.'

On 11 December 1941, Hitler appeared before the Reichstag and in a lengthy, vitriolic tirade against Roosevelt and America declared war on the United States, whilst revealing that the Axis powers had signed an agreement under which they resolved 'to wage the common war forced upon them by the United States and England' and not to make a separate peace or armistice with these adversaries.

At 2.30 p.m. that afternoon, Ribbentrop summoned Leland Morris, the American Chargé d'Affaires in Berlin, to his office and read out Germany's formal declaration of war to him. This mentioned Roosevelt's 'shoot on sight' policy in the Atlantic and claimed that the United States Government had gone from 'initial violations of neutrality' to the point where it had 'virtually created a state of war'. On handing the declaration to Morris, Ribbentrop said, 'Your President has wanted this war, now he has it.'

Hitler, who had tried to avoid war with America, at least for as long as possible, ended up declaring it on her. There is clear evidence that this paradox preyed on Hitler's mind. His aides noticed that he was uneasy about what had taken place. To one acquaintance he remarked that it was strange how Japan was at war to remove the white man from Asia while Britain was 'fighting against Europe with those swine the Bolsheviks'. On the day after declaring war, Hitler asked Grand Admiral Raeder if there was any possibility that, despite the humiliation of Pearl Harbor, America would give up East Asia for a while, in order to join Britain in defeating Germany and Italy first. Raeder thought this improbable.

Ribbentrop, on the other hand, who had lived in North America and therefore realized what war with the United States would entail, had a very different opinion. Unlike Raeder, he had always sought to avoid war with America and he now found it strange that the Japanese alliance, which had been designed to achieve that aim, had in fact had the opposite effect. With war a reality, he felt obliged to warn his Führer of the danger Germany now faced. 'We have just one year,' he told Hitler, 'to cut off Russia from her American supplies arriving via Murmansk and the Persian Gulf; Japan must take care of Vladivostok. If we don't succeed and the munitions potential of the United States joins up with the manpower potential of the Russians, the war will enter a phase in which we shall only be able to win it with difficulty.' Hitler did not make proper use of his year of grace and the difficulty foreseen by Ribbentrop became an impossibility. As a result, Germany was crushed between the two new superpowers.

Ribbentrop was not the only person who found it curious that the actions of Japan had brought about war between America and Germany. In the United States, there was widespread suspicion that Roosevelt had manipulated events in the Pacific in order to bring America into the war 'through the back door'. Six wartime investigations and one massive post-war Congressional inquiry were held into the surprise attack on Pearl Harbor, but no firm evidence emerged to substantiate the accusations levelled against Roosevelt. Nevertheless, the belief remains that the amazing turn of events in early December 1941 cannot be ascribed to mere fortune and that there is a very worldly solution to a seeming miracle. In his memoirs, Churchill explains it through the words of the English dictator Oliver Cromwell who, when assaulted by an army foolish enough to attack him rather than refuse battle, declared, 'The Lord has delivered them into our hands.'

The immediate question here is why did Hitler decide to drop the (from his point of view) sensible policy of ignoring Roosevelt's provocations and, while he was still fighting the Soviet Union and Britain, declare war on the most powerful country in the world, a step which undoubtedly sealed his fate? In *Germany's Self Destruction*, the distinguished German historian Sebastian Haffner describes this as the most puzzling of Hitler's wartime decisions, and confesses that he does not find any of the explanations advanced by historians very enlightening. And, in *Diplomacy*, Henry Kissinger, the former US Secretary of State, describes Hitler's decision to declare war on America as a 'bizarre' one which has never been 'satisfactorily explained'.

Hitler's contempt for America's moral fibre, his acceptance that war

Hitler declaring war on America in a speech at the Reichstag, 11 December 1941. (Ullstein Bilderdienst.)

with her was probably inevitable as long as Roosevelt was President, and the pressure from Japan were certainly all relevant factors. But there was something more, something which prompted him to take that fateful, and fatal, decision. Robert Sherwood, who knew more than most about what went on in FDR's White House (and indeed FDR's mind), believed that Hitler was so mentally exhausted from the years of psychological warfare with Roosevelt that he could not think rationally.

What is truly strange about this mystery is that it is in fact no mystery at all. In his speech to the Reichstag on 11 December, Hitler *did* give a reason for his decision to declare war on America — a last straw, so to speak, a matter which finally convinced him that war with the United States could not be avoided and that *it was safe for him to act at once to support an ally* and show the German people that their Führer was the dominant player on the international scene. To date, historians have neglected the key fact — simply because they did not study what Hitler actually said in his speech that day. To do this it is necessary to consult the original German speech. This is because anyone who compares Hitler's speech with the English translation of it which appears on page 1,072 of William Shirer's authoritative work, *The Rise and Fall of the Third Reich*, will immediately notice that *the vital sentence in which Hitler gave his reason for declaring war is omitted from the translation.*

Research into this sentence shows not only that Sherwood was correct when he attributed Hitler's decision to psychological pressure, but also that the truth about America's entry into the war is actually to be found not just in Tokyo and Pearl Harbor, but in Washington, Berlin and, of all places, Chicago, the bastion of isolationism. To demonstrate this, it is necessary to go back one year, to December 1940, and to another foreign trip Donovan undertook for his President.

THE TRAP

If your opponent is of choleric temper, seek to irritate him.

SUN Tzu,
ancient Chinese military philosopher

6

Donovan Visits the Balkans

The ungainly four-engined Sunderland flying boat droned on through the seemingly interminable night of the last day of 1940. On board this British plane was William Donovan, celebrating his 58th birthday as best he could on the cold, noisy, and circumspectly circuitous flight from London to the Rock of Gibraltar, the tiny but vital colony-cum-fortress which guarded the entrance to the Mediterranean from the Atlantic Ocean.

A fortnight before, Donovan, accompanied by 'Little Bill' Stephenson, had arrived in England from America, on a trip so mysterious that even Brigadier Lee, the Military Attaché at the US Embassy in London, did not know its purpose. Lee believed that it had to do with Ireland, which was neutral in the war, and that Donovan, of Irish extraction himself, had been sent by Roosevelt in an attempt to persuade the Irish Prime Minister, De Valera, to allow the British to use Irish naval bases, a concession which would be a great help in the battle against the U-boats. Lee believed that if De Valera did not prove accommodating, then 'steps will be taken in the United States to weaken the support which the Irish Free State has always drawn upon so freely'.

Lee was wrong. Donovan had not crossed the Atlantic just to visit Ireland. In London, he met Churchill with whom he discussed the increasing military co-operation between the United States and Britain, a matter on which Lee was heavily engaged. A military delegation was about to depart for Washington and, according to Lee, Churchill told Donovan that he had instructed the delegates to approach 'every question with a completely open mind' and 'to lay their proposals before the United States for the decision of the United States'. In these discussions, the Prime Minister emphasized that any invasion of German-occupied Europe by the Allies must not result in a repetition of the First World War battles in which huge numbers of young British lives had been lost. Donovan, a firm believer in the importance of cunning and deception in war, agreed. If the Germans could not be easily outfought, they could be outwitted.

These discussions, though, were secondary to Donovan's purpose in returning to London at this time. He had been asked by the British Government to visit the Mediterranean, an area which, in view of the greatly reduced threat of a German invasion of the United Kingdom following the RAF victory in the Battle of Britain, now seemed set to become a crucial theatre of operations. At present, the situation was to Britain's advantage. The Royal Navy had effectively crippled the Italian Navy, most notably in a surprise air attack on Taranto Harbour, an operation which was carefully analysed by the Japanese for a venture they had in mind. In North Africa, with a huge Italian army on the verge of being destroyed by a much smaller British force under General Wavell, there were signs that Hitler was preparing to intervene to help his beleaguered ally. Such a move could prove disastrous to Britain's strategic position, especially if the Suez Canal fell. Of immediate importance were the Balkans, where another Italian army was in serious danger of being destroyed by the Greeks and where an anti-Hitler alliance could feasibly be formed amongst the countries there. Donovan had agreed to tour the area, inspect the respective war zones, talk to the governments of the region and then report back to Roosevelt.

Following the success of Donovan's visit to London a few months before, the British Government saw 'Wild Bill' as a man who had Roosevelt's ear and who could help it get the supplies and aid it wanted from America. Indeed, the day after Donovan's arrival, Sir Alexander Cadogan, the head of the Foreign Office, told the Foreign Secretary by memorandum that, according to William Stephenson, Donovan exercised a 'vast degree of influence in the [US] administration' and that he had Colonel Knox, the Secretary of the Navy, 'in his pocket'. It is hardly surprising, then, that before leaving Britain, Donovan received Churchill's blessing and promise of full support. Accompanied by Churchill's military assistant, Colonel Dykes, Donovan boarded the flying boat and set off on his long and hazardous journey.

The Rock of Gibraltar has been recognized since ancient times as a natural fortress of great strategic importance. Rising at its northern side perpendicularly from the ground, the Rock, which is itself a peninsula, stands at the southern tip of Spain, a mere 14 miles from the clearly visible coast of North Africa. The country which controlled 'Gib' controlled the entrance and exit to the Mediterranean. Recognizing this fact, the British took the Rock from a weakened Spain in 1704 and fortified it to the point where it was able to withstand an epic siege during the eighteenth century. It was from its base in Gibraltar that the British fleet under Lord Nelson sailed in October 1805 to nearby Cape Trafalgar, where the great admiral destroyed for ever Napoleon's sea power, thereby laying the basis for the 'Pax Britannica' by which Britain maintained global harmony in the nineteenth century. In 1940, Gibraltar was more formidable than ever, a limestone promontory barely three miles long, but laced with over 30 miles of defensive tunnelling and bristling with guns. If Hitler wanted to turn the Mediterranean into an Axis lake, he would sooner or later have to storm the Rock. To do that successfully, he would need the help of General Franco, El Caudillo, the Fascist ruler of Spain.

The British assessments of Hitler's intentions were correct. After the defeat of the *Luftwaffe* in the Battle of Britain, Hitler concluded that he had no chance of conquering Britain in 1940 (an undertaking in which he probably never believed) and began instead to plan for his life's work — *Operation Barbarossa*, the destruction of the Soviet Union. To that end, he began to increase his military and economic influence in Romania, a neighbour of the Soviet Union and Germany's main supplier of oil. Nevertheless, the opportunity to pressure the British in the Mediterranean was an attractive one. If the British could not be defeated outright, a setback in the Mediterranean might at least force them to negotiate, which Churchill had always refused to do. With this in mind, Hitler met Franco on 23 October at the town of Hendaye on Spain's border with France.

This meeting did not go at all as Hitler had expected. Hitler proposed that Franco enter the war in January 1941 and allow a German detachment to transit Spain and take Gibraltar, which would then immediately revert to Spanish rule. However, to Hitler's surprise, Franco sidestepped these proposals. Spain — he reminded Hitler at great length in his squeaky, high-pitched voice which to the Führer's interpreter, Paul Schmidt, sounded like 'a muezzin calling the faithful to prayer' – was still recovering from a devastating civil war. The country needed, not the risks and hardships of another war, but immediate economic and financial assistance, which Germany might not be able to provide in sufficient quantities. Moreover, if anyone was to take Gibraltar, it would be Spain, not Germany.

Hitler found Franco's attitude infuriating. Franco had won the civil war against the Communist-backed Republicans largely because of the help he had received from Germany and Italy. And now Hitler, the Master of Europe, had flattered Franco by travelling all the way across France on his special train to meet him. Despite all of this, Franco was unwilling to show his 'gratitude'. At one point, Hitler jumped to his feet saying that there was no point in continuing the discussion – a move which would have put the fear of God into many people, as it was presumably meant to do here to Franco. However, El Caudillo refused to give way and Hitler actually returned to his seat. The discussions dragged on until dinner and continued afterwards, but to no avail. After some nine hours of talks, Hitler finally conceded defeat and left Hendaye with only a general declaration from Franco of his intention to enter the war at some unspecified date, provided that Spain first obtained the necessary weapons and supplies. So frustrating did Hitler find this experience that he said that he would rather have three or four teeth extracted than go through such an ordeal again.

If Franco's attitude was a setback for Hitler's plans in the western Mediterranean, the news from Mussolini which reached the Führer as he travelled eastwards through southern France was so serious that he immediately redirected his special train south to Italy and ordered Ribbentrop, the German Foreign Minister, to arrange an urgent meeting with the Italian dictator. But Hitler was too late. As the Führer stepped on to the railway platform in Florence on the morning of 28 October, Mussolini's corpulent frame strode forward with what he proclaimed to be glorious tidings: 'Führer, we are on the march! Victorious Italian troops crossed the Greco–Albanian frontier at dawn today!'

Mussolini had known that Hitler did not want any military adventures in the Balkans for the time being, but had decided to go against the Führer's wishes out of a sense of pique. He resented the fact that Hitler never took him into his confidence about his intentions, even though Germany and Italy were supposed to be close, formal allies. The surprise German move into Romania in early October had been the last straw for Mussolini. 'Hitler always faces me with a *fait accompli*,' he complained to Count Ciano, his playboy son-in-law and Foreign Minister. 'This time,' he declared, 'I am going to pay him back in his own coin. He will find out from the newspapers that I have occupied Greece. In this way the equilibrium will be established.'

Although inwardly furious, Hitler controlled his emotions remarkably well and promised Mussolini his full support in this new campaign. But as his interpreter, Paul Schmidt, noted, the Führer travelled home 'with bitterness in his heart' at the way he had been treated by 'ungrateful and unreliable friends'. No doubt, the likely consequences of Mussolini's actions were preying on Hitler's mind.

As Hitler had feared when he first heard of Mussolini's actions, the Italian invasion of Greece turned into a fiasco. Although greatly outnumbered, the Greek army savaged the Italians and pushed them back into Albania, which had been under Italian control since April 1939. This created a situation which threatened to engulf the whole Balkan peninsula (a notorious tinderbox) in turmoil and to endanger *Barbarossa*. Bulgaria and Yugoslavia might join the war for territorial gain and Russia might intervene to help her Slavic cousins, as she did at the outbreak of the First World War. Greece might seek help from the British, whose air force could attack the Romanian oil fields which were essential to Germany. Turkey might feel unable to stay out of a war where so much was at stake. Clearly, Hitler saw at once, this was a dangerous situation which had to be nipped in the bud.

On 12 November, Hitler issued Directive 12 in which he instructed his generals to organize an army group of some 10 divisions which should be prepared 'if necessary, to occupy the *Greek mainland* north of the Aegean Sea. This will enable the German Air Force to attack targets in the Eastern Mediterranean, and in particular those English air bases which threaten the Romanian oilfields [original italics]'. The British threat was so worrying to Hitler that on 13 December he issued

Directive 20, codenamed 'Marita', which outlined the German plan for the invasion of Greece in March 1941. Hitler also saw the need to write to Mussolini with his assessment of the situation in the Balkans.

In this letter, the Führer declared that, of all the countries in the area, Hungary and Romania had adopted the most 'clear-cut' (i.e. most pro-Axis) attitude. Bulgaria was reluctant to join the Tripartite Pact, due to pressure from the Soviet Union. Yugoslavia was playing for time, but did not look as if she were willing to join the Axis powers. Hitler was hopeful, though, that his military successes would 'improve the psychological climate' in that country. He assured Mussolini that plans were being drawn up and that all that was required from him 'was to stabilise your front in Albania so as to contain at least a part of the Greek and Anglo-Greek forces.' Hitler sent this letter to Mussolini on 31 December, the day that Donovan flew to Gibraltar to begin his grand tour.

For the next two months, Donovan criss-crossed the Mediterranean, inspecting any spot he thought of importance to the Allied cause. He visited Malta, that essential but much-battered British island base in the centre of the Mediterranean, which won the George Cross from the King for the gallantry it displayed against almost constant Axis aerial bombardment. From there he went on to the front line in North Africa, to the trouble spots in the Middle East, to the battlefields in Albania, to British headquarters in Egypt, and to Spain before returning to England. However, it was in the explosive arena of the Balkans that he devoted his greatest effort, for there both the British and American governments saw the chance to do Hitler harm.

Mussolini's rash attack on Greece not only presented the British Government with the opportunity to land an expeditionary force in the Balkans; it also gave Britain a chance to form an anti-Hitler pact amongst the Balkan states, which individually stood little chance against the Axis powers, but united together and allied with Britain could feasibly resist a German onslaught. This was in fact Donovan's prime aim as he toured the area.

Unfortunately, as Donovan reported to British staff officers on his return to England, he found in the Balkans a dispiritedness and a belief that Hitler's rule was preferable to Communism, which was seen there as the fate of the region if Germany were defeated. Turkey refused to join the war until she felt herself ready. King Boris of Bulgaria, for whom Donovan felt the utmost contempt, thought it unjust that peaceful nations like his own 'should be condemned to death'. Donovan shot back, 'I do not call it sentence of death. I call it suicide. If you let the Germans in, we shall not intercede for you at the peace.' Despite this threat, Bulgaria formally joined the Axis powers on 1 March 1941.

Donovan's last point to King Boris — that the democracies would eventually win — was the very essence of the message he sought to spread throughout his trip. He had told the former Grand Mufti of Jerusalem, whom he considered 'a shrewd but second rate crook', that he had only one thing to say: 'America is determined that England shall win this war.' The Spanish Foreign Minister (and Franco's brother-in-law), Surrano Suñer, had recorded his conversation with Donovan, who, convinced that these minutes would be handed to Hitler, said: 'You can tell whoever you are taking those notes for that for every ship England loses America will give her two; and for every destroyer another.' (Donovan may have been a bit unfair to Suñer, who attended the meeting with Hitler at Hendaye. After the meeting, a furious Hitler called Suñer 'a Jesuit swine'.)

Donovan's experience in Yugoslavia had been more promising, albeit not with the ruler of the country, the Oxford-educated Regent, Prince Paul, who was under such German pressure to join the Axis that he reminded Churchill 'of an unfortunate man in a cage with a tiger, hoping not to provoke him while steadily dinner-time approaches.' Paul's external problems were compounded by the patchwork nature of his country, which had been created, without thought of internal harmony, from the remnants of the former Austro-Hungarian Empire after the First World War. The governance of such a nation (if such a title can be applied here), simmering at the best of times in a stew of ancient vendettas, tribal hatreds, and petty enmities, could easily prove impossible if Hitler's pressure continued. As Paul knew very well, there were people in his country who would welcome an alliance with Germany, and there were others who would fiercely oppose such a move. In broad terms, the

Croats in the north were pro-German, while the Serbs, of which General Simovic was one, in the south were not.

Donovan met Prince Paul in late January in the Yugoslav capital, Belgrade, but failed to obtain a promise from him not to join Hitler, even though 'Wild Bill' made it clear that Yugoslavia would receive aid from the democracies if she showed herself willing to resist Germany. However, Donovan found a much more sympathetic ear in General Dusan Simovic, the head of the Yugoslav Air Force, an organization already known to the British Government as, in Churchill's words, 'a clandestine centre of opposition to German penetration into the Balkans and to the inertia of the Yugoslavia Government'. Simovic was impressed with Roosevelt's anti-Hitler broadcasts and was attracted by the promise of aid against the Axis. He told Donovan that he would resist any German encroachment on Yugoslavia and that he would not permit the passage of German troops through his country. In fact, Simovic assured Donovan, Yugoslavia would fight to protect Bulgaria or Greece from the Germans.

As far as British involvement in Greece was concerned, Donovan was strongly in favour of the idea, and before leaving Britain for America he submitted a letter to Churchill saying so. Donovan believed that the Balkans were the one theatre in which the British could beat the Germans, but only with the assistance of Turkey, Yugoslavia and, if possible, Bulgaria. President Roosevelt, Donovan pointed out, could help build up this 'Balkan Front' through direct appeals to the leaders concerned and the promise of war supplies. Another important, indeed decisive, factor in favour of an expedition was the beneficial effect British help to Greece would have on Britain's standing in America. This was especially important at a time when the Lend-Lease Bill was being discussed by Congress. In short, if Britain was not willing to help others who were threatened by Hitler, then Americans might feel that Britain did not deserve any help from Uncle Sam.

In early March, the British War Cabinet, after much debate and anguish, ordered General Wavell, the British Commander-in-Chief in the Middle East, not to advance on Tripoli in an attempt to expel the Axis powers from North Africa (as Wavell's army could probably have done with ease), but instead to send an expeditionary force of over 50,000 men, about half of them New Zealanders and Australians, from Egypt to Greece. On 10 March, Churchill imparted this information to Roosevelt, stating that 'we have felt it our duty to stand with the Greeks, who have declared to us their resolve, even alone, to resist the German invader.' Churchill added ominously: 'Mr. President, you can judge these hazards for yourself.' Churchill did not forget Donovan's contribution and at the end of his message wrote: 'In this connection I must thank you for magnificent work done by Donovan in his prolonged tour of Balkans and Middle East. He has carried with him throughout an animating, heart-warming flame.'

In this crisis, the importance of Yugoslavia was obvious to both sides. Churchill was not content with the pro-British neutrality of the country; he wanted the Yugoslav army to attack the Italians in Albania. In his message to Roosevelt, Churchill wrote with emphasis: '*At this juncture the action of Yugoslavia is cardinal. No country ever had such a chance. If they will fall on the Italian rear in Albania there is no measuring what might happen in a few weeks.*' Hitler, as already shown, wanted Yugoslavia to join the Axis Powers, and knowing that he needed her roads and railways in his forthcoming campaign against the Greek and British armies, he increased the pressure on Prince Paul, to become his formal ally. Churchill, aware of this, wrote to the Yugoslav Prime Minister, Dr Cvetkovic, urging him to resist Germany and insisting that 'the eventual total defeat of Hitler and Mussolini is certain'. Churchill also contacted the British representative in Belgrade and told him 'to pester, nag and bite' the Yugoslav Government to ensure that it did not join the Axis.

However, Hitler was too close and his power too great for Prince Paul's Government to withstand German pressure for long. On 5 March, Hitler met Paul secretly at the Berghof and in a lengthy discussion effectively told him that unless he signed the Tripartite Pact, war between Yugoslavia and the Axis could not be avoided. Paul knew that his country could not survive a German invasion, and that, even though his heart lay with the democracy in which he had been educated, he had to give way. 'I cannot lead [Yugoslavia] to slaughter, and that is what we must expect if we precipitate a war with Germany,' he told his Government. On 25 March, the Yugoslav Premier signed the Tripartite Pact at a special ceremony in Vienna attended by the beaming Führer himself. Hitler had got what he wanted at last. Or so he thought.

Around noon two days later, Field Marshal Keitel and his deputy, General Jodl, were summoned urgently by Hitler to the Reich Chancellery in Berlin. When they arrived, they found their Führer in such a fury that at first he could not speak sensibly. There had been a coup in Belgrade, Hitler raged. Prince Paul had been overthrown and replaced by the anti-German General Simovic. There were signs that Simovic wished to live in peace with Germany, but Hitler did not care what the new 'government' had to say. This was a personal affront which had to be avenged. Gathering his top military advisers around him, Hitler announced his intention to destroy Yugoslavia with 'unmerciless harshness'. So determined was to he do this properly, that he was prepared to postpone *Barbarossa,* the attack on the Soviet Union which had been scheduled to commence on 15 May. He turned to his generals. 'How much military force do you need?' he asked them 'How much time?'

General Simovic had indeed kept his word to Donovan. During the night of 26–27 March, Simovic and his followers removed the 'traitors' who had signed the Tripartite Pact and seized control of the capital, Belgrade, and all important military installations. Prince Paul was forced to abdicate. He fled to Greece with his wife, and the 17-year-old boy-King was installed as Peter II. As dawn broke, Belgrade began to celebrate wildly, with people dancing and singing in the streets. German interests were attacked. Hitler was burned in effigy. Union Jacks and the Stars and Stripes were everywhere to be seen.

The role played by Britain and America in this coup, indeed in the Balkans as a whole, was partly responsible for Hitler's rage. Sir Alexander Cadogan, the head of the British Foreign Office, confirmed in his diary that Anthony Eden, the British Foreign Secretary, had authorized the British representative in Belgrade, Sir Ronald Campbell, to bring about regime change by any means, including a coup. He also disclosed that the British had been giving money to a Serb party which had left the government when the majority decided to concede to

German demands. Of the coup itself, Cadogan recorded: 'General Simovic, to whom Col. Donovan had spoken confidently of the allies' prospects on his visit, became Prime Minister...'

Goebbels, the Nazi propaganda chief, recorded in his diary on 29 March, two days after the coup, that the American Government had admitted giving help to what he termed the 'operetta revolution' in Belgrade. Goebbels concluded that this assistance would not do the Serbs much good, for the USA was far away and retribution was about to follow.

Hitler took seriously the possibility that the Yugoslav army would do as Churchill wished and attack the Italian army in Albania from the rear. After signing, on the evening of 27 March, Directive 25, which outlined his plan to destroy Yugoslavia, Hitler rushed a telegram to Mussolini informing him of the developments in Belgrade. These, Hitler believed, had created a difficult situation: '...we on our part must avoid any mistake if we do not want, in the end, to endanger our whole position.' To this end, Hitler advised his ally to 'cover and screen the most important passes from Yugoslavia into Albania with all available forces' and 'to reinforce your forces on the Italian–Yugoslav front with all available means and with the utmost speed.' Hitler was sure that, if these measures were carried out in silence, his forthcoming operation would be a resounding success. 'That,' he assured Mussolini, 'is my granite conviction.'

On 6 April, Hitler again showed the world what his *Wehrmacht* could do. His *Luftwaffe* bombers, carrying out *Operation Punishment,* began to flatten Belgrade, a defenceless city, in an attack which lasted for three days and killed over 17,000 people. At the same time, the German army invaded both Yugoslavia and Greece. The outcome of this greatly uneven struggle was never in doubt. Yugoslavia surrendered on 17 April, and Greece six days later, forcing the British army to evacuate the European mainland, as it had done at Dunkirk the previous summer. By 27 April, the swastika was flying over the Acropolis in Athens. Yugoslavia was wiped off the map and her territory divided up amongst the Axis powers.

On 4 May, Hitler appeared before the Reichstag and told the delegates that he had never wanted war in the Balkans and that his aim had been to prevent the British entrenching themselves in that region. But the revolution in Belgrade was a matter which had to be dealt with severely: 'You will understand, gentlemen, that when I heard the news of the *coup d'état* in Belgrade, I at once gave orders to attack Yugoslavia. To treat the German Reich in this way is impossible.' On the face of things, it appeared that Donovan's visit had been a total failure. The 'Balkans Front', of which so much had been expected, had been crushed by Hitler with almost contemptuous ease, and Britain had suffered another humiliation through her clear inability to match, let alone beat, the Germans on the field of battle. And yet the venture had not been in vain, for it paid a large bonus by highlighting Hitler's great weakness – his own brand of temper, which Churchill described as 'that convulsive anger which momentarily blotted out thought and sometimes impelled him on his most dire adventures.'

As a result of the decision Hitler took whilst in a blind rage on 27 March, to postpone *Barbarossa* until Yugoslavia was destroyed and the Balkans occupied, the German attack on the Soviet Union did not take place until 22 June – ominously the anniversary of Napoleon's invasion. Historians are generally agreed that this delay was a dreadful mistake, pointing out that it was the ferocious Russian weather which prevented the *Wehrmacht* from destroying Stalin's regime in 1941 and not the Red Army. William Shirer, in his *The Rise and Fall of the Third Reich*, states that this postponement was probably the most catastrophic decision Hitler ever made.

Shirer's judgement here must be qualified. Damaging as the delay in the attack on the Soviet Union was, Hitler's fatal decision was to declare war on America, which, as already shown, he did on 11 December 1941 whilst the battle with Stalin was still raging through the frozen Russian wastelands. However, it is not easy to separate the two decisions, for they both stemmed, in part at least, from the rabid determination Hitler displayed on 27 March that year to annihilate a small country which had wronged both him and his precious creation, the Third Reich.

As Hitler ranted and roared that day to his generals in the Reich Chancellery, ordering death and destruction on a grand scale, there was waiting in an adjoining room a very important visitor to the Reich — Yosuke Matsuoka, the Foreign Minister of Japan. It is no exaggeration to state that what Hitler imparted to this man during his time in Germany sealed the fate of the Axis powers.

7

Except in Case of Attack

On 27 September 1940, the Tripartite Pact between Germany, Italy and Japan was signed in the Hall of the Ambassadors in the Reich Chancellery in Berlin. Under this treaty, Japan joined the Axis powers, recognizing 'the leadership of Germany and Italy in the establishment of a new order in Europe', while receiving the same recognition from those powers for her position of leadership in East Asia. Under a different section of the treaty, the three powers undertook 'to assist one another with all political, economic, and military means, if one of the three Contracting Powers is attacked by a Power at present not involved in the European War or in the Chinese–Japanese conflict.' To emphasize this point, Ribbentrop, Germany's Foreign Minister, announced in a preamble to the signing ceremony: 'Any State, should it harbour the intention of mixing in the final phase of the solution of these problems in Europe or Eastern Asia, or attacking one State signatory to this three-power pact, will have to take on the entire concentrated might of three nations with more than 250 million inhabitants.'

The nation to which Ribbentrop was referring, but diplomatically did not mention, was of course the United States. The main purpose of the Tripartite Pact was to keep America out of the war by threatening her with a two-ocean conflict should she intervene militarily in only one continent. An attack on Germany or Italy by America would mean war in the Pacific with Japan, while an attack on Japanese interests in Asia by the United States would mean war with the Third Reich and Mussolini's Italian empire. There had been friction between Japan and the USA since 1937 when the Japanese army, in a bid to obtain vital strategic material, invaded China, a country long favoured by America and by Roosevelt personally. In 1940, in protest against Japanese actions in China, the American Government imposed a limited embargo on oil and a formal embargo on steel and iron scrap against Tokyo.

As already shown, the creation of the encircling Axis alliance against the United States caused Roosevelt to order an assessment of the strategic threat facing America, an undertaking which culminated in General Marshall's estimate of September 1941, which recommended that America should defeat Germany first, while holding Japan in check. Brigadier Lee, the US Military Attaché in London, reached this conclusion very early on. On 5 October 1940, only a few days after the signing of the Pact, he wrote in his diary: 'The enemies of the world consist of one great and ominous nation and two second-rate ones. The way to deal with the trio is to concentrate on the strong one. When he is knocked out, the others will throw up their hands in a hurry.' Few would fail to identify Lee's 'great and ominous nation' as Nazi Germany. The modern-day reader, though, must surely find it strange to see Japan described by Lee as 'second-rate'. Japan is now a massive economic power and one of the most advanced countries on earth. However in 1940, Raymond Lee, a senior US Army staff officer involved in war planning, seriously equated Japan with Mussolini's Italy, a military joke, and thought that she would rush to surrender once Germany was beaten, an estimation which was wide of the mark. Japan's military performance in the war was impressive, to say the least, and it took the use of atomic weapons against her cities to force her to capitulate, even though her position was by then hopeless.

Nevertheless, it is important to note Lee's opinion here, for the great events of 1941 cannot be fully comprehended unless the gross underestimation of Japan by the western democracies, then still bearing Kipling's 'white man's burden', is appreciated. Before the war, the Japanese were depicted in the west as funny, little yellow men who all wore glasses and who could therefore not shoot straight, let alone fly aeroplanes properly. British army officers posted to the Far East prior to the war were even heard to complain that their men deserved better opponents than the Japanese. This racist nonsense permeated to the highest levels of the British and American governments. In other words, during the crucial diplomatic negotiations between Washington and Tokyo in 1941, it almost certainly never entered Roosevelt's mind that the Japanese Navy had the skill and (as Ernest Hemingway would have said) the *cojones* to sail in secret from Japan to Hawaii, a distance of over 3,000 miles, and attack Pearl Harbor by surprise, any more than it ever occurred to Churchill that in early 1942 a Japanese army of 30,000 men would come rampaging down the Malayan Peninsula and, with humiliating ease, force a British Empire army three times its size to surrender the supposedly impregnable fortress of Singapore.

As a consequence of this failure to understand the true nature of the Japanese people, the western democracies never seriously considered the possibility that Japan would decide to attack not just the vulnerable European empires in Asia, but also America — a country with twice her population and 10 times her war-making capacity. This attitude can be seen reflected in a paper submitted to Harry Hopkins in July 1941 by Sumner Welles, the US Under-Secretary of State, in which he suggested that Japan might seek to expand either into Russia, or deeper into China, or southwards against the European empires in southern Asia. Welles did not even bother to include American targets, for it seemed absurd that Japan would deliberately start a war she could not seriously expect to win.

For obvious reasons, Hitler did not encourage the Japanese to attack America. His aim, as already mentioned, was to use his alliance with Japan to keep America *out of the war* in Europe. To this end, he issued on 5 March 1941 his Directive 24, which was entitled 'Co-operation with Japan', and which sought to '*induce Japan to take action in the Far East* as soon as possible [original italics]'. Such a move, Hitler believed, would 'tie down strong English forces and ... divert the main effort of the United States of America to the Pacific'. Hitler ordered that the common strategy of the Axis powers 'must be represented as the swift conquest of England in order to keep America out of the war'. 'Apart from this,' Hitler wrote, 'Germany has no political, military, or economic interests in the Far East which need in any way inhibit Japanese intentions.'

In immediate practical terms, Hitler wanted the Japanese to take Singapore, Britain's Gibraltar in the east. This was the message that was awaiting Matsuoka, Japan's sophisticated, pro-German Foreign

Minister, who arrived to a great reception in Berlin on 26 March 1941. The importance of the visit can be discerned from the diary of Joseph Goebbels, who was immediately struck by the intelligence of the Foreign Minister when he helped to receive him at the railway station. In accordance with Goebbels's instructions, the streets of Berlin were lined with thousands of dutiful, cheering citizens of the Third Reich. Goebbels recorded in his diary that Berliners welcomed their visitor warmly because they knew how much depended on the success of his visit.

During his meetings with Matsuoka on 27 and 28 March, Ribbentrop sought to impress upon his Japanese counterpart the need to seize Singapore, the key to Britain's vast possessions in Asia. Apart from the damage this would do to Britain, whose morale was thought to be already low, Ribbentrop claimed that the taking of Singapore by the Japanese 'with one decisive stroke' would face Roosevelt with a *fait accompli* in the Pacific and make it difficult for him to take any decisive action against Japan, as he would be sending his fleet into an area already under the control of Japan. Relations with America after Britain was defeated, Ribbentrop declared, would depend on Roosevelt's attitude. When pressed further on this point by Matsuoka, Ribbentrop said that Germany did not have 'the slightest interest in a war with the United States'. The minutes of the meeting record that Ribbentrop elaborated on this: 'The Reich Foreign Minister replied that each [power] would exercise dominion in her own sphere. Germany, together with Italy, would do this in the Euro-African sphere; the United States would have to limit hers to the American continent; and the Far East was reserved for Japan...'

Hitler first saw Matsuoka on the afternoon of 27 March, having recovered somewhat from the rage he experienced that morning on receipt of the news of the coup in Yugoslavia. Britain, the Führer insisted, had already lost the war and was only struggling on because she believed America or Russia would enter the conflict. America, the Führer went on, found herself facing three choices — arm herself, help Britain, or wage war on another front. She could not, according to Hitler, arm herself and help Britain. If she abandoned Britain, however, the latter would be defeated and the United States left to fight the

Axis on her own. All of this, the Führer maintained, presented Japan with a golden opportunity to strike in Asia. Matsuoka agreed that it would be necessary to take Singapore if Japan were to solve her problems in southern Asia — which he was sure she would eventually do, although he could not give a date. He was, he added defensively, not in charge of Japan which, he pointed out, was then under the control of pro-Anglo-Saxon intellectuals with very different views on Japan's future. Matsuoka likened these intellectuals to 'a person who would like to capture the tiger cub but was not prepared to go into the den and take it away from its mother.'

Matsuoka left Germany on 31 March for a visit to Rome, where he was told by Mussolini that America and not the Soviet Union was the main enemy of the Axis. He did not meet Hitler again until his return to Berlin on 4 April. At this meeting, Hitler, who had spent the intervening period planning the annihilation of Yugoslavia and the German occupation of the Balkans, again called for Japan's immediate entry into the war against Britain. On this occasion, though, he spoke at greater length on how he regarded the threat posed by America:

> Germany's warfare against shipping tonnage represented an appreciable weakening not only of England but of America also. Germany had made her preparation so that no American could land in Europe. She would wage a vigorous war against America with her U-boats and her Luftwaffe, and with her greater experience, such as the United States still had to achieve, would be more than a match for America, entirely apart from the fact that the German soldiers were, obviously, far superior to the Americans...

What Hitler said next so surprised Matsuoka that the Führer had to explain what he meant. Here, *Hitler made a historic commitment which the Japanese Government, quite understandably, would one day call upon him to honour.* If Japan attacked Singapore, and war with America resulted from this move, then Germany, Hitler assured his guest, 'on her part would take the necessary steps at once'. It made no difference, Hitler maintained, whether America went to war with Germany first or with Japan. The United States would in any case seek to defeat one country at a time. The Third Reich, Hitler assured his guest, 'would promptly take part in the case of a conflict between Japan and America because the strength of the Allies in the Tripartite Pact lay in their acting in common. Their weakness would be in allowing themselves to be defeated separately.'

Anyone who has studied the Second World War will know that the Axis powers, unlike their much more powerful enemies, signally failed to co-ordinate their strategy and were, as a result, defeated one by one. A prime example of this fatal feature of the Pact can be found in the talks with Matsuoka, where Hitler made a point of not mentioning his planned attack on the Soviet Union. Matsuoka, who left Berlin without committing himself to anything, travelled on to Moscow where, to the astonishment of the diplomatic world including the Third Reich, he signed a five-year neutrality pact with Stalin. The surprise German attack on the Soviet Union on 22 June caused Matsuoka to lose face in Japan and led to his replacement on 16 July by Admiral Toyoda, a pro-American figure who was much less sympathetic to Germany. In this outlook, he shared the views of Admiral Kishisaburo Nomura, the Japanese Ambassador to Washington, who since March 1941 had been carrying on secret discussions with Cordell Hull, the US Secretary of State, in an attempt to reconcile the differences between the two countries over Japan's presence in China and her intentions in Asia.

This is not the place to give a blow-by-blow account of these nego-tiations, which lasted until the very day of the attack on Pearl Harbor. It is sufficient here to draw attention to two salient features of these discussions. The *first* and most obvious was the uncompromising nature of Roosevelt's diplomacy, which made no serious attempt to lure Japan away from her lukewarm German alliance or make any provision for the vital role of face in Asiatic politics.

In his autobiography, *Yankee from the West*, Senator Burton Wheeler, the arch-isolationist, records his belief that war with Japan could have been avoided if Roosevelt had told Cordell Hull 'to negotiate seriously and realistically with the Japanese'. According to Wheeler, Hull's tactic of rejecting and ridiculing the Japanese position, and his use of economic sanctions against Japan, made Tokyo conclude that war, not diplomacy, was the only solution.

Before being hanged as a war criminal in Nuremberg in 1946,

Ribbentrop wrote his memoirs, a document which must be seen as a form of dying declaration and therefore as an attempt by Ribbentrop to bare his soul before meeting his maker. Here, Ribbentrop states that in view of Roosevelt's 'absolute enmity' towards the Third Reich, Germany had no choice other than to seek to ensure that America entered the war as late as possible and that, when that happened, Japan would be on Germany's side. Indeed, so fragile was the Tripartite Pact that Ernst von Weizsäcker, the deeply perceptive head of the German Foreign Office, gained the impression during Matsuoka's visit in March 1941 that Japan might suddenly join the Anglo-Saxon camp, on whose side she had fought in the First World War.

Raymond Lee noticed this sentiment only a few days after the signing of the Tripartite Pact when, on 3 October 1940, he had a conversation with Major-General Tatsumi, his Japanese counterpart in London. Tatsumi told Lee that the Japanese people did not understand the war in China and that the German-trained Japanese officers in charge of policy had signed the Pact with Hitler and Mussolini merely to give the impression that Japan was doing something positive. Tatsumi did not understand how the Germans and Italians could be of assistance to Japan for, as he told Lee, 'they are at such a distance and have so much on their hands that we will have gained nothing by our bargain.'

Roosevelt, however, made no attempt to drive a wedge between Germany and Japan or to entice Japan away from Hitler, a real possibility in view of the economic gifts which he could have used to influence Japanese foreign policy, and the undoubted fact that there were groups within Japan which wanted a peaceful settlement with America.[1] On the contrary, Roosevelt adopted a series of measures which forced the Japanese Government, increasingly under the control of military extremists, to choose between war and national humiliation. The most important act was the oil embargo he imposed on Japan in late July 1941, in which the British and Dutch governments joined, and which left Japan with only a few months' supply of fuel before her

---

[1] By contrast, Roosevelt used these economic gifts to help keep *Spain* out of the war, an important fact considering that Franco's Spain was ideologically (as well as geographically) much closer than Japan to Hitler's Germany.

economy would literally grind to a halt. Consequently, the real possibility arose that the Japanese Government would feel forced to occupy the vulnerable European empires in southern Asia, areas which could provide Japan with the oil and other strategic supplies she needed to survive as an industrial power. So serious did this Japanese threat appear, that it featured as a major point of discussion at the Atlantic Conference between Roosevelt and Churchill in August 1941.

After the famous church service attended by the two leaders on the deck of the *Prince of Wales* in Placentia Bay on 10 August, Sir Alexander Cadogan, the head of the British Foreign Office, held a meeting with Sumner Welles, the US Under-Secretary of State, to discuss documents drawn up by the British Government entitled 'Parallel Communications to the Japanese Government'. These were meant to warn Japan that any further encroachments by her into the south-western Pacific would lead to war, not just with the European powers concerned, Britain and the Netherlands, but also with America. As Welles was leaving the *Prince of Wales* to accompany Roosevelt back to his ship, Churchill took him aside to say that this joint declaration was 'in the highest degree important' and that, without it, there was not much hope left for a peaceful settlement.

Roosevelt took a different view. Although at the conference he seemed to agree with Churchill over the need to issue a joint Anglo-American-Dutch warning, he changed his mind once back in Washington. On 17 August, he issued a vague statement telling the Japanese Government that if it continued to pursue a policy of aggression in Asia, the American Government would 'be compelled to take immediately any and all steps which it may deem necessary toward safeguarding the legitimate rights and interests of the United States and American nationals and toward ensuring the safety and security of the United States.' Nowhere did Roosevelt suggest that he would fight to protect British or Dutch possessions in Asia.

As the situation in the Pacific deteriorated over the next few months, Churchill continued to press for a clear, united statement which would leave the Japanese in no doubt as to America's position. For example, on 5 November, Churchill told FDR that what was needed was 'a deterrent of the most general and formidable character'. Although,

Churchill went on, Japan had not yet taken a final decision, the joint embargo imposed on her was 'steadily forcing the Japanese to decisions for peace or war'. Churchill was willing, though, to follow Roosevelt's lead. 'No independent action by ourselves will deter Japan... But of course we will stand with you and do our utmost to back you in whatever course you choose.'

The course Roosevelt chose was to pressure Japan even further, in fact into a position where she had to decide quickly between resorting to violence and suffering a monumental loss of face – a choice which, given the nature of Japanese society and the character of its new Government under the samurai warrior Hideki Tojo, was entirely predictable. On 26 November, Secretary of State Cordell Hull handed Ambassador Nomura a note entitled 'Outline of Proposed Agreement Between the United States and Japan', under which Japan was required to leave the Tripartite Pact and sign a non-aggression pact with the British Empire, the Soviet Union and the United States. The note also called upon the Japanese Government to withdraw all its forces from China, to surrender all extraterritorial rights in China and not to support any regime in China other than the Nationalist Government under Chiang Kai-shek. These demands were such a slap in the face for Japan that Nomura apparently found it difficult to report them to his Government.

In his memoirs, Ernst von Weizsäcker, the head of the German Foreign Office, asked why America did not seriously try to detach Japan from the Tripartite Pact, thereby averting armed hostilities in the Pacific. He concluded that Hull's note of 26 November must be seen not as a miscalculation on Washington's part, but as a deliberate, and successful, attempt to manoeuvre the Japanese into firing the first shot in a Pacific war.[2]

Weizsäcker's suspicions are in fact confirmed by no less a figure than Henry Stimson, the US Secretary of War, who recorded in his diary what took place during a lunchtime discussion Roosevelt had

---

[2] In the aftermath of this note, the German Ambassador in Tokyo told his Government on 5 December 1941 that, according to Toshio Shiratori, an adviser to the Japanese Foreign Ministry, 'in the leading circles of Japan, they had come to the conclusion that Roosevelt now wants to enter the war by way of conflict in the Far East.'

with his senior advisers on 25 November 1941, on Japan's intentions in the Pacific. According to Stimson, FDR thought it likely that the Japanese would launch a surprise attack by the following Monday (8 December). Stimson quotes Roosevelt as saying that the question was how to manoeuvre the Japanese into firing the first shot 'without too much danger to ourselves'.

Churchill, in Volume III of his memoirs (pages 473–4), *actually admits that Roosevelt provoked the Japanese into firing first.* FDR and his advisers, Churchill writes, 'had long realised the grave risks of United States neutrality in the war against Hitler and all that he stood for, and had writhed under the restraints of Congress...' The President and his men saw, Churchill goes on, that Japanese victories in the Pacific against the British and Dutch empires 'combined with a German victory over Russia and thereafter an invasion of Great Britain, would leave America alone to face an overwhelming combination of triumphant aggressors.' Churchill has no doubts as to the wisdom of the policy pursued by Roosevelt and his advisers: 'Future generations of Americans and free men in every land will thank God for their vision.'

In a reference to Hull's note to the Japanese Government on 26 November 1941, Churchill even went so far as to warn against portraying Japan as 'an injured innocent' suddenly 'confronted by the United States with propositions which her people, fanatically aroused and fully prepared, could not be expected to accept.' After all, Churchill pointed out, the behaviour of the Japanese army in China had been wicked and Japan had willingly thrown in her lot with Hitler by signing the Tripartite Pact. 'Let her do what she dared and take the consequences,' Churchill concluded.[3]

Roosevelt's motive in conducting this forceful diplomacy is obvious. Before his election in 1940, he had promised the American people that he would not send their sons to fight in a foreign war *except in case of*

---

[3] On the subject of FDR's proposals to the Japanese, Henry Kissinger, the former US Secretary of State, remarks in his book *Diplomacy*: 'Roosevelt must have known that there was no possibility that Japan would accept.' In his essay on Churchill as a military strategist in *Four Faces and the Man*, Basil Liddell Hart writes that Churchill's account makes 'vividly clear' the process by which Roosevelt, intent on getting at Hitler indirectly, forced Japan through economic and diplomatic pressure to strike in the Pacific. (See pages 190–1.)

attack. Provoking, or 'manoeuvring', Japan into attacking the British and Dutch would reduce that obstacle, and an assault on an American possession would remove it altogether. How, though, would a conflict in the Pacific secure Roosevelt's ultimate aim — war with Hitler's Germany?

To begin to answer this question it is necessary now to introduce the *second* important feature of the negotiations carried on between the US and Japanese governments in 1941 — the existence of *Magic*, the codename given to the successful US cryptographic operation which broke Japan's diplomatic codes and enabled the American Government to read in clear the secret messages which passed between Tokyo and the Japanese embassies around the world, including not just Washington *but also Berlin*. By late November 1941, this invaluable source was reporting two important and connected facts to the American Government. Firstly, the Japanese Government, irrespective of what Ambassador Nomura was saying to Cordell Hull in their negotiations, had secretly decided to go to war. Secondly, Tokyo was pressuring Hitler to honour the oral commitment he had made in March to Foreign Minister Matsuoka to support Japan in the event of a conflict in the Pacific.

Magic, however, did not provide all the answers Roosevelt was seeking. On the vital question of where Japan would attack, this source — impressive and important though it was — remained as silent as the radios of the Japanese fleet which on 25 November sailed from its native shores for Pearl Harbor in total secrecy. The highly respected American statesman Dean Acheson, who in 1941 was Assistant-Secretary of State, records in his memoirs, *Present at the Creation*, that the US Government knew by late 1941 that a Japanese attack was imminent, but that 'several spots on the Siamese, Malayan, British and Dutch territory seemed more likely to be struck than any on ours.' Harry Hopkins left behind a fascinating account of the conversations he had with Roosevelt on Japan's intentions in 1941:

> I recall talking to the President many times in the past year [1941], and it always disturbed him because he really thought that the tac-tics of the Japanese would be to avoid a conflict with us; that they

would not attack either the Philippines or Hawaii, but would move on Thailand, French Indo-China, make further inroads on China itself and possibly attack the Malay Straits. He also thought they would attack Russia at an opportune moment. This would have left the President with the very difficult problem of protecting our interests.

This last sentence is extremely significant, for Hopkins is effectively saying that it was in America's interest to enter the war. In fact, the great worry felt at that anxious moment by Churchill and Roosevelt was that a Japanese attack on only British and Dutch possessions in Asia would not be enough to bring America into the war. After all, why should the actions of the Japanese in some remote spot on the globe rouse the American people to martial fury when all that had happened on the Atlantic Ocean had signally failed to achieve this? As Robert Sherwood pointed out, if the killing of US sailors by Germans in the North Atlantic had not enraged the American public, how much 'will to battle' could be generated by reports that the 'Japanese were establishing a beach-head at Khota Baru on the Gulf of Siam'?

The Japanese attack on Pearl Harbor was therefore, as Churchill said, 'a vast simplification' of Roosevelt's problem. Harry Hopkins described Roosevelt's own feelings on the subject:

He always realized that Japan would jump on us at an opportune moment and they would merely use the 'one by one' technique of Germany. Hence his great relief at the method Japan used. In spite of the disaster at Pearl Harbor and the blitz-warfare with the Japanese during the first few weeks, it completely solidified the American people and made the war upon Japan inevitable.

However, the attack on Pearl Harbor did not make war with *Germany* inevitable, which was FDR's aim. Given the power of the isolationists in the American Congress, Roosevelt had little chance of securing a declaration of war against Germany, which had known nothing in advance about the attack on Pearl Harbor. This meant that only Hitler, *personally*, could bring about war between the United States and the Third Reich. To date, though, he had refused to allow himself to be drawn by Roosevelt's provocations. Would he now comply with the requests for support in any forthcoming war which were being made to him by the Japanese and which *Magic* was reporting to Roosevelt?

The first serious indication that something was afoot came in mid-November when the Japanese Government asked the German Government whether the Reich was prepared to sign a treaty with Japan undertaking not to make a separate peace against a common foe. On 21 November, Ribbentrop indicated to General Eugen Ott, the Reich's Ambassador in Tokyo, that the Reich was willing to make such a commitment to Japan in respect of America. On 28 November, he discussed this matter further with the Japanese Ambassador, Baron Oshima, a militaristic firebrand who struck William Shirer, the Berlin-based American journalist, as 'more Nazi than the Nazis'. Here, Ribbentrop repeated the promise Hitler had made to Foreign Minister Matsuoka: 'Should Japan become engaged in a war against the United States, Germany, of course, would join the war immediately. There is absolutely no possibility of Germany's entering into a separate peace with the United States under such circumstances. The Führer is determined on that point.' After reporting this message to his Government, Baron Oshima was instructed by Tokyo on 30 November to inform Hitler that 'there is extreme danger that war may suddenly break out between Japan and the Anglo-Saxon nations through some clash of arms', and to ask him to translate his promise to support Japan into a formal treaty. At this point the discussions between Berlin and Tokyo stalled, and understandably so. A declaration of war by Germany upon the United States was an enormous bargaining chip and one that Hitler would naturally be expected to use to the maximum benefit of the Third Reich in his negotiations with the Japanese.

Ernst von Weizsäcker, the head of the Foreign Office, advised his Führer that these talks should proceed on a quid pro quo basis, and that Germany should declare war on America only if Japan attacked the Soviet Union from the rear. This was a joint strategy which might well have caused the Soviet Union to collapse, an event which would have dealt the Allied cause a real body blow. At the very least, Japanese intervention would have been greatly welcomed by the *Wehrmacht*, which had encountered far stronger opposition from the Red Army than it had anticipated. However, Weizsäcker's proposal did not find much favour with Tokyo. War with the Soviet Union was apparently a price which Japan was not willing to pay for Hitler's support against America.[4]

As December 1941 arrived, with the Japanese fleet sailing ever closer to Pearl Harbor, no real agreement had been reached by the Japanese and German governments. All that was clear to the leaders in Tokyo and Berlin, as well as in Washington and London, was that, for the first time in history, man stood on the brink of a truly global conflict and that, incredible as it might seem, the exact nature of that *world* war would to a large extent hinge on the mind of one man – Adolf Hitler. What he decided to do once Japan had shown her hand would decide the course of the war and the destiny of mankind. Anything was still possible. Hitler might renege completely on his promise to support Japan; he might, as Ribbentrop urged him to do, stick to the letter of the defensive Tripartite Pact and refuse to help Japan in her war of aggression; he might insist on a Japanese invasion of the Soviet Union in return for his declaration of war on the United States; or he might decide to stand by his daring ally and declare war on the country whose President was the Third Reich's greatest foe. A historic decision would soon have to be made by the Führer of the German people.

To familiarize his Government with the situation in the United States, Hans Thomsen, the Acting German Ambassador, sent off a telegram to Berlin at 2.00 a.m. on the morning of 4 December, in which he stated that the US press campaign was being manipulated by the Government with the intention of gaining time for America and intimidating Japan. Thomsen listed a number of points for his superiors to consider, amongst them being the probability that a war between America and Japan would involve Germany. Thomsen also mentioned

---

[4] Churchill had a high opinion of Weizsäcker. In his memoirs, he describes the German diplomat as 'a highly competent Civil Servant' who 'certainly wrote good advice to his superiors, which we may be glad they did not take.' (Volume III, page 294.) Nevertheless, Weizsäcker was imprisoned by the Americans after the war. His son, Richard, who won an Iron Cross on the Eastern Front, became President of the German Federal Republic.

that, 'contrary to the views of frivolous American "experts" ', a war with Japan would be no easy matter and might well drag on for years, to the great detriment of US industry, which would be starved of vital raw materials.

There was certainly much to think about in this message. But before the German Foreign Office officials had time for a proper analysis of its contents, Thomsen flashed off another telegram to Berlin. There had been a sensational newspaper scoop, he declared. The fiercely isolationist *Chicago Daily Tribune* had published a leaked copy of a secret report drawn up by US Chief of Staff George Marshall on the instructions of President Roosevelt. According to this, Roosevelt intended to raise an Expeditionary Force of five million men and send it to invade Germany by 1 July 1943.[5]

---

[5] See *Documents on German Foreign Policy*, Series D, Vol XIII, No. 541. This telegram, No. 4250 of 4 December 1941, was sent at 4.05 p.m. and received at 2.45 p.m. on 5 December.

8

Red Rag to a Bull

Senator Burton Wheeler was home at his Washington address on Wednesday 3 December 1941 when the Army Air Corps captain called. Wheeler had known the mysterious captain, a 'clean cut and intelligent looking' officer, since the previous summer when he began to provide the senator with classified information on American air power. But what the captain brought with him this day was far more important than aeroplane statistics. He had in his hands a brown-paper package 'as thick as an average novel' and labelled 'Victory Program'.

Wheeler wondered whether the captain was not worried about handing over 'the most closely guarded secret in Washington to a senator'. The soldier's answer was firm. Congress was a branch of government, he declared, and it had the right to know what was really going on in the White House.

After seeing the captain out, Wheeler opened the package and felt his blood pressure rise as he scanned through its contents, which were nothing less than a copy of the 'Joint Board Estimate of United States Over-all Production Requirements' drawn up by General Marshall and submitted to Roosevelt on 11 September. There had been rumours in Washington that such a document existed and that FDR was secretly planning to take America into the war. Wheeler now had proof. In fact, the package also contained a letter of 9 July 1941, in which Roosevelt asked the Secretary for War, Henry Stimson, to prepare the estimate. Wheeler clearly had political dynamite in his hands. What was he to do with it?

Wheeler considered showing it to the Senate Foreign Relations Committee, but such was that body's reputation for subservience to the White House that he feared the report would never see the light of day. After satisfying himself that disclosure of the document would not constitute a criminal offence or jeopardize the lives of American servicemen, Wheeler decided that the report had to be brought to the attention of the American public via the Fourth Estate. To that end, Wheeler showed General Marshall's estimate to Chesly Manly, a Washington correspondent with the fiercely isolationist *Chicago Daily Tribune*, the rival of the *Chicago Daily News* owned by Frank Knox, the Secretary of the Navy.

Chesly Manly's article, which appeared the following morning in the *Chicago Daily Tribune* and was reproduced in its sister paper, the Washington *Times Herald*, is without doubt one of the greatest journalistic scoops of all time. The huge banner headline ran, 'F.D.R's WAR PLANS!' with the sub-title, 'GOAL IS 10 MILLION ARMED MEN; HALF TO FIGHT IN AEF [American Expeditionary Force]: Proposes Land Drive by July 1, 1943 to Smash Nazis; President Told of Equipment Shortage.' Reproducing FDR's letter to Secretary for War Stimson in its entirety, to establish the authenticity and background of the Estimate, Manly went on to quote liberally from General Marshall's document over several pages. It was described in the article as 'a blueprint for total war on a scale unprecedented in at least two oceans and three continents, Europe, Africa and Asia' which 'represents decisions and commitments affecting the destinies of peoples throughout the civilized world.'

As Hans Thomsen reported to Berlin, the publication of this document caused a sensation throughout America. According to Wheeler, the scoop brought official Washington to a standstill, with people far more concerned with the contents of Manly's article than their usual business. Roosevelt declined to comment on the leak and delegated this task to Stimson, who called a press conference where he asked what the American public would think if, given the state the world was in, the US General Staff did not prepare for every conceivable emergency the country might have to face. He also denied that the document ever 'constituted an authorized programme of the government', and denounced those responsible for Manly's article as so lacking in patriotism that they would publish material which could be of benefit to a potential enemy. Spokesmen for the White House in Congress denied the claim in the article that FDR was planning to raise an

Chicago Daily Tribune, 4 December 1941.

expeditionary force of five million men and send it to attack Germany by 1 July 1943, pointing out that there was nothing in General Marshall's paper to warrant such a firm conclusion.

In the Cabinet, Stimson advised the President to use the Conspiracy Statute to prosecute the McCormick family, the owners of the *Chicago Daily Tribune*. Harold Ickes, the Secretary of the Interior, supported the Attorney-General in calling for a prosecution of those responsible for the leak under the Espionage Act. However, Ickes was surprised at the reaction he encountered. While he got the impression that Roosevelt was angry about the publication, it did not seem to him that FDR and other members of the Cabinet were particularly interested in the matter.

In fact, nothing seems to have been done about this leak. Senator Wheeler claimed that the Federal Bureau of Investigation (FBI) carried out an investigation into the matter during which Manly was questioned about his source, which he protected, and Major Albert Wedemeyer, one of the compilers of General Marshall's Estimate, 'grilled'. However, the present author contacted the FBI for information on any inquiry that was carried out into this matter and was told by the 'Unit Chief of the Office of Public and Congressional Affairs' that her staff had been 'unable to locate any public source information concerning [this] incident...'

It is understandable that the attack on Pearl Harbor only three days after the appearance of Manly's article should have pushed even that sensational publication into the background and distracted people's attention. However, there has never been a satisfactory explanation as to why so serious a leak was never investigated properly, *if it was investigated at all*, and why this amazing journalistic scoop was allowed to fade away into its present-day obscurity. What is the truth behind this curious episode?

In his autobiography, Senator Wheeler mentions that some people in Washington thought that Roosevelt had leaked the report himself, in an attempt to boost the flagging morale of the British by assuring them 'the Yanks are coming'. Wheeler also says that, as there were only five original copies of General Marshall's Estimate, with every one numbered, it seems probable that a top-ranking officer or official had authorized the disclosure. Wheeler's conclusion raises two questions. Which high ranking member of Roosevelt's administration leaked the Estimate? And, even more importantly, why?

In the book *A Man Called Intrepid*, which was published in 1976, William Stephenson, the head of the British Intelligence network in North America, says that he had General Marshall's report forged and leaked it, via the mysterious captain, to Senator Wheeler with the intention of infuriating Hitler and provoking him into declaring war on America. The appearance of these 'plans' in the *Chicago Daily Tribune*, Stephenson claims, 'tripped a wire in the minefield of Hitler's mind'.

As the bogus map of South America showed, Stephenson was certainly capable of producing forgeries (and, via Donovan, of persuading Roosevelt to make use of them). However, Stephenson's claim here cannot be taken seriously because the plans leaked to Wheeler were undoubtedly genuine, as Roosevelt's letter alone proves beyond doubt. In any case, it is unlikely in the extreme that the British Government would have been stupid enough to interfere so grossly in the internal affairs of a country upon which it was coming to rely for its survival. This does not mean that Stephenson's story should be dismissed totally. As anyone who knows anything about intelligence work will confirm, a cover story should resemble the truth as closely as possible.[1]

The circumstances of the leak and its timing, together with Wheeler's suspicions and 'Little Bill' Stephenson's 'confession' combine to make it virtually certain that General Marshall's Estimate was leaked by Stephenson's crony, William Donovan, with Roosevelt's prior knowledge. In short, this whole incident is a clear example of the old political adage, 'The Ship of State is the only vessel that leaks from the top'.

By late 1941, Hitler was long known to have an Achilles heel in his temper, which could throw him into such a rage that he could not think and behave rationally. William Shirer records in his *Berlin Diary* that even before the war, the Führer was known in Germany as 'der Teppichfresser' (the carpet eater) — a reference to Hitler's habit of

---

[1] See *A Man Called Intrepid*, pages 317–20.

flinging himself to the floor when angered and chewing the carpet. These rages seemed to strike during times of national emergency. A good example of this was provided by Birger Dahlerus, a Swedish business friend of Hermann Göring, who acted as a neutral messenger for both London and Berlin during the pre-war crisis in the summer of 1939. In his book *The Last Attempt*, Dahlerus describes in some detail Hitler's behaviour at that time.

After arriving in Berlin from London with a message from the British Government around midnight on 26 August, Dahlerus was taken to meet Hitler, who had been woken up. Hitler at first listened to the Swede, but then he stood up abruptly and began to pace up and down excitedly, muttering that Germany was 'irresistible'. Then he suddenly stopped in the middle of the room and stared into space. Dahlerus goes on:

> [Hitler's] voice was blurred and his behaviour that of a completely abnormal person. He spoke in staccato phrases: 'If there should be war, then I shall build U-boats, build U-boats, U-boats, U-boats, U-boats.' His voice became more indistinct and finally one could not follow him at all. Then he pulled himself together, raised his voice as though addressing a large audience and shrieked: 'I shall build aeroplanes, build aeroplanes, aeroplanes, aeroplanes, and I shall annihilate my enemies.' He seemed more like a phantom than a real person. I stared in amazement and turned to see how Göring was reacting, but he did not turn a hair.

Later in these negotiations, when it became likely that Britain would go to war with Germany over Poland, Hitler threw another fit in front of Dahlerus:

> He grew more and more excited, and began to wave his arms as he shouted in my face: 'If England wants to fight for a year, I shall fight for a year; if England wants to fight two years, I shall fight two years...' He paused and then yelled, his voice rising to a shrill scream and his arms milling wildly: 'If England wants to fight for three years, I shall fight for three years...'

The movements of his body now began to follow those of his

arms, and when he finally bellowed: 'And if necessary, I will fight for ten years' he brandished his fist and bent down so that it nearly touched the floor.

It has already been shown that the *coup d'état* in Yugoslavia in March 1941 hurled Hitler into such a fury that he postponed his attack on the Soviet Union in order to take revenge on a small country which had crossed him, a rash action for which the Third Reich would pay dearly. This was the temper which, in Churchill's phrase quoted earlier, 'blotted out thought and sometimes impelled [Hitler] on his most dire adventures.'

William Donovan, as already shown, played no small role in this coup. It should come as no surprise therefore that one of 'Wild Bill's' first steps after becoming Roosevelt's spymaster in the summer of 1941 was *to recruit into his organization a German-speaking psychoanalyst who would carry out a study of Hitler's mind.*

William L. Langer, the distinguished Harvard historian, worked for Donovan during the war and was struck by 'Wild Bill's' imagination and resourcefulness. Donovan, Langer writes, 'had a low tolerance for uncertainty' and always sought to understand his enemy and learn what made his adversary act and react in the way he did. To achieve this, Donovan was quite willing to consult academic and business experts whenever he felt that his own expertise was lacking. It was this no-nonsense approach which led Donovan to conclude that he required a professional, psychological analysis of Hitler's mind. Langer was certainly in a position to comment on Donovan's methods, for the psychiatrist tasked by 'Wild Bill' to carry out this study was his own brother, Walter.

Towards the end of August 1941, Walter Langer was convalescing after an operation in a New England hospital when he read in a newspaper that William Donovan, the head of the newly established 'Coordinator of Information' (COI), was looking for suitable recruits. Noting that part of the COI's brief was the conduct of psychological warfare, Langer, a psychiatrist who had served in the First World War and had not been impressed by the crude 'good versus evil' tactics used in that conflict, sent off a letter to Donovan in which he expressed his opinion that, to be successful, a campaign targeted against the mind had to be 'imaginative, cunning and bold' and involve the use of 'unconscious and irrational strengths, for these were by far the most powerful'. He expected his letter to be thrown into the bin, and was much surprised therefore to receive a telephone call from Washington inviting him to have breakfast with Donovan. At the breakfast meeting, which lasted for almost two hours, Donovan displayed a knowledge of psychological theory and a willingness to apply that theory to his work. This made it easier for Langer to explain his views, and these impressed 'Wild Bill' so much that he offered his visitor a job with his new organization, which the following year grew into the Office of Strategic Services.

In early 1943, Donovan asked Langer to prepare a formal study of Hitler's mind. As Donovan knew, Langer had been studying in Vienna when Hitler annexed Austria with Germany. Langer had actually seen Hitler enter the Austrian capital, the city in which the Führer had spent much of his youth, and had heard him speak to the crowd. Langer had witnessed at first hand the machinery of the Third Reich and could not help but find himself professionally interested in what he saw. Donovan wanted to know what sort of man Hitler was, what ambitions he had, what his relationship with his subordinates was like, what drove him, what he would do if the war began to turn against him, and above all what his physical condition was. Langer duly completed his study, which was designed to be read by a layman, and handed it over to Donovan. Given the highly secretive nature of Donovan's organization, Langer never learned exactly to what use his study was put, but he had good reason to believe that it was read by Roosevelt and by the British Ambassador to Washington. In the late 1970s, Langer received permission from the US Government to publish his work, which appeared under the title, *The Mind of Adolf Hitler*.

Langer's work was produced well after the attack on Pearl Harbor, but it is clear that, even before America entered the war, Donovan was giving serious and active thought to the effective use of psychological warfare. Moreover, Langer's study is still obviously of importance in assessing the effect which the leaked report and the subsequent *Chicago Daily Tribune* article had on Hitler. The accuracy of Langer's findings can be assessed by reference to the prediction he made about Hitler's end. Langer considered various possibilities before concluding that the Führer would choose to die in a spectacular suicide – an impressively accurate description of Hitler's death in the *Götterdämmerung* of his wrecked capital.

In his study, Langer devotes a chapter to Hitler's rages, and quotes certain authorities to justify his conclusions. According to François-Poncet, the former French Ambassador to Berlin, these outbursts were caused by something that Hitler 'considers a challenge of his superman personality'. When faced with such a challenge, which might be very minor or even a figment of his imagination, Hitler felt the need to 'display his primitive character'. Langer cites François-Poncet's study, *The Yellow Book*, where the author claims that Hitler had reached the point where he considered himself both 'infallible and invincible' and had become totally intolerant of any form of dissent. According to François-Poncet, Hitler saw any opposition as a sacrilege to which the only response was 'an immediate and striking display of his omnipotence'.

These points were demonstrated in the aftermath of the Yugoslav coup when Hitler threw reason out of the window and postponed the attack on the Soviet Union in order to crush and dismember the country that had wronged him – an obvious display of his 'superman personality'. As he told his Reichstag deputies, 'To treat the German Reich in that way is impossible.' It was during this period that he assured the Japanese Foreign Minister that Germany would support Japan in a war with America – another example of his omnipotent feelings when angered.

Clearly, there were lessons to be learned here by anyone interested in Hitler's moods and it is in this context that the *Chicago Daily Tribune* article should be seen. There probably could not have been a greater challenge to Hitler's 'superman personality' than Roosevelt's publicly quoted intention to attack the Third Reich by 1 July 1943 – a statement which does not actually feature in General Marshall's paper and *seems to have been manufactured with the newspaper article in mind*. What indeed could have been more likely to throw the Führer into one of the tempers which would compel him to lash out blindly at the man who had been tormenting him? In other words, the leaked report was the proverbial red rag to a bull.

In fact, this incident is highly reminiscent of the ploy used by Bismarck, the Prussian Chancellor, to bring about war with France in 1870. Anxious to spark a conflict with his country's ancient enemy, Bismarck rewrote a telegram from his King to Napoleon III, the French Emperor, rendering the language diplomatically offensive, and then leaked the doctored message, known to history as the Ems Despatch, to the press. An outraged Napoleon III responded with a declaration of war, a step which, as Bismarck had calculated, proved disastrous to France and her imperial regime.

At this point, it is necessary to introduce another fact about William Donovan: in the autumn of 1941 he was engaged in an intelligence operation involving none other than Hans Thomsen, the Acting German Ambassador, who claimed that as Hitler's onetime secretary he had come to know the Führer intimately.[2] This operation, which became known only when the FBI's file on Donovan was declassified in 1980, is still shrouded in mystery. However, there is no doubt that Thomsen was in touch with Donovan via an American Quaker called Malcolm Lovell, and that Thomsen asked for the then enormous sum of $1 million from the US Government and for a private meeting with Roosevelt. Donovan's file indicates that the purpose of these requests, which as far as is known were never granted, was to help Thomsen defect or even organize a *coup d'état* against Hitler.

In a lengthy letter to Donovan on 19 September 1941, Lovell said that Thomsen claimed that it had always been his intention to bring about friendship between Germany and the United States. According to Lovell, Thomsen believed that with 'unlimited funds' as well as 'moral and physical' assistance, he could overthrow Hitler and establish a government in Berlin which would pursue policies 'consonant with the aims of the United States, and the true interests of the German people'.

---

[2] See Anthony Cave Brown's *Donovan: The Last Hero*, Chapter 12. Thomsen's service record shows that he served in the Reich Chancellery from 1933 to 1936, when he was posted to Washington. He therefore had the opportunity to observe Hitler at close quarters.

To prepare for all of this, Lovell explained, Thomsen needed to meet Roosevelt and Donovan, preferably at night in the President's home in Hyde Park, New York (not the White House). According to Lovell, Thomsen insisted that no written records whatsoever of these meetings be made, and maintained that he was a patriotic German who was simply interested in saving his country from 'disaster and chaos'.

There is no evidence that any attempt was made in late 1941 to unseat Hitler, and Thomsen definitely returned to Germany after war broke out between his country and the United States. (He was subsequently posted to neutral Sweden, where he saw out the war.) However, this operation does raise the fascinating possibility, indeed likelihood, that during the crucial pre-Pearl Harbor period, Hitler's representative in Washington *was acting under the influence of the American Government.*

Certainly the two telegrams which Thomsen sent to Berlin on 4 December 1941, one about the imminent Pacific war and the other on the *Chicago Daily Tribune* article, are suspicious not just in their timing, but also in their content, which gave the impression that a two-ocean war would be a disaster for the United States in that it would give Germany a free hand in Europe for the foreseeable future — claims which were music to Hitler's ears.

In his first telegram, Thomsen reported that America was unprepared for a two-front war, and that a conflict between the United States and Japan, which 'might drag on indecisively for years', would be 'hard to take for England and Russia from the standpoint of their material situation' and 'would mean a drastic cut in lend-lease aid to both nations as a result of the American requirements for carrying on the war in the widest sense; the closure of the port of Vladivostok to American supplies; and likewise as a result of disruption of the shipping route to the Persian Gulf.' In his second telegram, concerning the leaking of General Marshall's report, Thomsen told Berlin that Roosevelt's planned Expeditionary Force 'would require enormous sums of money and be attended by a serious shock to the American economy.' Thomsen also mentioned: 'The elimination of the Soviet Union as a fighting power by the summer of 1942 at the latest and the collapse of the British Empire are soberly included in the calculations of the American General Staff so that the publication of the document will hardly cause any special rejoicing among the allies.'

In his first telegram to Berlin after the attack on Pearl Harbor, which was sent at 8.36 p.m. on the evening of 7 December, Thomsen referred to the *Chicago Daily Tribune* article in order to illustrate his claim that a conflict in the Pacific was good news for Germany.

> All the American war plans which, as was demonstrated in the recent article in the *Chicago Tribune*, were oriented toward Europe and calculated to gain time for at least another year or two, have suddenly been scuttled. A war in the Pacific 2 to 3 years before the completion of the two-ocean navies, at a time when one's own army has not been equipped and the great armament industry has only just started up, must come at an extremely inopportune time for the American Government.

In view of all that has been mentioned above about psychological pressure on Hitler and his need to demonstrate his omnipotence, it is interesting to scrutinize the telegram which Thomsen sent to Berlin on the evening of 8 December 1941, in which he described the mood in America following the Pearl Harbor attack and suggested that Roosevelt, in an attempt to restore his injured pride, might steal Hitler's thunder by declaring war on Germany first. In this telegram, Thomsen said that Roosevelt 'could count on the solid backing of the nation in a war against Japan', although 'the American people were not as yet ripe for war on European soil'.

Thomsen went on to say that it was uncertain as to whether Roosevelt would also ask for a declaration of war against Germany and Italy, pointing out that it would be logical for America to avoid a war on two fronts. However, he added: 'Roosevelt may attempt at least in this regard to anticipate the decisions of Germany and Italy, if only to make up for some of the loss of prestige throughout the whole world and particularly in South America resulting from the inadequate preparations against the Japanese operation.'

Hitler, who of course knew nothing about Thomsen's dalliance with Donovan and Roosevelt, certainly valued the opinion of his man in Washington. On 18 May 1942, the Führer told luncheon guests that

Hans Thomsen, Hitler's Chargé d'Affaires. (Ullstein Bilderdienst.)

Thomsen had shown the Americans that he was a diplomat 'who could not be bluffed'. So impressed was Hitler that he intended to task Thomsen with 'a post of exceptional difficulty' when the war was over. On the work carried out by his Embassy in Washington under Thomsen's direction, Hitler commented: 'The reports they sent us must be regarded as models of their kind, for they invariably gave us a perfectly clear picture of the situation.' As events showed, Thomsen's reports to Berlin were far from accurate portrayals of America's ability and willingness to wage war. Indeed, a close study of the evidence supports the view that Thomsen – for genuine, patriotic reasons of his own – *deliberately misled his master about Roosevelt's intentions and America's war-waging capacity.* Clearly, Hitler relied heavily on Thomsen's opinion and advice. In this instance at least, such counsel appears to have been intentionally misleading, with the result that Hitler concluded, quite wrongly, that a Pacific war would spoil Roosevelt's reported plans to attack Germany.

What can be stated as a fact is that, at one of the meetings between Thomsen and his contact, Lovell, the German diplomat made a statement which Donovan, on learning of it, found so important that he passed it on to his President. On 13 November 1941, Donovan told FDR by written message: 'The following is the substance of statements made by Dr. Hans Thomsen on Thursday afternoon, November 6th, to Mr. Malcolm R. Lovell: "If Japan goes to war with the United States, Germany will immediately follow suit."' By this route, therefore, Donovan and Roosevelt heard from an impressive source, *Hitler's own representative in the United States and a man who knew Hitler well*, that the Führer would support his Japanese ally and declare war on America. Here would have been more reason for FDR to conclude that the best, perhaps even the only, way to force war between the United States and Germany in late 1941 was to anger Hitler through the leaking of General Marshall's report and then wait for the outbreak of hostilities somewhere in the Pacific to test the Führer's loyalty to his Japanese allies.

The proof of the pudding is in the eating. It is time now to examine a valuable source on the Second World War, but one which, strangely, historians have largely ignored. This is, of course, Hitler's speech to the Reichstag on 11 December 1941 in which he finally took the plunge and declared war on the United States.

It is clear that Hitler did not consult any of his subordinates about declaring war on America, and that he did not take long to decide to honour his oral commitment to Japan, without even asking for Japanese reciprocity in the form of a commitment to attack the Soviet Union. His main aim, as he stated to Ribbentrop in the conversation mentioned earlier, was not to support his ally, but to unleash his pent-up wrath on the United States. On 8 December, the day after the attack on Pearl Harbor, he instructed his navy to fire on American ships 'whenever and wherever they may encounter them'. That same day, he travelled back to Berlin by train, arriving there around 11.00 a.m. the following morning. He had intended to address the Reichstag then, but chose instead to postpone the meeting for two days whilst his speech was prepared with the help of Hans Dieckhoff, the former German Ambassador to Washington.

During this period, Hitler gave the impression of being worried that America would declare war on him first, as Hans Thomsen suggested Roosevelt might do for reasons of prestige. In fact, Dr Paul Schmidt, Hitler's interpreter, noted Hitler's mood and concluded that the Führer 'with his inveterate prestige . . . wanted to get his declaration in first'. In the telegram to the German Embassy in Washington ordering Thomsen to hand the Reich's notice of hostilities to the American Government, Ribbentrop wrote at the end: 'Please ensure, before carrying out the foregoing instruction there is no contact whatsoever between the Embassy and the State Department. We want to avoid absolutely the American Government's stealing a march on us by taking a step of that kind.' According to Ernst von Weizsäcker, Ribbentrop commented: 'A Great Power does not permit any power to make war on it. It declares war itself.' Here, Ribbentrop was surely reflecting the opinion of his Führer, who, by declaring war on America, was out to reassert his 'superman personality' and repair his damaged ego.

Predictably, Hitler's address to his Reichstag delegates on 11 December, which was much awaited both within Germany and abroad, was a lengthy tirade against Roosevelt and the United States. Hitler asked why it was that Roosevelt was so hostile to Germany, a country which had done no harm to him personally or to America. Between the German and American peoples, there were, he maintained, no territorial or political matters which affected the interests or the existence of the United States. Moreover, the differences between capitalist America and Bolshevik Russia were considerably greater than those separating the United States and the Third Reich. Why then, Hitler asked, did Roosevelt see it as his mission to bring about war between Germany and America?

To answer this question, Hitler compared his career with that of the American President. Roosevelt came from a wealthy, establishment family and moved naturally into a position of power. He himself, by contrast, came from a humble background and had to work his way to the top through diligence and hard work. He and Roosevelt moved into office in the same year and had to deal with the same problems of mass unemployment and a collapsing economy. Posterity would prove, Hitler maintained, that his Third Reich tackled these issues far more successfully than Roosevelt did with his 'New Deal', a project which Hitler scorned and mocked. This project had been such a failure, Hitler claimed, that Roosevelt was seeking a foreign diversion in order to prevent the collapse of all his plans. Roosevelt now feared a peaceful settlement in Europe, for that would reveal his rearmament programme to be a fraud. As nobody will attack America, Roosevelt must provoke the attack himself, Hitler claimed.

Hitler went on to outline what he described as Roosevelt's campaign to force Germany into war with America. He listed the help that Roosevelt had given to Britain and the examples of Roosevelt's 'interference' in Europe's affairs, meddling which Roosevelt would not tolerate in his own hemisphere. Here, Hitler took the opportunity to vent his feelings on the Yugoslav coup. Early that year, Hitler mentioned, Roosevelt had sent Donovan, whom he described as 'an utterly worthless creature', to the Balkans in order to try and bring about a rising against the Axis powers. Roosevelt, Hitler claimed, 'incites war, then falsifies the causes, puts forward arbitrary assertions, wraps himself in a cloud of Christian hypocrisy and leads mankind slowly but surely to war, not without then, as an old Freemason, calling to God as witness to the honesty of his actions.'

To Hitler, Roosevelt's aim was plain: he intended to annihilate one Axis country after another. Hitler was now prepared to do what Roosevelt, 'this provocateur', had been trying for years to achieve. And he was now prepared to go to war not only because he was an ally of Japan, but because he had sufficient insight and strength to see that what was at stake was the existence of his nation, perhaps for all time. Roosevelt and his kind, Hitler exclaimed, 'had once tried to starve democratic Germany; now they intend to destroy National Socialist Germany.'

For this reason, Hitler had that day ordered the American representative in Berlin to be handed his papers and told the following:

In pursuit of President Roosevelt's policy, which is aimed at establishing world supremacy, the United States, in union with Britain, have shrunk from nothing in denying the German, Italian and Japanese peoples the prerequisites of their livelihood. For this reason, the British and American Governments have opposed, not just for the present but for all time, every just attempt to bring about a new world order.

Since the beginning of the war, the American President Roosevelt has been guilty of the worst crimes against international law. Illegal attacks on shipping and other property of German and Italian citizens were made in conjunction with the threat to deny those concerned of their personal freedom through internment. These increasing attacks on German shipping continued to the point where he issued the order, against all the efforts of international law, to attack, fire upon and sink German and Italian ships. American ministers have busied themselves in this criminal way, in which they have destroyed German U boats. German and Italian merchant ships were attacked by American cruisers, captured and their peaceful crews puts in prison. Without any attempt at an official denial of the part of the American Government, President Roosevelt's plan has been published, under which Germany and Italy are to be attacked with military force in Europe by 1943 at the latest.

In this way have the sincere and unprecedented forbearance of Germany and Italy and their attempt to prevent an extension of the war and to maintain relations with the United States – despite President Roosevelt's provocations, which have been successfully borne for years – been frustrated.[3]

Hitler, it will be noted, mentioned the *Chicago Daily Tribune* article and in a manner indicating that he saw the leaked plan as clear evidence that Roosevelt was out to destroy Nazi Germany. Whatever one thinks of Hitler, the point he made in this sentence about no attempt being made by the American Government to offer an official denial *must be conceded*. The publication of such a plan would be a serious diplomatic incident at any time. However, disclosure of it in the highly charged atmosphere of early December 1941 could only serve to heighten tension still further. If Roosevelt had really wanted to avoid trouble with Germany at this juncture, he would have hurriedly provided

---

[3] The full text of Hitler's speech is given in Domarus, *Hitler's Speeches & Proclamations*, volume 4.

Hitler with an explanation for the leaked plan in an attempt to calm an explosive situation. That Roosevelt did not do so is open to only one interpretation – *that he wanted the leaked plan to goad Hitler into declaring war on the United States.*[4]

The leaking of this plan at a moment when Roosevelt knew that the Japanese were about to attack somewhere in the Pacific, thereby sparking off an exchange of war declarations, cannot be accepted as a coincidence. Premeditation, intent and design lay behind the *Chicago Daily Tribune* article. The leaking of the plan to Senator Wheeler was an inspired move in that Roosevelt used one enemy to negate another. Wheeler, the arch-isolationist and personal foe of Donovan, handed the plan over to an isolationist newspaper, which published it, thereby angering Hitler so much that he at last decided to declare war on America, a step which in turn silenced the isolationists for fear of being labelled traitors. William Stephenson and his colleagues in British intelligence may have played a part in the planning of this trap. They may even have suggested it. The British, who have been playing this game for centuries, have the reputation of being masters at such ruses. However, there can surely now be little doubt that the plan was executed, not by William Stephenson, as he himself claimed, but by Roosevelt's spymaster, William Donovan.[5]

It is strange that the sentence in which Hitler commented on the

---

[4] Hitler's declaration of war was not enthusiastically received within Germany. Max Domarus, in his *Hitler's Speeches & Proclamations*, describes the applause of the Reichstag members to Hitler's speech as 'dutiful but thin' and the assurance of loyalty to the Führer by Göring, the Reichstag President, as 'very routine'. On the Government bench, according to Domarus, 'serious and pensive faces were to be seen'. German Government reports on morale stated that the German people, mindful of what had happened in the First World War, regarded war with the United States as an ominous development.

[5] In *A Man Called Intrepid*, William Stephenson claims that a secondary purpose in leaking General Marshall's Estimate was to convince Hitler that an Anglo-Saxon invasion of Western Europe would take place in 1943, thereby persuading him to divert troops from Russia, where the Red Army was under severe pressure, to France and the Low Countries. It is a fact that on 14 December 1941, only a few days after reading the leaked document, Hitler ordered the construction of the 'New West Wall', in order that we can be sure of repelling any landing attempt, however strong, with the minimum number of permanently stationed troops.' The following March, Hitler issued Directive 40, which outlined in detail how Western Europe was to be defended from invasion.

leaked American plan is omitted from the English translation of his speech to the Reichstag which appears on page 1,072 of *The Rise and Fall of the Third Reich* by William Shirer, a close friend of Douglas Miller. Not only is the sentence a startling one in its own right; it can also be used as a guide through the tortuous and confusing process of miscalculations and design by which the European war was transformed into a global affair.

As has been seen, Hitler welcomed the news of Pearl Harbor, wantonly confident in the ability of his Japanese ally to divert America's attention away from Europe to the Pacific arena. Churchill knew better. 'So we had won after all,' he thought to himself after learning of America's entry into the war. Given the strength and unity of the Allied coalition, he saw at once that, although a hard fight lay ahead, there could be no doubting the eventual outcome of the war. To secure victory, all that was required of the Allied powers was, in Churchill's famous phrase, 'merely the proper application of overwhelming force'.

However, as will now be shown, even Churchill did not foresee the degree of force Roosevelt had in mind.

THE RESOLUTION

O brave new world, that has such people in't!
William Shakespeare, *The Tempest*

9

A World To Gain

Sunday 24 January 1943 was a watershed in the Second World War, indeed in the history of the modern world. By this date, the superior strength of the Allies was beginning to show on the battlefields around the world. On the Pacific island of Papua New Guinea, the American and Australian forces under General MacArthur had finally broken the ferocious resistance of the Japanese defenders. The epic siege of Leningrad, in which the inhabitants of the city had suffered almost unbelievable hardships, had been temporarily lifted. In the city of Stalingrad, in the south of Russia, the trapped German Sixth Army was in its death throes. In Tunisia the remnants of Rommel's Afrika Korps were being driven into the Mediterranean. The tide of war was turning clearly and inexorably in favour of the Allies. It was not, though, a field of conflict which provided the setting for the importance of this day, but a placid, sunlit garden in the Moroccan city of Casablanca, which was then under the control of the United States army.

An élite group of some 50 war correspondents was brought there that morning by the military authorities to attend a press conference about which the newsmen had been told little in advance. The correspondents gathered on the lawn and were mingling with military personnel when, to their amazement, Roosevelt and Churchill appeared from the house. Roosevelt was carried out to his chair, while Churchill, wearing his trilby (presumably as protection against the sun), crossed the lawn and sat down beside the President. The astonishment of the correspondents was even greater when they learned that the two leaders had been in Casablanca for 10 days, discussing the future of the war in a conference which had been a closely guarded secret.

Roosevelt and Churchill were accompanied by two rival French generals, Henri Giraud and the giant figure of the future President of France, Charles de Gaulle. In an effort to show that some sort of understanding had been reached between them, the two Frenchmen posed for the cameras and then moved off, leaving Roosevelt and Churchill to talk to the newspapermen, who stood informally around or sat cross-legged on the grass near the two leaders.

Using briefing notes, Roosevelt spoke first. He described what had been achieved during the conference and then abruptly changed the subject:

Another point. I think we have all had it in our hearts and our heads before, but I don't think that it has ever been put down on paper by the Prime Minister and myself and that is the determination that peace can come to the world only by the total elimination of German and Japanese war power.

Some of you Britishers know the story – we had a General called U.S. Grant. His name was Ulysses Simpson Grant, but in my, and the Prime Minister's early days, he was called 'Unconditional

President Roosevelt and Prime Minister Churchill at the Casablanca Conference, 24 January 1943. (Imperial War Museum.)

Surrender' Grant. The elimination of German, Japanese and Italian war power means the unconditional surrender by Germany, Italy and Japan. That means a reasonable assurance of future world peace. It does not mean the destruction of the population of Germany, Italy or Japan, but it does mean the destruction of the philosophies in those countries which are based on conquest and the subjugation of other peoples.

This meeting may be called the 'Unconditional Surrender' meeting.

As Roosevelt spoke, Churchill's Chief of Staff, General Sir Hastings Ismay, noticed the startled look on the Prime Minister's face, as did Captain John L. McCrea, Roosevelt's naval aide. Churchill recovered from the surprise, but nevertheless began his address in a somewhat rambling manner: 'I agree with everything the President has said and I think it was a very happy decision to bring you gentlemen here to Casablanca to this agreeable spot ... the scene of much the most important and successful war conference which I have ever attended or witnessed.'

Over a game of cards that evening, Churchill privately expressed his anger at Roosevelt to Averell Harriman, the American millionaire turned diplomat, who had never before seen the Prime Minister so angry with the President. According to Harriman, Churchill was upset that Roosevelt had made such a 'momentous announcement without consultation'. Harriman, who gained the impression that Churchill thought the President's statement would toughen German resistance, mentioned the Prime Minister's feelings to Roosevelt the following morning. But FDR merely spoke once again of the American Civil War and General Grant's insistence on 'Unconditional Surrender'.

Amazing as it may seem, Roosevelt's announcement also came as news to Cordell Hull, the American Secretary of State, who was not present at Casablanca (and who was apparently denied access to the conference minutes by the President). Hull records in his memoirs that the principle of Unconditional Surrender had not originally been a part of State Department thinking, and that he was as much surprised as Churchill when FDR announced it at Casablanca. Hull adds, 'I was told the Prime Minister was dumbfounded.'[1]

Churchill's reaction is not difficult to understand. The phrase 'Unconditional Surrender', which, it is important to note, did *not* appear in the official press communiqué, fundamentally altered the nature of the war. Until Roosevelt used the expression that morning, the professed aim of the allies had been the destruction of Hitler and his regime. Even Stalin, whose country had suffered monstrously at the hands of the German invaders, was then drawing a distinction in his propaganda between the 'Hitlerites' and other Germans. The message to the German people was, 'Get rid of Hitler and his gangsters and we can talk.'

Clement Attlee, the leader of the Labour Party and by the time of the Casablanca Conference, Churchill's deputy, spelled this out in an address to the German nation on 9 January 1940:

> We are opposed to any attempt from outside to break up Germany. We do not seek the humiliation or dismemberment of your country. We wholeheartedly desire to welcome you without delay into the peaceful collaboration of civilised nations. We must warn you, however, that Hitler and his system prepared and started this war. He could not continue if you ceased supporting him. Until this accursed Nazi regime is overthrown there is no hope of peace between us. If you establish a Government willing that Germany should be a good neighbour and a good European, there shall be no humiliation or revenge.

Roosevelt's *public* announcement changed that. From then on, the target was Germany herself, whatever government she had – a fact which greatly weakened internal resistance to Hitler and which, given the legendary fighting power of the German army, condemned the

---

[1] The State Department Security Committee on Security Problems, which was chaired by Hull's friend Norman Davies, is reported as having concluded in May 1942: 'On the assumption that the victory of the United States will be conclusive, unconditional surrender rather than an armistice should be sought from the principal states except perhaps Italy.' It would appear that Hull never learned about this recommendation. Or is there a less innocent explanation to this discrepancy?

European mainland to widespread death and destruction. There was now to be a fight to the finish, in which the ancient continent of Europe would be the battlefield. This fact was made clear the following month, when Goebbels, Hitler's propaganda chief, responded with a speech in which he told the German people that the Allies were out to enslave them, and called upon them to wage 'Total War' in order to ensure the preservation of their nation. As Chester Wilmot points out in his classic book *The Struggle For Europe*, Roosevelt's statement enabled the Nazis to tell the German people with conviction, 'It is you, as well as we, that they intend to destroy.'

'Unconditional Surrender' also meant the abandonment of a policy which the British Government had pursued since the rise of the nation state in the sixteenth century – namely, the maintenance of a balance of power in Europe which enabled Britain to prevent any one country from dominating the continent. To this end, the British Government had formed alliances over the centuries against Spain, France and Imperial Germany (and would, after 1945, against the Soviet Union). However, suddenly an exception was made in respect of Germany, despite the enormous implications such a policy had for the character of post-war Europe. If Germany was to be battered into rubble, as indeed happened, the country most likely to fill the gap left by her disappearance was the Soviet Union. Now, if the British Government was fighting, as it claimed, for liberty and democracy, why should it adopt as its major war aim a policy which would swap Stalin for Hitler – in effect, exchange one form of terror in Europe for another?

It can hardly be claimed that the British Government was unaware of what the consequences of Roosevelt's policy were likely to be. Even before hostilities began, Basil Liddell Hart, the military writer and Government adviser, issued warnings:

> ...I had many times pointed out that another unlimited effort like 1914–18 was bound to end in bankruptcy even if it ended in victory, and result in Britain declining into a poor dependant of the U.S.A. Secondly, I pointed out that there was no prospect of Britain and France, however unlimited their effort, being strong enough to conquer Germany; that this would only become possible if Russia

joined our side — in which case she would be able to dominate Europe. While I was anxious to see Russia brought into a collective security plan as a check on war, and Hitler, I thought it folly to commit ourselves blindly to the aim of total victory if war came.

One would have expected the British Government to explain why it had abandoned its traditional policy for what Liddell Hart considered to be one of folly, but this was not the case. On his return to London, Churchill merely told Parliament that he had concurred with Roosevelt's statement as the 'agent' of the War Cabinet. In fact, Churchill did not speak in public about the adoption of the Unconditional Surrender policy until 21 July 1949, when the matter was debated in the House of Commons. In this debate, Ernest Bevin, the Foreign Secretary, spoke of the difficulties the former Allied powers faced in rebuilding a Germany which had been reduced to rubble as a result of the policy:[2]

> ... it left us with a Germany without law, without a constitution, without a single person with whom we could deal, without a single institution to grapple with the situation, and we have had to build right from the bottom with nothing at all. We have had to build a State which has over 20 million displaced persons scattered about it, and we had to build it while something like 5 million people were driven out of one part of the country into the other.

All of this, Bevin said, stemmed from the policy of Unconditional Surrender 'on which neither the British Cabinet nor any other Cabinet had a chance to say a word.'

The young Michael Foot (the future leader of the Labour Party) was so astonished at this statement that he asked Bevin to confirm that the 'British Cabinet never had notice of the matter at all'. This sparked off the following exchange between Bevin and Churchill [author's italics]:

---

[2] During the war, Britain was run by a coalition government in which Churchill, as leader of the Conservative Party, was Prime Minister, while Attlee, the leader of the Labour Party, was his deputy. Immediately after the defeat of Germany, Churchill called an election, which he lost. He appeared in the 1949 debate as Leader of the Opposition.

Mr. Bevin: The first we heard about it was in the press.

Mr. Churchill: The first time I heard that phrase used it was from *the lips* of President Roosevelt.

Mr. Bevin: ... I say that I never heard of that phrase until I saw it in the Press, and that, if it had been put to me, as a Member of the British Cabinet, *I would never have agreed to it.*

Mr. Churchill: The statement was made by President Roosevelt *without consultation with me.* I was there on the spot, and I had very rapidly to consider whether the state of our position in the world was such as would justify me in not giving support to it. I did give support to it, but that was not the idea which I had formed in my own mind. In the same way, when it came to the Cabinet at home, *I have not the slightest doubt that if the British Cabinet had considered that phrase, it is likely that they would have advised against it,* but, working with a great alliance and with great, loyal and powerful friends from across the ocean, we had to accommodate ourselves.

Later in the debate, Churchill added:

> ... I must say that the phrase 'unconditional surrender' was not brought before me to agree to *in any way* before it was uttered by our great friend, our august and powerful ally President Roosevelt. But, I did concur with him after he had said it, and I reported the matter to the Cabinet, who accepted the position.

From this, Churchill's position seems clear enough: he knew nothing at all about Roosevelt's policy of Unconditional Surrender until the press conference itself. However, in Volume IV of his memoirs, which was published in 1951, the year Ernest Bevin died, Churchill relates an entirely different version of events. Here Churchill states that, after the above debate, he checked his records and found that he *had* in fact discussed Unconditional Surrender officially with Roosevelt at the Casablanca Conference and that the War Cabinet, which he said he contacted by telegram about this subject, *did* in fact approve the policy in principle. Churchill admits being surprised by Roosevelt's use of the phrase at the press conference on 24 January, but only because they had already agreed not to mention the policy at that time, which, Churchill states, is why it did not appear in the official communiqué.

In his memoirs, Churchill produces two documents to support this volte-face. The first is a telegram, STRATAGEM 98, which he says he sent to the War Cabinet in London on 20 January 1943 (pages 547–9). Paragraph 6 reads:

> We propose to draw up a statement of the work of the conference for communication to the press at the proper time. I should be glad to know what the War Cabinet would think of our including in this statement a declaration of the firm intention of the United States and the British Empire to continue the war relentlessly until we have brought about the 'unconditional surrender' of Germany and Japan. The omission of Italy would be to encourage a break-up there. The President liked this idea, and it would stimulate our friends in every country.

Churchill says that, according to War Cabinet minutes, this last paragraph was discussed by the War Cabinet at their afternoon meeting on 20 January, and that he was sent the following telegram, TELESCOPE 212, in reply by the Deputy Prime Minister, Clement Attlee, and the Foreign Secretary, Anthony Eden:

> The Cabinet were unanimously of opinion that balance of advantage lay against excluding Italy, because of misgivings which would inevitably be caused in Turkey, in the Balkans, and elsewhere. Nor are we convinced that effect on Italians would be good. Knowledge of all rough stuff coming to them is surely more likely to have desired effect on Italian morale.

It is extraordinary that the Cabinet should have accepted so readily such a break with traditional British policy. It is even more extraordinary that no other member of the Cabinet ever referred to this decision. Anthony Eden, who is supposed to have sent the telegram, makes no mention of it in his memoirs. On page 376 of *The Reckoning*, Eden states that he did receive a telegram from Churchill on 20 January 1943, but says that it concerned the Prime Minister's desire to fly from Casablanca to the Eastern Mediterranean in a bid to lure

Turkey into the war on the side of the Allies. There is no reference here to the subject of 'Unconditional Surrender'. Nor is there in the diary of Eden's Private Secretary, Oliver Harvey, who in his entry for 25 January 1943 mentions only the Turkish telegrams. Moreover, Clement Attlee, the Deputy Prime Minister, when reminiscing about 'Unconditional Surrender' in *A Prime Minister Remembers*, records that Roosevelt 'more or less blurted it out' at Casablanca, forcing the British Government to agree. Attlee did not recollect whether the phrase 'Unconditional Surrender' had been referred to in an earlier document, but is adamant that *it had never been discussed.*

The matter is made even more confusing by a note on 'Unconditional Surrender' which Churchill includes on pages 552–3 of his memoirs. Churchill wrote this note for his Cabinet colleagues on 15 January 1944, and actually submitted it to the full Cabinet on 13 March of that year. This note described in some detail what the policy of 'Unconditional Surrender' meant in practice. What is essential to register here is that, in his memoirs, Churchill *omits the first paragraph of the original document*, which is to be found in the Government file Prem 3/197/2 in the Public Record Office, and which was not made available to the public until recently. The omitted paragraph reads:

1. The expression Unconditional Surrender was used by the President at Casablanca *without previous consultation*, but I thought it right to endorse what he said and it *may well be* that at that period of the war the declaration was appropriate to the circumstances [author's italics].

How can this paragraph be reconciled with the version of events Churchill gives in his memoirs? The whole Cabinet could surely not have forgotten that they had approved the principle of 'Unconditional Surrender' only a year before. How then can Churchill's deliberate omission of the above paragraph be explained? Any doubts as to what Churchill meant in the paragraph are removed by a second note on 'Unconditional Surrender' which Churchill wrote to Sir Alexander Cadogan, the Head of the Foreign Office, in April 1944: 'This matter is on the President. He announced it at Casablanca *without any consultation*. I backed him up in general terms [author's italics]...'

Moreover, on 26 January 1944, the British Chiefs of Staff Committee issued a report on 'Unconditional Surrender' which begins with the following paragraph:

> The formula of unconditional surrender was first used at Casablanca by the President and endorsed by the Prime Minister. It has subsequently been accepted as our first war aim and appears in the final Sextant Report as the overall objective of the war.

This document was signed by Field Marshal Sir Alan Brooke and Air Chief Marshal Sir Charles Portal, both of whom were present at Casablanca with Churchill and therefore knew exactly what was said at the plenary sessions attended by the President and the Prime Minister.

Not surprisingly, historians have accepted Churchill's second version of events, which means that any standard history of the Second World War will state that, prior to the press conference at Casablanca on 24 January 1943, Roosevelt and Churchill agreed on the policy of 'Unconditional Surrender' and that Churchill received the support of the British War Cabinet in London. However, the discrepancies listed above show that this version is hardly satisfactory. Clearly, the best way to clarify this confusing matter is to scrutinize the official documents on 'Unconditional Surrender' in the Public Record Office.

The first volume to consult in such a case is 'The Cabinet Office Index to Minutes & Memoranda Cab 65 & Cab 66' for 1943. This contains a reference to every subject discussed by the War Cabinet in that year. *There is no listing in this volume for 'Unconditional Surrender', 'Surrender', or 'Peace Terms'.* Churchill claims that the War Cabinet discussed 'Unconditional Surrender' on 20 January 1943. A Cabinet meeting (or Conclusions as they are called) did indeed take place on that day at 5.30 pm. The index to War Cabinet No. 12 of 1943, Confidential Annex, Cabinet papers, 65/37 lists the following topics:

12th Conclusions

    Minute 1.   French North Africa: General de Gaulle and General Giraud.

    . . .

    Minute 2.   Air Policy: Targets in France.

...

Minute 9.   Casablanca Conference: Proposed Meeting between the Prime Minister and the Representatives of Turkey.

The above Minute 9 refers to the subject mentioned by Anthony Eden in his memoirs. However, *there is no mention here in the index that 'Unconditional Surrender' was ever discussed.* The minute sheet itself is a different matter.

The relevant minute sheet contains the following:

MOST SECRET

CASABLANCA CONFERENCE

Proposed Meeting between Prime Minister and Representatives of Turkey.

The War Cabinet considered STRATAGEM No. 102 from the Prime Minister, as to his further movements.

The FOREIGN SECRETARY gave reasons why he thought it was expedient, on grounds of foreign policy, that the Prime Minister should seek a meeting in Cyprus with representatives of Turkey.

As regards the visit to Cairo, the view of the War Cabinet was that they doubted whether there were any matters of sufficient importance in Cairo to justify the Prime Minister incurring the risks of the further flights involved.

From the point of view of opinion in parliament and in the country, there would be great advantage in the Prime Minister returning home as soon as his conference with the President was over.

The Foreign Secretary was invited to prepare a draft embodying these points.

(The Foreign Secretary's draft was read to the War Cabinet at the conclusion of the Meeting and approved – See TELESCOPE 182.)

What is immediately striking about this page is that *an addition has been made to the bottom of it by someone unskilled in the use of a typewriter.* This addition, which is typed so badly that it is in parts difficult to decipher, reads as follows:

Reference was also made to paragraph 6 of STRATAGEM No. 98. In this paragraph the Prime Minister stated that it was proposed to draw up a statement of the work of the Conference for communication to the Press at the proper time. The Prime Minister added that he would like to know what the War Cabinet would think of the inclusion in this statement of a declaration of the firm intention of the United States and the British Empire to continue the war relentlessly until we have brought about the 'unconditional surrender' of Germany and Japan. The suggestion was that the omission of Italy would encourage a break-up in that country.

The War Cabinet thought that the omission of Italy was liable to be misunderstood in, for example, the Balkans. Generally, the War Cabinet thought that it was a mistake, at any rate at this stage, to make any distinction between the three partners in the Axis.

It was agreed that the Foreign Secretary should send a communication in this sense to the Prime Minister. (See TELESCOPE 212.)

This addition can simply not be accepted at face value. Its shabby appearance and its absence from the index are clear indications that *it is a false entry*. However, before one jumps to conclusions, the telegrams which Churchill includes in his memoirs must be examined.

A copy of the telegram containing the reference to 'Unconditional Surrender' to which Churchill refers in his memoirs, STRATAGEM 98, is to be found in Cabinet Papers 120/76. According to this, the telegram was sent at 14:23 hrs on 19 January and received in London at 02:40 hrs the following morning. Like the addition in the Cabinet minutes, the beginning of the telegram is badly typed. But what is of immediate interest is the first sentence:

Admiral Q [i.e. Roosevelt] and I called a plenary conference this afternoon...

This is a *factual error*. File CAB 99/24 shows that there were three plenary conferences held at Casablanca: on 15 January at 17:30 hrs, on 18 January at 17:00 hrs, and on 23 January at 17:00 hrs. *Contrary to what the telegram says, there was* no *plenary conference on 19 January –*

virtual proof that the telegram was written some time after the event by someone with a defective memory.

Cabinet papers (Cab 120/76) show that a telegram, STRATAGEM 102, was sent by Churchill to the War Cabinet at 18:59 hrs on 19 January – only *a few hours* after the 'Unconditional Surrender' telegram is reported to have been sent. This is the telegram which is mentioned by Anthony Eden in his memoirs and which was discussed by the War Cabinet on 20 January. There can therefore be no doubt as to the legitimacy of this document, which means that it can be used to test the authenticity of STRATAGEM 98.

The first point which must be noted is that this telegram *makes no reference to previous correspondence on the same subject.* This is extraordinary in view of the fact that Churchill repeats information *already contained in the suspect first telegram.* In paragraph (4) of STRATAGEM 98, Churchill wrote: 'Thought it a good opportunity to broach on plenary session the question that at the right time Alexander should become Deputy Commander in Chief to Eisenhower...' However, a few hours later, Churchill, in paragraph 2 of STRATAGEM 102, informed the War Cabinet: 'Yesterday in plenary session it was unanimously agreed that Alexander should become Eisenhower's deputy C.-in-C. of the whole of North Africa...' This does not make sense, unless, of course, *the first telegram was never sent – because it was written years after the event.*

The records also show that Churchill sent a telegram to the War Cabinet at 22:03 hrs on 20 January (STRATAGEM 126), enclosing a draft of the statement which he and Roosevelt proposed to release to the press at the end of the Casablanca Conference. Churchill told his Cabinet colleagues that it was essential that he heard from them by the following day, 21 January. The relevant part of the draft statement concludes: 'The meetings held during past week in North Africa make clear the only purpose which can be considered at this time – the winning of the war against Axis powers and with it the liberation of France.' What is important to note here is that the phrase 'Unconditional Surrender' is *not mentioned in this draft statement, or indeed anywhere in the telegram.* This is quite astonishing in view of the fact that, according to the timetable in Churchill's memoirs, the above telegram was sent *after* Churchill asked the Cabinet to consider including the phrase 'Unconditional Surrender' in the press statement and *before* he received the Cabinet's reply on 22 January. *Once again the version of events mentioned by Churchill in his memoirs does not stand up to scrutiny.*

The minutes of the plenary meeting which took place at the Casablanca Conference on 18 January contain the following paragraph:

> The Prime Minister suggested that ... we release a statement to the effect that United Nations are resolved to pursue the war to the bitter end, neither party relaxing in its efforts until the unconditional surrender of Germany and Japan has been achieved. He said that before issuing such a statement he would like to consult with his colleagues in London.

In the light of the revelations made above, the sad significance of this paragraph is obvious. *The minutes of the Casablanca Conference have also been doctored to conceal the truth about Unconditional Surrender.*

Lord Moran, Churchill's wartime physician, noticed that Churchill found it so difficult to accept that he was wrong or had made a mistake that he sometimes sought to conceal the error. Moran believed that this trait stemmed from Churchill's fits of depression and states in *Winston Churchill: The Struggle for Survival* that the Prime Minister's refusal to recognize a mistake had grown to the point where he himself was probably not aware of the fact that this influenced both his speech and his 'way of thinking'. Moran also records that Churchill found it difficult to live with the consequences of allowing Stalin to dominate Europe. Churchill, according to Moran, feared that there would be an even bloodier war which might destroy civilization and for which he would be held responsible.

Perhaps it is also useful to record here a statement made at the Tehran Conference in November 1943 by Roosevelt's adviser, Harry Hopkins, who declared, 'I have learnt that the provisions of the British Constitution and the powers of the War Cabinet are just whatever Winston Churchill wants them to be at any given moment.' Hopkins doubtless meant this comment to be taken in a light-hearted manner. However, the implications of the above revelations are in no way funny.

There is, of course, no intention here to 'blame' Churchill for what he (and others) did in respect of these forgeries. He was an old man when these 'revisions' were made and he doubtless felt great embarrassment at the way he had been treated by his wartime comrade-in-arms. Doubtless, too, he would have come under political pressure to conceal what had happened.

After all, by the time Churchill produced his memoirs, the fears he had expressed during the war about the consequences of Roosevelt's policy had become dreadful reality. Europe was divided into two camps, the democratic West and the Communist East, separated by an 'Iron Curtain', a phrase made famous by Churchill himself, although actually coined by Joseph Goebbels in the dying stages of the war. Behind this barrier which ran from the Baltic in the north to the Adriatic in the south, Stalin — the wartime ally turned evil ogre in the eyes of Washington — was said to be plotting the complete takeover of the continent. All that kept him at bay, so official policy had it, was the protection afforded to western Europe by the United States and the recently formed North Atlantic Treaty Organization. In short, America, which had invaded Europe to liberate the continent from Hitler, had felt the need to stay in western Europe after the war to keep that part free from Stalin, who had occupied the eastern half of the continent as a result of FDR's decision to remove Germany from the diplomatic chessboard. Given this situation, Churchill was in no position to do or say anything detrimental about this American-led western alliance whose proclaimed purpose was the defence of (what was left of) 'democracy and freedom' in Europe.

What is immediately important here is not the attribution of blame, but the authority to state with certainty that Roosevelt did *not* discuss the policy of 'Unconditional Surrender' with Churchill beforehand, and that he sprang the phrase on Churchill in such a manner and under such circumstances that the Prime Minister had no choice but to express agreement. To display any dissent or division in front of the world's press could have been highly damaging to the war effort, as Roosevelt, a master of press conferences, well knew.

The undeniable conclusion is that, through a simple but outrageous trick, *Roosevelt hijacked Britain's war effort for his own ends*. From the moment he announced the policy of 'Unconditional Surrender', all the blood, toil, tears and sweat expended by the British people and all the money spent by the British Government, which plunged headlong into enormous debt to the United States through Lend-Lease, went *in the pursuit of a war aim decided by Roosevelt and by Roosevelt alone.* Roosevelt's Cabinet did not know of this announcement in advance, nor did, as will shortly be shown, his Joint Chiefs of Staff. At most, a very few of Roosevelt's closest advisers, who apparently did not even include Harry Hopkins, were aware of what FDR intended to announce to the world at the press conference that sunny day in Casablanca.

Whether 'Unconditional Surrender' was a wise policy is an important issue in its own right. However, the British obviously had the right to discuss that policy beforehand and decide for themselves whether to adopt it or not. Roosevelt denied the British that right, almost certainly because he knew that they would reject the policy, as Churchill and Bevin admitted in the House of Commons. That was why FDR at Casablanca presented the world with a *fait accompli* which would not permit debate on the policy of 'Unconditional Surrender', let alone its rejection.

It is interesting to record here what impression De Gaulle drew of Roosevelt from their brief meeting in Casablanca. Roosevelt, the Frenchman declared, was out to secure 'an American peace' which would be determined by Washington and to which all the states overrrun in the war would be subjected. France in particular, De Gaulle concluded, was meant to see Roosevelt as her 'saviour and arbiter'.

Ironically, Hitler, of all people, saw clearly what had happened. In his *Testament*, which he dictated to his secretary, Martin Bormann, in his Berlin bunker on 4 February 1945, he recorded his view that Britain was not fighting her own war, but that which had been 'imposed on her by her implacable allies'.

Roosevelt's mendacity was obvious from the moment of the press conference itself. He told Harry Hopkins that the phrase just 'popped into my mind' as he was talking, *even though the words 'Unconditional Surrender' appeared in the briefing notes from which he read.* In fact, these notes, through the use of clever phraseology, leave the reader with the impression that Churchill had already agreed with Roosevelt to adopt the policy of 'Unconditional Surrender', *which is untrue*. The notes read:

> The President and the Prime Minister, after a complete survey of the world war situation, are more than ever determined that peace can come by a total elimination of German and Japanese war power. This involves a simple formula of placing the objective of this war in terms of an unconditional surrender by Germany, Italy and Japan. Unconditional surrender by them means a reasonable assurance of world peace for generations...

Robert Sherwood, in his book on Hopkins and Roosevelt, dismisses Roosevelt's version of events. Whilst preparing his book in 1948, he sought Churchill's version of what happened at Casablanca and received much the same account as Churchill was to give in the House of Commons the following July – that he first heard the phrase 'Unconditional Surrender' from Roosevelt at the press conference. After considering all the available evidence, Sherwood states categorically that the 'Unconditional Surrender' announcement 'was very deeply deliberated' and that Roosevelt made it 'with his eyes wide open', although he offers no more detail.

It is *reported* – and Chester Wilmot, who agreed with Sherwood's conclusions, refers to this in his *Struggle for Europe* published in 1952 – that Roosevelt discussed the policy of 'Unconditional Surrender' with his Joint Chiefs of Staff on 7 January, before leaving Washington for Casablanca. The minutes of this reported meeting read: 'The President said he was going to speak to Mr Churchill about the advisability of informing Mr Stalin that the United Nations were to continue on until they reach Berlin, and that their only terms would be unconditional surrender.'[3] In view of the forgeries mentioned above,

---

[3] Admiral William Leahy, an old friend of the President, was Roosevelt's representative on the Joint Chiefs of Staff (JCS) and would therefore have surely known if the issue of 'Unconditional Surrender' was ever discussed by the JCS. It is important to note therefore that in his autobiography, *I Was There*, Leahy states: 'A surprising development at the Casablanca Conference was the announcement at the final news conference held by the President and the Prime Minister of the principle of 'unconditional surrender'. As far as I could learn, this policy had not been discussed with the combined Chiefs and, from a military viewpoint, its execution might add to our difficulties in succeeding campaigns, because it would mean that we would have to destroy the enemy.' All of the above merely adds to the suspicion that this entry is yet another forgery.

one is surely justified in suspecting that the above entry is also a fake. Roosevelt, as already shown, did not discuss 'Unconditional Surrender' with Churchill, let alone the role Stalin was to play in this policy. It follows, then, that Roosevelt did not discuss this with his Joint Chiefs, either.

It is not surprising, though, that FDR is at least reported to have discussed this announcement with his top military men, for the thinking behind 'Unconditional Surrender' can be seen in General Marshall's Estimate of September 1941. This, it will be remembered, listed America's 'first major objective' as 'the complete military defeat of Germany' and pointed out that the destruction of the Nazi regime was an insufficient war aim because it was 'not at all certain' that the new German government would agree to America's peace terms. These terms, FDR made clear at Casablanca, were Unconditional Surrender.

The fact that FDR chose to make this public when Hitler's *Wehrmacht* was suffering its first serious defeats at Stalingrad and in North Africa can only mean that his statement was directed primarily at the German resistance to Hitler. FDR's public, inflexible statement was designed to tell the German conspirators, who were in fact plotting Hitler's death or arrest at that very moment, that overthrowing the Nazi regime would not be enough for America. Germany, and not Hitler's regime, was FDR's target.

Although Marshall's Estimate provided no details, there is no doubt that, from an early stage, Roosevelt prepared for the construction of the post-war world which would be brought into being by the execution of the 'Unconditional Surrender' policy. Post-war reconstruction was the responsibility of 'Wild Bill' Donovan, who was answerable to the Joint Chiefs headed by General Marshall. In fact, there is evidence that Donovan was involved in this aspect of his work *even before America entered the war.*

On 18 September 1941, Brigadier Lee, the US Military Attaché in London, received a visitor newly arrived from Washington, a British intelligence officer called 'Jones' who worked alongside Lee's old friend Hayes Kroner, who was then Chief of the Intelligence Branch of the Military Intelligence Division (G2). The ostensible reason for Jones's visit was to deliver an estimate drawn up by Kroner. However,

Jones took the opportunity to complain about Donovan. According to Jones, Donovan had become very mysterious and, as a result of this, people were afraid to deal with him. Jones added that Donovan had apparently mobilized a group of professors. In his diary, Lee stated that if Donovan and his professors were indeed planning post-war reconstruction, they had better make a better job of drawing 'the boundary lines' than they had done after the First World War: otherwise they would simply make 'another mess of it'.

The intelligence unit to which Jones and Lee were referring was almost certainly the 'Research and Analysis' branch of Donovan's organization. According to Anthony Cave Brown in his *Donovan, The Last Hero*, this unit was also known as the 'College of Cardinals'. A senior member of this unit, and its head from September 1942, was William L. Langer, the brother of Walter Langer, the man tasked by Donovan to produce the psychological portrait of Hitler mentioned earlier. In his autobiography, *In and Out of the Ivory Tower*, William Langer describes Donovan as 'a truly charismatic personality' with 'an exceptional gift for arousing the interest and enthusiasm of others and of enlisting their loyalty and devotion'. Here, Langer also sheds light on the people Donovan recruited for his organization, 'a veritable galaxy of prominent lawyers and bankers, manufacturers, foreign service officers, and merchants'. The man chosen by Donovan initially to lead his analysts was the diplomatic historian James Phinney Baxter III, the President of William College, who in turn established a staff of experts in various fields.

It is interesting at this juncture to examine some of the people recruited by Donovan, not because these people were necessarily themselves policy-makers, but because their very selection indicates that what they had already said or written found favour with Donovan and, by extension, Roosevelt.

Not surprisingly, one business expert recruited almost immediately by Donovan was Douglas Miller, the former Commercial Attaché to the US Embassy in Berlin and author of *You Can't Do Business with Hitler*, which called for the United States to attack Germany before Hitler had the time to organize his 'New Order' in Europe, and which was publicly praised by Roosevelt himself. Expecting war to break out in

Europe that summer, Miller resigned his diplomatic post in May 1939 and returned to the United States, where he took up a position as Assistant Professor of Economics in the School of Commerce of the University of Denver. After publishing his book on Hitler in mid-1941, Miller obtained leave of absence from his university to begin a study of the economy of Nazi Germany, under the auspices of the Rockefeller Foundation in New York. Shortly afterwards, and before America entered the war, he joined Donovan's newly formed organization in a very senior capacity. *Current Biography 1941* listed Miller's occupation as 'assistant to William J. Donovan, United States coordinator of defense information'. It is important therefore to examine what Miller had to say about the future in his best-selling book.

In line with the suspicion raised by Raymond Lee in his diary, the last chapter in Miller's book is entitled 'Our Post-War Policy'. In this chapter, which can seriously be viewed as a blueprint for the modern world once the United States had defeated Germany and established her global hegemony, Miller makes one crucial point early on to his American readers: '... in thinking a long way ahead towards a final world settlement, it seems to me that there are only two alternatives. There is no use for us to consider a stalemate or regulated peace... This leaves us two alternative settlements for a future world – a German settlement or an American settlement.' This quotation can surely be seen as the origin of Roosevelt's insistence on 'Unconditional Surrender'. There was to be no compromise with Hitler, *indeed with Germany*. The war was to be fought until America had established her unquestioned supremacy.

What role, however, would the British play in this American settlement? As Churchill found out to his great surprise at Casablanca, the British would have no say in the major decisions and would be expected to tag along. Machiavelli warns of this danger when he writes: '... a prince should never join in an aggressive alliance with someone more powerful than himself, unless it is a matter of necessity... This is because if you are the victors, you emerge as his prisoner.' Writing hundreds of years later, Douglas Miller showed that time had not diluted the truth of Machiavelli's caveat: 'We must not worry unduly about the British peace aims; by the time this war is over the chief

British aim will be their aim to please us. Right now we could undoubtedly secure the British assent to any and all peace proposals that we had in mind.' With the British in their place, Miller issues a clarion call to his fellow Americans: 'The more difficult task is for us to make up our minds what kind of post-war world we wish to see, and how we are going to create it. No one is going to prevent us; we shall be elected to this task by a unanimous ballot. We must perform it – not to save the world, but to save ourselves.'

And what sort of world did Miller envisage?

> In thinking about the post-war world, after an American victory, we must imagine Europe almost completely stripped of peacetime production, her peacetime industries shattered, worn out from years of effort without installation of new equipment, and blown to bits by aerial bombs and land artillery... Only one great country will possess the mechanical equipment, the raw materials, the finances, and the energy to rebuild a post-war world. America alone will have the strength, the resources, and the leadership which are needed... We want to give employment to our own people, to maintain our price level, expand our world trade, create thousands of interesting and well-paid jobs for Americans in foreign countries; and all this will cost us only one thing – increased effort. After all, that is what we want. We all desire interesting, stimulating, well-paid employment. We Americans do not desire to stagnate and allow our machines to rust. We like activity and enterprise. We shall have nothing to lose in such a programme, and, in very truth, *a world to gain* [author's italics].

Miller seems here to be saying that it does not matter how much Europe will suffer in the bringing about of an *American peace*, because the United States will repair the damage. That is to say, the total subjugation of Germany will involve a fight to the finish from which America will emerge as the last man standing, with all other combatant countries bankrupt or devastated, or both. This prediction, which Miller made in early 1941 before any substantial fighting had taken place, was certainly accurate. As Lord Hankey, himself a one-time member of Churchill's Cabinet, points out in his book *Politics, Trials and Errors* published shortly after the war, the policy of Unconditional Surrender left not only enemy countries, but *everyone*, except America, 'impoverished and in dire straits'.

Churchill was himself well aware that it was in Britain's financial interest to end the war as quickly as possible. In a letter to Roosevelt on 4 March 1944 about Britain's parlous economic position, Churchill pointed out that the British 'alone of the Allies will emerge from the war with great overseas debts' and urged the President to help keep Britain's dollar reserves above one billion dollars, adding 'the shortening of the war *even by a month* would far exceed the sums under consideration [author's italics].'

In considering the behind-the-scenes influence which *You Can't Do Business with Hitler* had on Roosevelt at Casablanca and in the formulation of any hidden agenda, one should note that Douglas Miller's book clearly influenced the *official agenda* of the conference. It will be remembered that Miller calls in his book for an American land offensive against Germany 'from the West', as opposed to one launched via Italy or the Balkans, which was suggested by the British at various times during the war. The groundwork for *Operation Overlord*, the Allied landings in France, was indeed laid at Casablanca. It will also be remembered that Miller calls in his book for this invasion to be preceded by a lengthy bombing campaign against Germany, a strategy which was adopted at Casablanca in the form of the Combined Bombing Offensive.

The aim of the bombing offensive, as envisaged by the Allied commanders at Casablanca, was 'the progressive destruction and dislocation of the German military, industrial and economic system, and the undermining of the morale of the German people to a point where their capacity for armed resistance is fatally weakened.' On page 119 of his book, Miller states that the invasion of Germany should only be carried out after she had been subjected to a massive aerial bombing campaign which would last for years. Miller explains what he envisages:

... an ever-increasing supply of bombers and fighting 'planes which can swarm over the heart of Germany's industrial regions, destroying land and sea communications, harbours, docks, factories, railways stations, and public buildings. We can smash the vulnerable factories for manufacturing ersatz materials. We can effectively cripple the huge German war machine by stopping its production of synthetic fuel and lubricants. We can destroy the plants manufacturing cotton and wool substitutes. We can prevent the Germans from securing adequate supplies of fats and vegetable oils. We can cause Hitler's machine to crumble by pulling out the pin at critical points. Only then, when the German army is starved, immobilized, and bewildered, will a final attack of mechanized land forces upon the Continent be necessary to clinch the victory.

As anyone who has studied the Second World War will be able to see from the above, Miller's 1941 plan, with some modifications, is what came to pass. (A major modification in Miller's plan to secure an American peace derived from the role played by Stalin who, it must be stressed, was not involved in the war when Miller published the first edition of his book.)

Another person recruited by Donovan was Edgar Ansel Mowrer, a foreign correspondent of the *Chicago Daily News*, the newspaper owned by Roosevelt's Secretary of the Navy, Frank Knox. Mowrer accompanied Donovan on his trip to London in the summer of 1940 when 'Wild Bill', at Roosevelt's request, assessed the British will and ability to resist Hitler. (Donovan travelled under the guise of a *Chicago Daily News* reporter.) On their return to America, Mowrer and Donovan wrote a series of articles on German fifth-column tactics based, according to H. Montgomery Hyde in his book *The Quiet Canadian*, on material supplied by William Stephenson, head of the British intelligence network in North America. The gist of these articles, which were published by Knox and offered free by him to editors as part of America's defence program, was that Hitler had been helped in his conquests by German sympathizers and expatriate Germans living in the countries invaded by the Third Reich. In these articles, Mowrer concluded that the United States probably possessed the 'finest Nazi-schooled fifth column in the world, one which, in case of war with Germany, could be our undoing'. Donovan discussed these articles in a nationwide radio 'link-up', the first such opportunity given to anyone other than the President.

In 1928, Mowrer wrote *This American World*, in which he outlined how, in his view, American influence would inevitably spread throughout the globe. In the chapter entitled 'Europe Becomes Americanized', Mowrer asked, 'What is plainer in American history than the cultural drawing power of military success?' By way of explanation he went on to describe America's performance in the First World War when the United States raised and equipped a huge army at 'Myrmidon speed' and then shipped it to Europe to inflict the *coup de grâce* on Imperial Germany. If America's successes in engineering and economics were added to this military achievement, Mowrer maintained, it became obvious why the United States was beginning to impose its lifestyle on both Europe and Asia and why the country was 'loved and hated accordingly'. To reinforce his argument, Mowrer quoted Machiavelli, using a phrase which, the American maintained, was 'worth many books' – *Vincere fu sempre mirabil' cosa*. Vincere fu sempre mirabil' cosa! To win has always been a wonderful thing! To win unconditionally is, of course, even more wonderful.

The concept of a united Europe did not worry Mowrer. He conceded that such an entity could well defeat America in a war. However, as he pointed out with remarkable prescience, a united Europe could only be created 'under pressure of atrocious fear' and, in any case, the Americans could still win by 'buying out of the European block a major ally or two'.

Mowrer is best known as the author of the Pulitzer Prize-winning *Germany Puts the Clock Back,* in which he describes the ruthless nature of the Nazi movement. He also criticizes at length the principle of *autarky* (self-sufficiency) which Hitler, in order to free his country from the grip of international financiers, made the basis of his economic policies. Referring to the German economists Hans Zehrer and Ferdinand Fried, who propounded this principle through the journal *Die Tat*, Mowrer argues that the views of these men 'strengthened the suspicion that Germany – Prussia at least – was hardly part of the western world at all'. In fact, Mowrer concludes that what was wrong with Germany was not Hitler, or the Nazi movement, but *Prussia*, the home of militarism. As he says in the final chapter of the first edition of his book, 'with the possible exception of Japan, the entire civilised world had outgrown the Prussian conception of society.'

The refusal to draw any distinction between Nazis and Germans was certainly a prime characteristic of Roosevelt's policy. Indeed, unlike Churchill, Roosevelt harboured a deep personal dislike of Germans, a sentiment which may have stemmed from his Dutch ancestry or possibly from the time he spent as a schoolboy in Germany. Roosevelt expressed his true feelings about Germans during the Munich crisis when, despite the conciliatory message he was spreading in public, he privately urged the British and French governments to bomb Germany into submission. Certainly, in his first major statement on 'Unconditional Surrender' in December 1943, Roosevelt declared it the intention of the United Nations to 'rid Germany once and for all of Nazism and Prussian militarism and the fantastic and disastrous notion that they constitute the "Master Race".' On 1 April 1944, he told his military commanders that, while he was not out to destroy the German people, he was not willing to say then that 'we do not intend to destroy the German nation'. When he heard in late August 1944, from his Secretary of the Treasury and long-time friend Henry Morgenthau, that Churchill had plans to rebuild Germany's economy after the war – thus enabling her to pay reparations – Roosevelt told Morgenthau that all he needed was a half-hour with Churchill and he would 'correct this', adding that they had 'to be tough with Germany and I mean the German people, not just the Nazis'. It was a case, Roosevelt stated, of castrating (sic) the Germans or finding a way of stopping them from behaving as they had in the past.

The phrase 'Unconditional Surrender' was itself not new: General Grant had, of course, coined the phrase during the American Civil War and it had been in use in America during the First World War. In fact, Roosevelt's distant cousin, the former President Theodore Roosevelt, had urged President Wilson to adopt this policy against Imperial Germany. This did not happen, and hostilities were brought to an end in the First World War through an armistice and then the Versailles Peace treaty, a settlement that Hitler denounced as a 'dictated peace' which he was determined from the very beginning of his rule to overthrow.

Defenders of the adoption of the policy of 'Unconditional Surrender' in the Second World War have pointed to Hitler's success in building the myth amongst his people that Germany had not been defeated in 1918. According to Hitler's version of events, the Imperial German Army was stabbed in the back by its own Government and Germany was cheated by the Allies at the Peace Congress at Versailles. There is no doubt that the circumstances surrounding the end of the First World War allowed this myth to develop in Germany. The Armistice of 1918 came into effect while the German army was still in France, and allowed the German soldiers to march home with their weapons and colours to a home front which, until the Government suddenly sued for peace, had been misled by official propaganda into believing that victory was imminent. 'Unconditional Surrender' in the Second World War, Roosevelt's defenders have argued, carried the war right into Germany and left the Germans in no doubt that they had been well and truly defeated in a war which their Government started.

However, the impression must not be given that Roosevelt's policy was uncritically accepted. Chester Wilmot, in his *Struggle for Europe*, writes that by publicly announcing the policy at Casablanca, 'the Anglo-Saxon powers denied themselves any freedom of diplomatic manoeuvre and denied the German people any avenue of escape from Hitler.' Admiral Canaris, the head of Hitler's counter-intelligence service and a leading anti-Nazi, told a subordinate that the policy disarmed the German resistance to Hitler of its last weapon. From then on, the German resistance movement had no incentive to overthrow Hitler if the new government would be faced with the same inflexible policy. No government could ever be expected to hand over its people unconditionally to another country, let alone to a tyrant like Joseph Stalin. Allied military commanders tried in vain to have the policy altered, or at least watered down, because of the fierce resistance the German army was putting up. Eisenhower, the Supreme Allied Commander in Europe, has been quoted as saying that if a man had to choose between being hanged and charging 20 bayonets, he would choose the latter course. In typical fashion, Eisenhower's British subordinate, Field Marshal Montgomery, bluntly called the policy a 'tragic mistake'.

Roosevelt's own Secretary of State, Cordell Hull, opposed the policy on two grounds: firstly, that it could lengthen the war by 'solidifying Axis resistance into one of desperation'; and secondly, that it would require the victorious nations to occupy and govern Germany after the war. Hull concluded, 'We and our Allies were in no way prepared to undertake this vast obligation.'

In May 1943, James P. Warburg, a banker in civilian life who as Deputy Director of the Overseas Branch of the Office of War Information was responsible for propaganda warfare in the European theatre, became so alarmed at the way in which German propaganda was using 'Unconditional Surrender' that he put up a paper to Roosevelt entitled 'State of Mind of German People and the Need for a Statement of American Policy'. He pointed out that this inflexible policy was enabling Goebbels to tell the German people that the Allies intended 'to destroy them utterly and dismember their country', and he called for a public statement which would show the Germans that whatever they suffered in defeat would not be as bad as what a continuation of the war would mean for them. Warburg attached a seven-paragraph draft statement which, amongst other things, sought to assure the Germans that America would not take part in mass reprisals against them and that after the war German resources would be 'held in trust' for the German people and order maintained in the country by the United Nations. Warburg claimed that Roosevelt at first looked favourably upon this paper, but then sent it back with a note saying that a further statement should be 'held in abeyance for a short time at least'. (Warburg, mistakenly, attributed this attitude to Churchill, who was visiting Washington at the time.)

Roosevelt did not need a new paper to examine Hitler's own state of mind. In the study of Hitler's psychology drawn up by Walter Langer, Langer stated with certainty that Hitler would not surrender. Langer was sure Hitler meant what he said when he uttered the following words: 'We shall not capitulate – no, never. We may be destroyed, but if we are, we shall drag a world with us ... a world in flames.' In his authoritative *History of the Second World War*, Basil Liddell Hart, regarded by some as a military historian of genius, goes so far as to say that the greatest obstacle the Allies faced in beating Hitler was 'their leaders unwise and short sighted demand for "unconditional surrender"'. Liddell Hart maintains that if the Allies had provided the German people with serious peace terms, then Hitler would have been overthrown long before 1945. As it was, the German resistance was given no encouragement by the Allies and therefore found it difficult to persuade people to take 'a leap in the dark'.

One can only surmise as to what Liddell Hart would have said if he had learned the truth about how the policy of 'Unconditional Surrender' came to be accepted as Allied policy. What *is* known is the opinion of Heinz Guderian, a German general who studied and mastered the principles of *Blitzkrieg* first outlined by Liddell Hart, and who was obviously in a position to describe accurately what it was like to be on the receiving end of Roosevelt's policy.

Guderian writes in his memoirs, *Panzer Leader,* that 'this brutal formula' had a great effect on the German nation and even more so on the German Army which concluded that the Allies were intent on the 'utter destruction of Germany' and were fighting not just against the Nazi regime, but against 'their efficient, and therefore dangerous, rivals *for the trade of the world* [author's italics]'.

No sane person could question the need to destroy Hitler's regime and, as General Marshall pointed out in his Estimate of September 1941, that could not be achieved with certainty without America's active involvement in the war. But, by the same token, could a fair-minded person read Douglas Miller's book and doubt that there is truth in what Guderian says? 'A world to gain' and 'for the trade of the world' do indeed sound like two ways of expressing the same point. Moreover, Miller's book and Marshall's Estimate both make clear one important fact about the Second World War, namely that Roosevelt's target was not just the Nazi regime, but Germany herself.

Anyone who questions this need look no further than the notorious Morgenthau plan which Roosevelt persuaded Churchill to initial at the Quebec Conference in September 1944.

```
W.M. (43) 6th Conclusions,
              Minute 2.        Air Policy:  U-boat Bases in the Bay of
                               Biscay.

            9th Conclusions,
              Minute 1.        French North Africa:  General de Gaulle
                               and General Giraud.

           11th Conclusions.   French North Africa:  General de Gaulle
                               and General Giraud.

           12th Conclusions,
              Minute 1.        French North Africa:  General de Gaulle
                               and General Giraud.

              Minute 2.        Air Policy:  Targets in France.

              Minute 9.        Casablanca Conference:  Proposed
                               Meeting between Prime Minister and
                               Representatives of Turkey.

           13th and 14th       Casablanca Conference:  Proposed
              Conclusions.     Meeting between Prime Minister and
                               Representatives of Turkey.

           15th Conclusions,
              Minute 1.        Casablanca Conference:  Proposed
                               Meeting between the Prime Minister and
                               Representatives of Turkey.

           18th Conclusions,
              Minute 1.        Casablanca Conference:  Proposed
                               Meeting between the Prime Minister and
                               Representatives of Turkey.

           19th Conclusions,
              Minute 1.        France:  The French Fleet at Alexandria.

           20th Conclusions.   France:  The French Fleet.

           22nd Conclusions.   France: The French Fleet.

           25th Conclusions,
              Minute 1.        India:  Detention of Mr. Gandhi.
```

The Index to War Cabinet No. 12 ('Conclusions') which took place on the afternoon of 20 January 1943 (CAB 65/37). It will be noted that there is no reference here to the subject of 'Unconditional Surrender' being discussed.

The Cabinet Office Index to Minutes & Memoranda Cab 65 & 66 for 1943 confirms that the subject of 'Unconditional Surrender' was not discussed by the War Cabinet at any time that year. (Crown Copyright PRO.)

(THIS DOCUMENT IS THE PROPERTY OF HIS BRITANNIC MAJESTY'S GOVERNMENT).

TO BE KEPT UNDER LOCK AND KEY.

It is requested that special care may be taken to
ensure the secrecy of this document.

20

MOST SECRET.

COPY NO. 5

W.M.(43) 12th CONCLUSIONS, MINUTE 9.

Confidential Annex.

(20th January, 1943 - 5.30 p.m.)

CASABLANCA
CONFERENCE.
————
Proposed
Meeting
between
Prime Minister
and Representa-
tives of Turkey.

The War Cabinet considered STRATAGEM No. 102[†] from the Prime Minister, as to his further movements.

THE FOREIGN SECRETARY gave reasons why he thought it was inexpedient, on grounds of foreign policy, that the Prime Minister should seek a meeting in Cyprus with representatives of Turkey.

As regards the visit to Cairo, the view of the War Cabinet was that they doubted whether there were any matters. of sufficient importance in Cairo to justify the Prime Minister incurring the risks of the further flights involved.

From the point of view of opinion in Parliament and in the country, there would be great advantage in the Prime Minister returning home as soon as his conference. with the President was over.

The Foreign Secretary was invited to prepare a draft embodying these points.

(The Foreign Secretary's draft was read to the War Cabinet at the conclusion of the Meeting and approved - See TELESCOPE 182)[†]

Reference was also made to paragraph 6 of STRATAGEM No. 96. In this paragraph the Prime Minister stated that it was proposed to draw up a statement of the work of the Conference for communication to the Press at the proper time. The Prime Minister added that he would like to know what the War Cabinet would think of the inclusion in this statement of a declaration of the firm intention of the United States and the British Empire to continue the war relentlessly until we have brought about the "unconditional surrender" of Germany and Japan. The suggestion was that the omission of Italy would encourage a break-up in that country.

The War Cabinet thought that the omission of Italy was liable to be misunderstood in, for example, the Balkans. Generally, the War Cabinet thought that it was a mistake, at any rate at this stage, to make any distinction between the three partners in the Axis.

It was agreed that the Foreign Secretary should send a communication in this sense to the Prime Minister. (See TELESCOPE 212).

Offices of the War Cabinet, S.W.1.

† copies attached

The Minute Sheet for the 12th meeting of the War Cabinet in 1943 (CAB 65/ 37). The index shows that the subject of 'Unconditional Surrender' was not discussed. However, a badly typed false entry stating that this subject was raised and approved in principle has been added to the bottom of the page. (Crown Copyright PRO.)

CASABLANCA
CONFERENCE:
———
Proposed
Meeting
between
Prime Minister
and Representa-
tives of Turkey.

The War Cabinet considered STRATAGEM No. 108 from the Prime Minister, as to his further movements.

THE FOREIGN SECRETARY gave reasons why he thought it was inexpedient, on grounds of foreign policy, that the Prime Minister should seek a meeting in Cyprus with representatives of Turkey.

As regards the visit to Cairo, the view of the War Cabinet was that they doubted whether there were any matters of sufficient importance in Cairo to justify the Prime Minister incurring the risks of the further flights involved.

From the point of view of opinion in Parliament and in the country, there would be great advantage in the Prime Minister returning home as soon as his conference with the President was over.

The Foreign Secretary was invited to prepare a draft embodying these points.

(The Foreign Secretary's draft was read to the War Cabinet at the conclusion of the Meeting and approved - See TELESCOPE 189).

Reference was also made to paragraph 6 of STRATAGEM No. 98. In this paragraph the Prime Minister stated that it was proposed to draw up a statement of the work of the Conference for communication to the Press at the proper time. The Prime Minister asked would think of the inclusion in this statement of a declaration of the firm intention of the United States and the British Empire to continue the war relentlessly until we have brought about the "unconditional surrender" of Germany and Japan. The suggestion was that the omission of Italy would encourage a break-up in that country.

The War Cabinet thought that the omission of Italy was liable to be misunderstood in, for example, the Balkans. Generally, the War Cabinet thought that it was a mistake, at any rate at this stage, to make any distinction between the three partners in the Axis.

It was agreed that the Foreign Secretary should send a communication in this sense to the Prime Minister. (See TELESCOPE 212).

An enlargement of the false entry added to the Minutes of the 12th meeting of the War Cabinet in 1943 (CAB 65/37). This is so badly typed that it is difficult to decipher. What is clear, though, is that the documents mentioned in this false entry, STRATAGEM 98 and TELESCOPE 212 (CAB 120/76), are fakes. (Crown Copyright PRO.)

HUSH - MOST SECRET · · IN

HUSH MOST SECRET.   M E S S A G E   IN

1423/19 January.

From H.M.S.BULOLO.

Date 20.1.43.

Recd. 0249

NAVAL CYPHER SPECIAL (X) by W/T

Addressed Admiralty.

126.   From Prime Minister to Deputy Prime Minister and War Cabinet.   (STRATAGEM No. 98)

Admiral Q and I called a plenary conference this afternoon at which the Combined Chiefs of Staff reported progress. It was a most satisfactory meeting. After five days discussions and a good deal of apparent disagreement the Combined Chiefs of Staff are now I think unanimous in essentials about the conduct of the war in 1943 their final report is not yet ready but the following is the gist of the statement which C.I.G.S. made on their behalf. The security of sea communications was agreed to be the first charge upon our combined resources and the principle reaffirmed that we must concentrate first on the defeat of Germany. Full preparations for HUSKY are to go ahead at once with a view to carrying out the operation at the earliest possible moment. In addition we hope to mount ANAKIM towards the end of this year. The Americans have undertaken to supply the lion's share of the assault shipping and landing craft, which will be American manned and also to help us out with Naval covering forces. At home BOLERO is to go ahead as fast as our commitments allow with a view to a sledgehammer of some sort this year or a return to the continent with all available forces if Germany shows definite signs. of collapse. In the Pacific operations for the capture of Rabaul and the clearing of New Guinea are to continue in order to retain the initiative and hold Japan. Whether this offensive should subsequently be carried forward to Truk will be a matter for decision later in the year.

(1) Admiral Q and I were in complete agreement with the above outline.

(2) Having learned that in the course of the discussions of the Combined Chiefs of Staff the fear had been expressed by the American representatives that we might pull out once Germany was defeated, I thought it right to say in categorical terms that our interest and our honour were alike engaged and that the determination of British Parliament and

people.....

The first page of STRATAGEM 98 (CAB 120/76) mentioned in the false entry to the Minute Sheet for the 12th meeting of the War Cabinet in 1943. This doctored document purports to have been sent by Churchill in Casablanca to the War Cabinet in London. Note the untidy headings, all evidence of tampering. (Crown Copyright PRO.)

HUSH - MOST SECRET   IN

~ 2 ~

people to devote their whole resources to the
defeat of Japan after Germany had been brought to
her knees was not, in doubt. I added that I was
sure that the War Cabinet would be fully prepared
to enter into a formal treaty or pact with the
United States on this point. Admiral Q brushed
aside the idea since he was confident that the
United States and the British Empire were entirely
of one mind in this matter. He added however that
it would be very desirable if it were at all possible
to get a definite engagement - secret if necessary -
from Russia that they would join in the struggle
against Japan once Germany was out of the war.

(3) Having reached agreement on broad principles
the Chiefs of Staff will have to spend the next ten
days examining ways and means. There is a good deal
of detailed work to be done and I do not think they
ought to separate for several days. It will in any
event be necessary to have another conference of this
kind within the next six months the necessity for this
was particularly stressed by General Marshall.

(4) Thought it a good opportunity to broach on
plenary session the question that at the right time
Alexander should become Deputy Commander in Chief to
Eisenhower, see paragraph 4 of STRATAGEM NO.56.
It was warmly welcomed by Marshall and King. The
difficult question of air command is under active
consideration and will I am assured be settled
satisfactorily.

(5) The War Cabinet should know that General
Marshall asked to place on formal record his admiration
of the profound contribution which had been rendered to
the Allied cause in North Africa by Admiral Cunningham.
His Naval leadership and skill had been outstanding and
his wisdom and counsel had been of the greatest help
to General Eisenhower. Admiral Q also paid a warm
tribute to Field Marshal Sir John Dill. He had come to
be regarded by the Americans as an indispensable link
between the United States and British Chiefs of Staff
on military policy.

(6) We propose to draw up a statement of the
work of the conference for communication to the press
at the proper time. I should be glad to know what the
War Cabinet would think of our including in this
statement a declaration of the firm intention of the
United States and the British Empire to continue the
war relentlessly until we have brought about the
"unconditional surrender" of Germany and Japan. The
omission of Italy would be to encourage a break up
there. The President liked this idea, and it would
stimulate our friends in every country.

(7)....

Paragraph (6) of STRATAGEM 98 (CAB 120/76), which calls for a statement on 'Unconditional Surrender', is a fabrication. A similar paragraph in the Minutes of the plenary session of the Casablanca Conference held on 18 January (CAB 99/24) must also be a fake. (Crown Copyright PRO.)

HUSH - MOST SECRET IN

HUSH MOST SECRET.   M E S S A G E   IN

From H.M.S. BULOLO.   1859A/19 January.

                                       Date 20.1.43.

                                       Recd. 0312

           NAVAL CYPHER (O.T.P.) BY W/T

Addressed Admiralty.

IMMEDIATE.

129.   STRATAGEM No. 102.

          Prime Minister to Deputy Prime Minister
and Foreign Secretary.   IMMEDIATE Personal and
MOST SECRET.

     1.   It looks as if we shall finish up here
Friday January 22nd, and Admiral Q will depart
thereafter. He proposes on Friday to give a State
luncheon to the Sulton of Morocco to which I am
invited, and also contemplates a press conference
with all the British and American correspondents
available, at which he and presumably I will
answer questions as we did at the White House.
I see no difficulty in this. The release will not
take place until he has definitely quitted African
shores.

     2.   Yesterday in plenary session it was
unanimously agreed that Alexander should become
Eisenhower's deputy C. in C. of the whole of North
Africa. General Marshall proposed that the command
of any sledgehammer or round-up which may be
undertaken this year should be British.

     3.   I also raised the Turkish question, having
explored the ground beforehand, with Admiral Q.
It was agreed that we play the hand in Turkey whether
in munitions or diplomacy the Americans taking the
lead in China and of course in French North Africa.
You will be pleased at this.

     4.   As soon as Admiral Q has gone I shall, if
weather is good fly Marrakesh to Cairo, where I
propose to stay for 2 or 3 days and settle several
important matters.

     5.   I have no doubt, and C.I.G.S. agrees,
that Jumbo Wilson is far and away the best man to
take over the Middle East Command when it is vacated
by Alexander. I am arranging for him to meet me in

                                       Cairo.....

STRATAGEM 102 (CAB 120/76) which was sent by Churchill in Casablanca to the Deputy Prime Minister and Foreign Secretary in London only hours after STRATAGEM 98 is reported to have been dispatched. There is, though, no reference here to STRATAGEM 98 or to 'Unconditional Surrender'. (Crown Copyright PRO.)

HUSH - MOST SECRET · IN

2203A/20 January.

M E S S A G E   I N

From: H.M.S. BULOLO   Date: 21.1.43.

Recd. 0140

NAVAL CYPHER (OTP) by W/T

Addressed: Admiralty.

MOST IMMEDIATE

156. STRATAGEM NO. 126.

Prime Minister to Deputy Prime Minister and Foreign Secretary.

1. The President has shown me the enclosed draft statement. I invite your comment upon it and will very likely propose some changes in it myself. It is essential that I hear from you tomorrow 21st.

2. We have been waiting all day for a further reply from De Gaulle or for some explanation by you. If De Gaulle does not come President will make an arrangement very favourable for General Giraud which I shall not easily be able to resist. Giraud has made excellent impression on everyone here military and political alike.

3. The President proposes to raise rate of exchange from 75 francs to dollar to 50 and he asks whether we will alter our rate in Madagascar and elsewhere in reverse direction to have one unique rate of 50. On this point I seek your advice. Draft Statement begins:

Suggested joint Statement by the President and the Prime Minister. The President and the Prime Minister met in Northern Africa on January 14th. They were accompanied by or preceded by members of Combined Staff.

Since then there have been daily conferences relating to continuation and strengthening of war effort. The plans are progressing in every way, favourably.

They have received visits from Mr. Murphy and Mr. MacMillan, Generals Eisenhower, Clark and Spaatz of American Expeditionary Force in North Africa, and also from General Alexander and Air Marshal Tedder from British 8th Army operating in Tripoli.

The President was accompanied by Mr. Hopkins, and the meeting was joined by Mr. Averill Harriman and Lord Leathers of the British Shipping Administration, who came from London.

General.....

STRATAGEM 126 (CAB 120/76) which was sent by Churchill in Casablanca to the British War Cabinet in London late on 20 January 1943. This document, which concerns the draft of a press release at the end of the Casablanca Conference, makes no reference at all to previous correspondence on 'Unconditional Surrender'. This is not surprising for there had in fact been none. (Crown Copyright PRO.)

10

A Potato Patch

It was a hot, sticky day in East Prussia on 20 July 1944 and, as a result, the Führer Conference at the *Wolfsschanze* was held in the *Lagabaracke,* a wooden hut, and not the usual underground bunker (which was in any case being renovated). As Mussolini was arriving at the camp at 2.30 that afternoon, *en route* to visiting Italian divisions fighting on the eastern front, Hitler had brought the time of the meeting forward from 1.00 p.m. to 12.30.

These conferences were becoming increasingly gloomy. The encircling jaw of Germany's enemies was beginning to tighten around her. Six weeks before, on 6 June, the 'final attack of mechanized land forces' upon the continent of Europe, advocated in 1941 by Douglas Miller in *You Can't Do Business with Hitler,* had begun with the Allied landings in Normandy under the US command of General Eisenhower. The *Wehrmacht* had worked wonders in containing the thrusts of the British, American and Canadian armies, but it would be only a matter of time until the German units in Normandy broke under the terrible punishment they were taking each day. To coincide with the invasion of France by his allies, Stalin had launched a massive offensive along the eastern front which was finally sweeping the Germans from Russian soil, and by mid-July brought the Red Army to within 100 miles of the *Wolfsschanze* itself. Germany was staring disaster in the face. Only a miracle — or a dramatic act — could save the Fatherland now.

The conference was already a few minutes old when a ruffled Field Marshal Keitel entered the room, accompanied by the dramatic figure of Colonel Count Claus von Stauffenberg, the Chief of Staff of the Home Army, who had just arrived by air from Berlin. A lean, strikingly handsome man, Stauffenberg graphically displayed his courage in the wounds he had received on a North African battlefield, where he lost his left eye, his right arm and the third and fourth fingers of his left hand. What he did not display openly, though, was the hatred he carried for Hitler and all that Nazi Germany had come to represent. While recuperating in hospital from his wounds, he had told a trusted surgeon: 'I could never look the wives and children of the fallen in the eye if I did not do something to stop this senseless slaughter.'

Stauffenberg had been summoned to the *Wolfsschanze* to deliver a report on how the Home Army could be used to reinforce front-line units. However, this day was the chance which he and his fellow conspirators had long planned for. The crippled Colonel saw the trip as an opportunity to rid Germany once and for all of the man who had besmirched her name and was threatening to bring about her destruction. In the briefcase which Stauffenberg carried in the claw of his left hand was a bomb, primed to explode in a few minutes.

There were over 20 people in the conference room, which was about 30 feet long by 15 wide. In the middle of the room stood a specially designed oak map table which rested, not on legs, but on two heavy supports. Hitler was seated at the centre of the table with his back to the door, listening to a report on the collapsing Russian front from his Chief of Operations, General Heusinger, who, like every officer in the room, stood in his Führer's presence. Keitel brought Stauffenberg's arrival to Hitler's attention, but the Supreme Warlord wanted to hear all of Heusinger's report before considering what the Home Army could offer.

Stauffenberg moved to Hitler's right, where he joined General Korten, the *Luftwaffe* Chief of Staff, and Colonel Heinz Brandt, Heusinger's Chief of Staff. With only a few minutes to go before the acid in the bomb's timing mechanism would eat away the restraint on the detonator, he placed his briefcase under the table and shoved it casually with his foot towards Hitler's legs. Then, under the pretext of receiving an urgent telephone call from Berlin, he excused himself and hurried out of the hut towards a bunker a few hundred yards away, where a fellow plotter, General Fellgiebel, was waiting.

In the conference room, Heusinger intended to conclude his report with a warning. The Russian advance was proving so swift, he said, that unless the German Army Group 'around Lake Peipus is not immediately withdrawn, a catastrophe...' That was as far Heusinger got. At that point, 12.42 p.m., the bomb exploded with an orange flash, blowing the room apart and bringing the roof crashing down. Stauffenberg and Fellgiebel witnessed this spectacle and saw bodies come flying out of the hut on to the surrounding grass. Not doubting the success of their mission, the two men split up. Fellgiebel would inform their colleagues in Berlin by telephone that Hitler was dead, and then do his utmost to jam communications to and from the *Wolfsschanze* for as long as possible. Stauffenberg set off for Berlin to take part in Operation Valkyrie, the *coup d'état* which would sweep away the Nazi regime and replace it with a government ready and willing to negotiate with the Allies for an honourable peace.

It was almost 5.00 p.m. by the time Stauffenberg arrived back at the Home Army headquarters in Berlin's Bendlerstrasse, which the conspirators had made their own centre of operations. On his return to Berlin, Stauffenberg had been astonished to see that nothing had been done. There were no troops loyal to the coup on the street. The broadcasting stations had not been seized by the conspiracy. The senior Nazis in Berlin, such as Goebbels who rarely left the capital, had not been arrested or shot. Stauffenberg learned the reason for this inactivity when he entered the office of his superior, General Fromm, the Commander of the Home Army.

Fromm told Stauffenberg that earlier that afternoon he had telephoned Field Marshal Keitel at the *Wolfsschanze* and had been assured by him that Hitler was alive. The coup had failed, Fromm declared, and Stauffenberg must therefore shoot himself at once. Not surprisingly, Stauffenberg would have none of this and insisted that Keitel was lying. He had seen the bomb go off with his own eyes and was sure that nobody could have survived that blast. However, Fromm said that he had to believe Keitel, who had certainly survived the explosion, which meant that if Stauffenberg did not commit suicide he would be placed under arrest. Calling upon help from nearby conspirators, Stauffenberg announced that it was Fromm who was under arrest and, after a brief scuffle, disarmed the general and confined him to his room, from which he promptly escaped to round up his own supporters.

While this farcical scene was being acted out, Hitler was actually drinking tea in his private quarters at the *Wolfsschanze*, accompanied by Mussolini and the top Nazis who had rushed to their Führer's side with loyal utterances after learning of his miraculous escape from a bomb blast which, amazingly, had left him with only a few superficial injuries. The hut, which had all its windows open because of the heat, had offered little resistance to the bomb, and most of the blast had consequently been dissipated into the surrounding air. Another factor in Hitler's survival was Colonel Brandt who, on stubbing the toe of his boot against Stauffenberg's briefcase shortly before the explosion, moved the bag to the other side of the map table's thick wooden support, thereby shielding the Führer from the full force of the blast, which killed Brandt and three other men in the room. By contrast, Hitler only suffered minor bruising and lacerations, mainly to his lower back, and was fit to greet Mussolini when the Italian dictator arrived at the *Wolfsschanze* railway station at 2.30 that afternoon.

Eugen Dollmann, an SS general who served as Hitler's liaison with Mussolini, recorded for posterity what took place during this episode, which, but for its subsequent blood-letting, could bear comparison with a similar event in *Alice in Wonderland*. Whilst white-liveried waiters moved amongst Hitler and his guests, serving tea and pastries, Göring, Ribbentrop, and Dönitz began arguing with the generals and then with each other about why the war was going badly. Ribbentrop blamed the generals, who in turn blamed him and then Dönitz. Göring started hurling abuse at Ribbentrop, who insisted on being addressed as 'von' Ribbentrop. Göring reacted by taking a swipe at the Foreign Minister with his Reichmarshall's baton and calling him a jumped-up champagne salesman.

Hitler was initially content to sit quietly beside Mussolini sucking pastilles, but he suddenly erupted — as Dollman described:

The Führer leapt up in a fit of frenzy, with foam on his lips, and yelled out that he would be avenged on all traitors, that Providence had just shown him once more that he had been chosen to make world history, and shouted about terrible punishments for the women and children [of the conspirators] . . . He shouted about an eye for eye and a tooth for a tooth for everyone who dared to set himself against divine Providence.

Hitler's threats, as Alan Bullock says in his classic biography of the Führer, 'were rarely idle'. The world would soon learn what it meant to try to kill a monster and fail. Hitler's wrath extended far beyond Stauffenberg and the immediate ring of conspirators, most of whom were in any case shot that very night by Fromm in a vain attempt to save himself. Around 5,000 people were executed by Hitler's regime as a result of this botched assassination, many by being hung from butchers' hooks, with thousands more thrown into concentration camps. Guilt and innocence were of secondary importance in this process. Unquestioned public loyalty to the Führer was what mattered.

As Dollmann watched this 'mad tea party' unfold, he was so appalled by what he saw that he asked himself why he did not go over to the Allies there and then. In this, he was not alone. On the evening of 20 July, the subject of direct negotiations with the Allied commanders in France loomed large in the mind of Hitler's senior general on the western front, Field Marshal Hans von Kluge. For a few hours that day, von Kluge dithered on whether or not to end the suffering of his valiant but bleeding army by offering Eisenhower an immediate cease-fire.

Hans von Kluge had been badly injured in a car crash in late 1943 and returned to active duty in the post of Commander-in-Chief of the German Armies in the West only on 2 July, as replacement for the world-weary von Rundstedt, who was relieved from duty after telling Keitel that his solicited advice on what to do next was 'Make peace, you fools!' Von Kluge, though, had long been a peripheral member of the *Schwarze Kapelle* (the black orchestra), the codename given to the anti-Hitler movement. He had taken part in the aborted plan by senior members of the *Wehrmacht* to arrest Hitler during the Munich crisis of 1938, and in 1943 had known of the plot, in which his subordinates were actively engaged, to kill Hitler by planting a bomb in the Führer's plane when he flew from von Kluge's headquarters in Russia to Germany. (The bomb failed to detonate and had to be defused by fellow conspirators. By a fantastic coincidence, the bomb, which was disguised in a bottle of Cointreau, was addressed to Colonel Brandt, the officer who saved Hitler's life on 20 July by pushing Stauffenberg's briefcase to the other side of the table.)

In his new position, von Kluge was the immediate superior of Germany's most popular Field Marshal, Erwin Rommel, who had let it be known that he was prepared to play a leading role in the government which succeeded Hitler. In broad terms, Rommel, who initially favoured arresting Hitler and placing him on trial rather than assassinating him, sought to make peace with the western Allies but to continue the war against the Russians. Rommel's belief was that the western democracies would not turn down such an opportunity to end the war quickly, and would surely come to see that surrendering Germany unconditionally to a tyrant like Stalin was such an insane notion that no German could consider it. One can only speculate as to what would have happened if Rommel had been allowed to act, for, once again, the divine providence in which Hitler firmly believed struck, this time in the form of a British fighter bomber which on 17 July strafed Rommel's staff car on a French road, badly wounding the Field Marshal. When the attempt was made on Hitler's life three days later, the man who was supposed to have led Germany into a new era was lying unconscious in a military hospital.

This left von Kluge as the officer to whom the conspirators in France turned for guidance on 20 July. But 'clever Hans', as he was known (via a German pun on his surname), was not a man to make a rash decision. Like most members of the old German officer caste, he had an ambivalent attitude towards the Nazi regime, a condition which Hitler, in several instances, exploited through naked bribery. Von Kluge was of course a patriot, and there can be no doubt that he privately detested Hitler's methods. However, like any German soldier, he was nothing if not a loyal servant of the state, which in Nazi Germany was literally Adolf Hitler. To break the oath of loyalty to his Führer was a step which von Kluge was not prepared to take, and for that reason he had made it clear to the conspirators that he would move only when he was sure Hitler was dead.

At his headquarters on 20 July, von Kluge received a telephone call from a conspirator in Berlin telling him that Hitler had been killed, a message which was apparently confirmed by a teleprinter message announcing a *coup d'état*. Von Kluge turned to his Chief of Staff, Günther Blumentritt, and said, 'This is a historic moment, you know... If the Führer is dead we ought to get in touch with the people on the other side right away.' Then a telephone call came through from the *Wolfsschanze*, with the news that Hitler had survived the assassination attempt. Von Kluge's mood changed at once. 'Nothing more can be done,' he told the conspirators. 'The Führer is alive.' The unequal and predictable struggle would continue.

On the evening of 14 August, von Kluge began a battlefield inspection of his battered and outnumbered units, which were somehow still holding back the very best that the United States, Britain and Canada could hurl at them through the dense *bocage* of the Normandy landscape.[1] Near the town of Falaise, Sepp Dietrich, the one-time chauffeur of the Führer, now an SS general, warned von Kluge that his front would soon cave in. The following morning, von Kluge set out for a 10.00 a.m. rendezvous with two other generals in the village of Nécy, and almost suffered the same fate as Rommel had nearly a month before. *En route* to his meeting, his conspicuous vehicles attracted the attention of an Allied fighter bomber, which attacked the column, knocking out the radio truck and forcing the Field Marshal to take cover in a ditch. Von Kluge spent the rest of the day dodging air attacks, and it was not until the early hours of the following morning that he reported back to his headquarters at La Roche Guyon on the river Seine.

Hitler later described that day, 15 August, as the worst of his life. Von Kluge's disappearance, taken in conjunction with an intercepted Allied message asking about his whereabouts and the increasing evidence about the role of 'clever Hans' in the bomb plot, convinced Hitler that his Field Marshal had tried to hand his armies over to the Allies. As far as is known, this was not true. Nevertheless, von Kluge's days as Commander-in-Chief West were numbered. He was replaced by Field Marshal Model (who was nicknamed 'the Führer's fireman' for his

---

[1] Max Hastings, in his splendid account of the Normandy campaign, *Overlord*, points out that a major factor in maintaining German morale was two words – unconditional surrender. Hastings quotes one German as saying that he would sooner have died in Normandy than live as an Allied slave for the rest of his life.

ability to extricate German armies from seemingly hopeless positions) and told to report back to Germany. Knowing that arrest by the Gestapo awaited him, von Kluge took poison rather than return to his Fatherland.

Von Kluge left behind a letter to Hitler in which he told the Führer that the western front could not hold out for much longer. Von Kluge hoped that he was wrong and that Model could succeed where he and Rommel had failed. But should this not be the case, von Kluge begged Hitler to end the war: 'The German people have borne such untold suffering that it is time to put an end to this frightfulness. There must be ways to obtain this object and above all to prevent the Reich from falling under the Bolshevist heel.'

Von Kluge's plea was in vain. Hitler had no intention of surrendering, and the Allied position on 'Unconditional Surrender' was immutable. Shortly after von Kluge's death, his prediction came true. The German front line in Normandy burst like a dam, allowing the Allied armies to pour virtually unopposed across northern France into Belgium. Such was the extent of the German losses that the survivors of the Normandy units did not stop until they reached the borders of the Reich itself. Hitler had suffered a defeat far worse than Stalingrad and far closer to home. Surely the war would be over by Christmas.

This was certainly the feeling as the Allied delegations gathered in Quebec on 12 September 1944 for the second wartime conference held in that city. According to Sherwood, there was a 'general belief among the higher authorities assembled at Quebec that German surrender could come within a matter of weeks or even days.' As Sherwood recorded, those who remembered the first war, and there were of course many, held out the hope that the Germans would surrender now that they were fighting in their own country. Intelligence reports suggested that such thoughts were not fanciful and that there was a real chance of a total German collapse in the near future. It was against this background that Roosevelt and Churchill discussed the post-war treatment of Germany.

When Churchill arrived at the Quebec Conference, he found that there were two main items on the agenda – the extension of Lend-Lease to Britain until the defeat of Japan, and a plan drawn up by

Henry Morgenthau which was designed to turn Germany into 'a country primarily agricultural and pastoral in its character'. Some, including Secretary of State Cordell Hull and Secretary of War Henry Stimson, have suggested that the appearance of these two issues on the same agenda was not a coincidence, and that the Lend-Lease extension was in fact a bribe offered to Churchill to ensure his agreement to Morgenthau's plan. When Churchill explained to his assistant, John Colville, how much money was on offer (in fact billions of dollars), Colville commented, 'Beyond the dreams of avarice.' Churchill replied, 'Beyond the dreams of justice.'

Cato the Elder, the Roman statesman, ended every speech he made, regardless of the subject, with the sentence, 'Delenda est Carthago' – Carthage (Rome's greatest rival) must be destroyed. Cato would have approved of what Morgenthau had in mind for America's greatest rival. The salient features of the plan read as follows:

Program to Prevent Germany from Starting a World War III

Demilitarization of Germany

1. It should be the aim of the allied forces to accomplish demilitarization of Germany in the shortest possible period of time after surrender. This means completely disarming the German Army and people (including the removal or destruction of all war material), the total destruction of the whole German armament industry, and the removal or destruction of other key industries which are basic to military strength.

The Ruhr[2] was to receive special treatment:

4. The Ruhr Area.

Here lies the heart of German industrial power. This area should not only be stripped of all presently existing industries but so weakened and controlled that it cannot in the foreseeable future become an industrial area. The following steps will accomplish this:-

(a) Within a short period, if possible not longer than 6 months after

---

[2] This included the Rhineland, the Kiel Canal and all German territory north of the canal.

the cessation of hostilities, all industrial plants and equipment not destroyed by military action shall be completely dismantled and transported to Allied nations as restitutions. All equipment shall be removed from the mines and the mines closed.

(b) The area should be made an International Zone to be governed by an international security organization to be established by the United Nations. In governing the area the international organization should be guided by policies designed to further the above-stated objective.

In addition, Germany was to be dismembered into two autonomous, independent states, a South German state comprising roughly Bavaria, Württemberg, and Baden and a North German state comprising Prussia, Saxony, and Thuringia. Austria was to be restored to her pre-1938 borders. Furthermore, Poland would obtain Silesia and the part of East Prussia not given to the Soviet Union, while France would get the Saar and the territories adjoining the Rhine and Moselle rivers.

Churchill claimed that he was at first horrified by the plan. 'You can't indict a whole nation,' he maintained that he exclaimed on learning of Morgenthau's proposals. Cordell Hull quoted him as saying that, if this plan were implemented, Britain would find herself 'chained to a dead body'. However, he changed his mind when Roosevelt and Morgenthau told him that Britain would need to boost her exports after the war and that it was to her advantage to have Germany out of the way, a highly dubious economic (not to mention moral) proposition. 'How would you like to have the steel business of Europe for 20 or 30 years?' Roosevelt asked Churchill over lunch. Churchill's long-time friend, Lord Cherwell, who was present at Quebec and on whom Churchill relied heavily for advice on matters other than war and politics, urged him to adopt the plan. Churchill redrafted Morgenthau's memorandum himself, and initialled the revised version with Roosevelt on 15 September.[3]

---

[3] Churchill's doctor, Lord Moran, who was at Quebec, records in his memoirs, *Winston Churchill: The Struggle for Survival*, that Lord Cherwell ('the Prof') was responsible for the Prime Minister's volte-face. Moran also records that Churchill was less than totally candid in his own memoirs about this episode, and attributes the Prime Minister's refusal to admit a mistake to his long-standing fight with depression.

News of this caused a revolt in both the British and American cabinets. Eden, the British Foreign Secretary, told Churchill that the British Cabinet would never accept the plan. In a speech given in 1941, Eden had said that it was not the aim of the British Government to impose a peace on Germany which would cause her to collapse economically. He explained: 'I say that not out of any love for Germany, but because a starving and bankrupt Germany in the midst of Europe would poison all of us, who are her neighbours. This is not sentiment; it is common sense.' It would appear that common sense was now being discarded.

Cordell Hull, the American Secretary of State, was furious and immediately used his considerable influence to have the plan quashed. At a meeting with Roosevelt, he told the President that 'only 60 per cent of the German population could support themselves on German land and that the other 40 per cent would die.' (Hull's absence from the Casablanca Conference can perhaps be seen in a sinister light here.)

Henry Stimson, the US Secretary of War, called the plan 'blind vengeance', arguing that the destruction of German industry would have a highly detrimental effect on Europe's economy. Stimson recorded in his diary that when he finally outlined the plan in detail with Roosevelt, the President 'grinned and looked naughty and said "Henry Morgenthau pulled a boner on me" or an equivalent expression.' When Stimson drew attention to the economic and social consequences of the plan, Roosevelt, Stimson recorded, was 'frankly staggered' and said he did not understand how he could have initialled such an important document without much thought.

Given the manner in which Roosevelt duped Churchill into adopting the policy of 'Unconditional Surrender', FDR's reaction here simply defies belief. He and Churchill had initialled a document which would have thrust Germany back to the Middle Ages and done immense harm to the economy of Europe, but, when challenged on the matter, he claimed that he had not realized what he was doing – a defence which, given FDR's political skills, is surely difficult to credit.

If the Morgenthau plan had been buried in government files for historians to mull over years later, it would not have done much harm. However, on 24 September, the plan was mysteriously leaked to the press. In the same way that Roosevelt's announcement of 'Unconditional Surrender' at Casablanca had been followed by Goebbels's declaration of 'Total War', the publication of Morgenthau's plan produced a marked strengthening of German resistance on the western front, just as the British and American armies were poised to enter the Third Reich. They were in fact at that very moment heavily engaged in the Arnhem campaign, Field Marshal Montgomery's daring bid to cross the Rhine which ended in tragic failure. Cordell Hull thought that the leak – which he makes clear in his memoirs did not emanate from his State Department – could lead to bitter German resistance that would cost thousands of American lives.

The Germans, mindful of what they had done in the Soviet Union, knew they could expect no mercy from the Russians and were fighting back fiercely against the Red Army. The publication of the Morgenthau plan enabled Goebbels to say that Germany could expect no mercy from the western Allies, either. Since the 'Unconditional Surrender' announcement, Goebbels had been telling the Germans that the Allies were out to exterminate them 'root and branch as a nation and as a people'. Now, *quoting a document which bore the initials of both Roosevelt and Churchill*, Goebbels could announce authoritatively that the Allies were intent on turning the Reich into 'a potato patch', an assertion underlined by the continued destruction of Germany's cities through aerial bombing. Moreover, as Chester Wilmot points out in *The Struggle for Europe*, the fact that Morgenthau was a Jew could only have served to convince Germans that they were all about to reap the whirlwind of Hitler's lunatic racial policies, and that there was no real alternative but to fight to the bitter end alongside their Führer, whose grip on the German people after the botched assassination attempt of 20 July was probably greater than it had ever been.

To understand the control which Hitler was able to exercise, and the effect the Morgenthau plan would have on the German psychology, one must in fact delve deep into European history, to the atavistic nightmare of the Thirty Years War, the religious conflicts of the seventeenth century which devastated whole regions of Germany and reduced the population of the country by at least a third. This internecine conflict, caused by internal division and manipulated by external interests, convinced Germans that their salvation lay in unity and in their freedom to decide their own future. Morgenthau's plan suggested that history had come full circle and that Germany was once more to be used as an anvil to strike and a country to devastate for foreign gain. Clearly, this was a fate which the Germans would fiercely resist.

With the stiffening of resistance throughout the western front, as demonstrated in the ferocious battle for the city of Aachen, which lasted for most of October and which cost the Americans around 8,000 casualties, went any real hope that the Germans would hold back the Russians and allow the British and American armies to take over their country. As Goebbels wrote in Germany's national journal, *Das Reich*, on 21 October 1944, the day Aachen finally surrendered: 'It hardly matters whether the Bolshevists want to destroy the Reich in one fashion and the Anglo-Saxons propose to do it in another. They both agree on their aim: they wish to get rid of thirty to forty million Germans.'

In *The Other Side of the Hill*, Basil Liddell Hart states that, during the last nine months of the war, a number of German officers often tried to find a way of making contact with the Allies in order to discuss surrendering, but were prevented from doing so by the policy of 'Unconditional Surrender'. His book is based on post-war interviews he conducted with senior *Wehrmacht* officers, and he records that these officers told him that, had it not been for this policy, they – and their men – 'would have been prepared to surrender sooner, separately or collectively.' Liddell Hart continues:

> 'Black-listening' to the Allies' radio service was widespread. But the Allied propaganda never said anything positive about the peace conditions in the way of encouraging them to give up the struggle. Its silence on the subject was so marked that it tended to confirm what Nazi propaganda told them as to the dire fate in store for them if they surrendered. So it greatly helped the Nazis to keep the German troops and people to continue fighting – long after they were ready to give up.

As a result, the western Allies had to fight off a winter offensive by the

Germans, the so-called 'Battle of the Bulge', and then in the spring push their way into Germany to the Rhine, which they crossed in late March 1945. By this time, the German army in the west was on its last legs. Churchill travelled to Germany and watched the river crossing alongside the Supreme Allied Commander, General Eisenhower. Observing the light resistance to the Allied assault, Churchill turned to Eisenhower and said, 'My dear General, the German is whipped. We've got him. He's all through.'

Once across this major obstacle, Field Marshal Montgomery's men, in the execution of Eisenhower's own plan, prepared to race across the north German plain towards the major objective of the war – Berlin. To help him achieve this, Montgomery had been allocated two American armies, the Ninth and the Second. On 27 March, he sent a coded telegram on his plans for them to Eisenhower, informing the Supreme Allied Commander that the situation looked good and that the advance on the river Elbe by his two US armies would be made with the 'utmost speed and drive'. Montgomery added that his tactical headquarters would proceed by stages to Hanover and then, he hoped, 'by autobahn to Berlin'.

On the evening of 11 April, advance units of the US Ninth Army, under General William Simpson, reached the banks of the river Elbe, about 60 miles south-west of Berlin. Such was the low level of German resistance that the tanks of the 2nd Armoured Division had driven an incredible 57 miles in the previous 24 hours. There was good reason to believe that the division could roar down the autobahn and be in Berlin within two days. The German army was still fighting the Russians tooth and nail to the east and north of Berlin, but the area in front of the western Allies was now almost uncontested and there were indications that the Germans wished the Americans to proceed. Moreover, Simpson's army was in good shape. The morale of his men was high and his supplies were more than adequate. There was no military factor preventing a move on the German capital, which, there was good reason to believe, would fall to the western Allies without a serious fight.

However, on 15 April, Simpson, in the midst of his preparations to move his army across the Elbe, was suddenly summoned to an interview with his American superior, General Omar Bradley. What Simpson was told so shocked him that he had difficulty absorbing it. There had been a change of plan, Bradley said. Eisenhower wanted the Ninth Army to stop on the Elbe and advance no further. Berlin was to be left to Stalin.

11

Uncle Sam and Uncle Joe

It was at lunchtime on 23rd January 1943, the ninth day of the Casablanca Conference, that the phrase 'Unconditional Surrender' was thought up. There were four men at the table – Roosevelt, Churchill, Harry Hopkins and FDR's son, Elliott. Roosevelt coined the phrase, and Hopkins took an immediate liking to it. Churchill took longer to express an opinion. He ruminated for a while, chewing a mouthful of food. Finally, he grinned and announced, 'Perfect! And I can just see how Goebbels and the rest of 'em 'll squeal.' Elaborating on his phrase, FDR said, 'Of course, it's just the thing for the Russians. They couldn't want anything better. Unconditional Surrender.' Sucking on a tooth he added, 'Uncle Joe might have made it up himself.' Hopkins was so impressed that he immediately began to draft a statement. FDR, Churchill, and Hopkins, with Elliott Roosevelt present, hammered out the final draft after dinner, working until 2.30 a.m. by which time a satisfactory communiqué had been drawn up. Churchill raised his 'ever ready glass' and with determination in his voice called for a toast to 'Unconditional Surrender'.

According to Elliott Roosevelt in his book on his father's wartime Presidency, *As He Saw It*, this, in outline, is how the policy of 'Unconditional Surrender' was born and adopted. Elliott Roosevelt's book was published in 1946, after the death of both FDR and Harry Hopkins. However, it will be immediately noticed that what is mentioned above does not at all tally with Sherwood's account of the Casablanca Conference, which was based in part on the papers of Harry Hopkins. Churchill, of course, did have the chance to comment on Elliott Roosevelt's version, but he was restrained in his language. In his memoirs, Churchill merely states that he has 'no recollection of these private and informal interchanges where conversation was free and unguarded'.[1]

That Churchill disowned Elliott Roosevelt's account is hardly surprising, for the revelations contained in this book make it quite clear that what FDR's son wrote was *a total fabrication*. Roosevelt did not dream up 'Unconditional Surrender' over lunch. He came to Casablanca with the intention of duping Churchill into agreeing to this policy. Nor was the statement directed at Stalin; it was in fact a warning to the German resistance that removing Hitler would not lead to a negotiated peace with America. But at least it can be said that FDR acted in the pursuit of what he saw to be America's national interest, and that by securing 'Unconditional Surrender' as the major Allied war aim, albeit by unorthodox means, he took a major step towards eliminating his country's rival. What Elliott Roosevelt did on the other hand, was to try to cheat posterity for his own selfish ends. As a selling point for his book, he produced a story which has been accepted by historians, but which can, indeed must, now be dismissed as an invention.[2]

That Elliott Roosevelt should distort the historical record in this way about such an important subject is disturbing. But his fairy tale does make an appropriate introduction to an aspect of the war which has intrigued and confused students of it, and which must now be reconsidered in the light of the material contained in this book.

This is the relationship between President Roosevelt, the leader of the world's largest democracy, and the man he called 'Uncle Joe' – Joseph Stalin, the heir to Lenin, founder of the Bolshevik movement, and the ruthless dictator of the Soviet Union, in which capacity he probably killed more Russians than Hitler managed to do. Stalin was the embodiment of Soviet Communism, the very antithesis of the freewheeling capitalism which America champions, and the most

---

[1] Elliott Roosevelt also claims that his father suspected Churchill of trying to stop General de Gaulle from attending the Casablanca Conference. In his memoirs, Churchill describes this assertion as 'rubbish'.

[2] Elliott Roosevelt, a failed businessman who sought to make a living out of his father's name, claimed that he lost the diary which contained the source material on which his book is based.

potent symbol of a totalitarian state whose speedy containment after the war became by far the main foreign-policy concern of the US Government. However, during the war Roosevelt always sought to depict Stalin in friendly, avuncular terms, on one occasion even claiming that the dictator had something of the 'Christian gentleman' about him. How can a man as clever and as insightful as FDR have held such views about one of the great monsters of history?

The 'traditional' view is that Roosevelt did not foresee the consequences of the policy of 'Unconditional Surrender' and that, either through encroaching illness or the sheer inability to understand the mind of a totalitarian ruler, he allowed eastern Europe to fall into the hands of the Soviet tyrant. This picture is based on an *assumption* that the Second World War was purely a crusade of good against evil and that Roosevelt, as an exponent of democracy, would have no truck with the extension of totalitarian rule in any form. Is this assumption justified? Or is it just that — *an assumption*?

After all, Roosevelt was a master politician and no one who has studied his career would ever call him naive, let alone stupid. Moreover, it would be just silly to consider that the brilliant academics recruited by Donovan to plan for the post-war world, a task apparently started before America entered the war, did not appreciate the consequences of their country's policies. As Robert Sherwood said, Roosevelt's decision to announce the 'Unconditional Surrender' policy at Casablanca had been 'very deeply deliberated' and FDR made it with his 'eyes wide open'. A consequence of 'Unconditional Surrender', obvious to the discerning world from the moment of the press conference in Casablanca, was that the war would culminate in the meeting of the American and Russian armies in the wreckage of central Europe.

Evidence that Roosevelt had no delusions about the Soviet role in post-war Europe comes from no less a witness than a prince of the Catholic Church, Cardinal Spellman of New York, who discussed the future with the President at the Quebec Conference of 1944, at which, it will be recalled, the Morgenthau plan was approved by FDR and Churchill. According to Cardinal Spellman, Roosevelt told him: 'The world will be divided into spheres of influences: China gets the Far

East; the US the Pacific; Britain and Russia Europe and Africa. But as Britain has predominantly colonial interests it might be presumed that Russia will predominate in Europe...' Roosevelt hoped that the 'Russian intervention would not be too harsh', but conceded that this 'might be wishful thinking'. Elaborating on this point, Roosevelt said that 'the European people will simply have to endure the Russian domination in the hope that – in ten or twenty years – the European influence would bring the Russians to become less barbarous.'

That Roosevelt should envisage such a future for Europe may at first sound shocking, but it is entirely consistent with the material presented in earlier chapters, where it was shown that the American President found it necessary to transform the European war of 1939–41 into a world war in order to stop Hitler from conquering the Soviet Union and establishing his 'New Order' which, in time, would have outmatched America. It is useful to note here that, on learning of the likelihood of America's intervention in the war, Mussolini remarked, 'Thus we arrive at the war between continents which I have foreseen since September 1939.'

The point Mussolini made here is surely a valid one, albeit a neglected one, in understanding Roosevelt's Grand Strategy. For it is surely simplistic to think that people who live in Europe will have the same viewpoint as those who live outside the continent. The dilemma that bedevilled civilized Europeans in the 1930s was that there were *two* tyrants stalking their continent. Hitler was the more immediate threat because of his aggression, but that did not make the calculating Stalin any less of a menace. The way forward for Europe was to remove both tyrants, and not to knock down one in such a manner as to strengthen the other. That was why Churchill, for one, was appalled at the prospect of Stalin's occupation of central Europe after the total defeat of Germany demanded by Roosevelt.

Roosevelt and his advisers, sitting on the other side of the Atlantic, naturally had a different perspective on the continent of Europe from Churchill's. Britain is a small island with limited resources off the European mainland. America, on the other hand, is a continent-sized country in effective economic control of an entire hemisphere. The Second World War exhausted Britain and finished her as a world power. That war, on the other hand, established America as *the* world power. It is only to be expected therefore that the Washington Government should think in broad, global terms — 'the big picture' — and not in the parochial, almost tribal, manner so often adopted by British politicians. Kipling summed up this attitude neatly when he wrote, 'Winds of the World, give answer! They are whimpering to and fro — / And what should they know of England who only England know?'

To FDR, the only real threat to America emanating from Europe was Hitler and his expansionist Germany, which represented not just a military threat, but also the economic powerhouse and technological 'cutting edge' of the continent. As Douglas Miller pointed out, not being able to do business *on America's terms* with such an advanced country constituted an immense strategic danger to the United States. On the other hand, not doing business with Stalin was a relatively unimportant matter, for the simple reason that, *in the financial sense*, there was relatively little 'business' to be had with a backward Communist state. But doing *political* business with Stalin on how Europe should be controlled after Germany's defeat was for Washington another thing altogether.

All of this presumably explains why Douglas Miller, incredible as it may seem, did not feel the need to mention even the existence of Stalin in *You Can't Do Business with Hitler*, which appeared in May 1941, the month before Hitler attacked the Soviet Union. In this book, Miller paints a scenario strange to the modern-day reader, namely that of America, together presumably with Britain and Canada, attacking Germany 'from the West' without the help of Stalin, whose probable reaction to such a campaign Miller does not even discuss.[3]

It is of course far from clear that such an attack against a *Wehrmacht* unblooded by three years of internecine war against the Soviet Union would have been successful. After all, when Miller's plan was finally executed in the summer of 1944, it took the western Allies over two gruelling months to break out of Normandy. The casualties suffered by

---

[3] The May 1941 edition of Miller's book does not contain an index but, as far as this author can see, there is no mention of Stalin in this volume.

the western Allies against the full power of an intact and undamaged *Wehrmacht* would probably have been far in excess of those which a democracy could sustain. Indeed, it is often claimed that Britain has never recovered from the 60,000 casualties it suffered on the first day of the Battle of the Somme on 1 July 1916 during the First World War.

Stalin's totalitarian state was a different proposition. His country could take the casualties and, in Churchill's phrase, 'tear the guts out of the German Army'. This was dependent, of course, on the Soviet Union being suitably rewarded at the end of the war, which it was by Roosevelt. In short, Stalin's involvement in the war was seen by Roosevelt, not as the potential threat to Europe recognized by Churchill, but as an opportunity to help the United States achieve its 'American victory' with far less loss of American lives.

What that 'American victory' entailed – and this is central to understanding the Second World War and its aftermath – was spelled out in General Marshall's 1941 Estimate, where, it will be recalled, Marshall described America's objective in the war as, amongst other things, the 'eventual establishment in Europe and Asia of balances of power which will most nearly ensure political stability in those regions and the future security of the United States.' *What, it must be asked, was the post-war settlement reached by Washington and Moscow if not a balance of power between the two new superpowers?*

To comprehend the Second World War, one must accept that Roosevelt waged war not just on Hitler, or even Germany, *but on the very concept of a united Europe*. Abraham Lincoln fought the American Civil War, not to abolish slavery as is often claimed, but to preserve the Union and prevent America from becoming like Europe – a number of small, squabbling states which could be manipulated and played off one against the other by external powers. Roosevelt fought the Second World War to prevent Europe from becoming like America – a continent-sized, centrally controlled country, enjoying a large population, an immense economy and vast natural resources. Thomas J. McCormick surely has a point in his book *America's Half Century*, where he states that Roosevelt's aim was not simply the destruction of Nazi Germany, but 'the prevention of any one power from dominating Europe and limiting American access to it.'

All of this meant that, after Germany's unconditional surrender, Europe would be divided and ruled, directly or otherwise, by the only two men in the world who mattered – the President of the United States and, as a poor second, the dictator who ran the Soviet Union. West European countries would prosper under loose and, for the most part, benign American leadership, while eastern Europe would rot beneath the dead hand of Soviet Communism. Poland, for whose liberty Britain and France went to war against Hitler in 1939, would fall under Stalin's tyranny, as would Czechoslovakia, the country whose surrender to Nazi rule during the Munich crisis of 1938 was denounced by many, including of course Winston Churchill, as a disaster for peace and democracy.

The essential point, though, was that the strategic danger to America of a united Europe would be averted. The two victors of the war, Capitalist America and Communist Russia, would settle down to face each other over the divide of Europe during that period of political theatre known to history as the Cold War, in which Stalin, the 'Uncle Joe' who helped America *win* effective control of western Europe, would be speedily transformed into the bogeyman used by Washington to *maintain* its effective control of western Europe. Indeed, it was as early as March 1946, less than a year after the end of the war, that Churchill, whose public and implacable opposition to Communism dated back to the Russian Revolution itself, made his famous 'Iron Curtain' speech in the presence of Harry Truman, Roosevelt's successor – an event generally seen as the 'first shot' in the Cold War.

The basis for this arrangement, as indicated above, was General Marshall's Estimate of September 1941, whereby Marshall advised the creation of a 'balance of power' in post-war Europe in order to safeguard the security of the United States. An elaboration of this position appeared in a document that Harry Hopkins brought to the Quebec Conference of August 1943, which, it should be noted, was *three months before Roosevelt first met Stalin*. The document, entitled 'Russia's Position', was a 'very high-level United States military strategic estimate' by an unidentified source. It read as follows (with the original italics):

Russia's post-war position in Europe will be a dominant one. With Germany crushed, there is no power in Europe to oppose her tremendous military forces. It is true that Great Britain is building up a position in the Mediterranean vis-à-vis Russia that she may find useful in balancing power in Europe. However, even here she may not be able to oppose Russia unless she is otherwise supported.

The conclusions from the foregoing are obvious. Since Russia is the decisive factor in the war, she must be given every assistance and every effort must be made to obtain her friendship. Likewise, since without question she will dominate Europe on the defeat of the Axis, it is even more essential to develop and maintain friendly relations with Russia.

Finally, the most important factor the United States has to consider in relation to Russia is the prosecution of the war in the Pacific. With Russia as an ally in the war against Japan, the war can be terminated in less time and at less expense in life and resources than if the reverse were the case. Should the war in the Pacific have to be carried on with an unfriendly or a negative attitude on the part of Russia, the difficulties will be immeasurably increased and operations might become abortive.

It was surely this document – so redolent of power politics that it would have been immediately understood by Cardinal Richelieu or Bismarck – and not any high-flown notions about freedom, democracy and the like, which guided America's policy in the last period of the war and beyond. The logic of the situation is beyond question. Roosevelt's immediate aim was, in accordance with General Marshall's Estimate of September 1941, to bring about the 'complete military defeat of Germany'. Events since the Estimate was written had shown that the only force on earth capable of ensuring that aim was Stalin's Red Army, which, while unable to match the Germans professionally, was very big and very tough.[4]

---

[4] As Hitler should have known from his study of the campaigns of Frederick the Great, who fought the Russians on many occasions and who complained, 'Shooting these fellows is not enough; you have to knock them over as well.'

To help Stalin in this vital task and to *ensure that Stalin did not make a separate peace with Germany*, Roosevelt was willing to give Russia 'every assistance' and to do all he could to 'obtain her friendship'. In short, regardless of the consequences for Europe, FDR was prepared to pay Stalin's price for continuing the war, not just against Germany, but also, it must be noticed, for entering the war against Japan, thereby saving an incalculable number of American lives, which, naturally enough, was of prime interest to Roosevelt.[5]

One immediate problem for FDR was to persuade Stalin to accept the principle of 'Unconditional Surrender'. Clearly, he could not treat Stalin in the same way as he had Churchill. And *persuasion* was necessary, for Stalin did not at first approve of the policy. He considered it 'bad tactics' for the Allies to commit themselves publicly to such an inflexible objective, and in the summer of 1943 he himself set up the 'Committee of Free Germany' whose propaganda encouraged the German people to overthrow their 'Hitlerite' masters and discuss peace terms. Harry Hopkins recorded Stalin's comments on this subject at the Tehran Conference of November 1943, where the Soviet leader met Roosevelt and Churchill for the first time:

> As a wartime measure Marshal Stalin questioned the advisability of the unconditional surrender principle with no definition of the exact terms which would be imposed upon Germany. He felt that to leave the principle of unconditional surrender unclarified merely served to unite the German people, whereas to draw up specific terms, no matter how harsh, and tell the German people that this is what they would have to accept, would, in his opinion, hasten the day of German capitulation.

One factor in winning over Stalin on 'Unconditional Surrender' was lavish use of what General Marshal called America's 'trump card' –

---

[5] In securing Stalin's agreement at the Yalta Conference to join the war against Japan, Roosevelt gave the Soviet Union pieces of Chinese territory which he had no authority to grant. American interest in obtaining Stalin's help against Japan decreased once it became clear that *Operation Manhattan* – the construction of the atomic bomb – had been successful. In fact, it has even been suggested that the decision of the US Government to use atomic weapons against Japan was motivated by the desire to end the war quickly and prevent Stalin from securing too strong a position in eastern Asia.

Lend-Lease.[6] For the most part, the Red Army was armed with home-made weapons, which were generally of good quality and in some cases superior to anything possessed by the Germans. However, logistically the Russians were badly equipped, which meant that they were incapable of manoeuvring their forces properly and replenishing their units satisfactorily. With this handicap, they would probably have been unable to defeat the Germans. Uncle Sam came to the rescue. As the Red Army slogged its way towards Germany, it marched in American boots, fed itself off American rations, made its uniforms out of American cloth and, perhaps most importantly, carried and pulled its supplies and equipment on American trains and vehicles.

Behind this material help stood Roosevelt's willingness, in accordance with the document cited above, to win Stalin's friendship, regardless of the consequences for post-war Europe. So determined was Roosevelt to achieve this that, from the very outset, he sought to distance himself from Churchill in order to show Stalin that the Soviet Union was not facing an Anglo-Saxon alliance – even to the extent of turning down, as did his successor Harry Truman, an invitation from Churchill to visit London.[7]

Roosevelt did not hide from Churchill the fact that he wanted to build up a strong relationship with Stalin. In a letter to Churchill, he declared that he could 'personally handle Stalin better than either your Foreign Office or my State Department'. Without offering any evidence, he added: 'Stalin hates the guts of all your top people. He thinks he likes me better and I hope he will continue to.' What FDR *did* try to conceal from Churchill was his desire to meet Stalin *on his own*.

In April 1942, Roosevelt invited Stalin by letter to a meeting in the summer 'near our common border off Alaska'. FDR thought it 'of the utmost military importance that we have the nearest possible approach to an exchange of views.' Stalin did not respond to the President's

---

[6] In the 'Four Power Declaration' which was signed in Moscow on 30 October 1943, the foreign secretaries of the United Kingdom, the United States, the Soviet Union and China stated, inter alia, their resolve to bring about the 'Unconditional Surrender' of the Axis powers.

[7] Stalin, for his part, regarded both Churchill and Roosevelt as 'pickpockets', but with one distinction. Churchill, Stalin maintained, would dip into someone's pocket for a *copeck*, whereas Roosevelt would go only after a much bigger coin.

approach other than to make it clear that, in view of the military situation, he could not afford to leave the Soviet Union. In May 1943, Roosevelt tried again to meet Stalin, this time via a letter taken personally by Joseph E. Davies, a former US Ambassador to the Soviet Union. In this missive, Roosevelt suggested that he and Stalin 'would talk very informally and get what we call "a meeting of minds".' As far as a meeting place was concerned, FDR thought Africa 'almost out of the question in summer'. Iceland would involve difficult flights for both men and 'in addition, would make it, quite frankly, difficult not to invite the Prime Minister at the same time.' All in all, Roosevelt thought the best meeting place to be 'either on your side or my side of the Bering Strait'.

This démarche was also unsuccessful, but Churchill got to hear of it and felt the need to warn Roosevelt of 'the use the enemy propaganda would make of a meeting between the heads of Soviet Russia and the United States at this juncture with the British Empire and Commonwealth excluded.' Such a conference, Churchill went on, would 'be serious and vexatious and many would be bewildered and alarmed thereby'. In reply, Roosevelt told Churchill, 'I did not suggest to UJ [Uncle Joe] that we meet alone...' — an answer which indicates that Elliott Roosevelt's penchant for 'terminological inexactitudes' was hereditary.[8]

When the 'Big Three' arrived in Tehran for their long-awaited meeting, Roosevelt was invited by Stalin to stay in the Russian Embassy compound, on the strength of a report that a German assassination squad was in the city with orders to eliminate the American President. In view of FDR's attempts to meet Stalin privately, there are surely strong grounds for regarding this rumoured assassination attempt, of which nobody else had heard, as nothing but a ruse designed to ensure that Roosevelt and Stalin were able to hold meetings from which Churchill was excluded — a practice repeated at the second meeting of the 'Big Three', which took place at Yalta in February 1945, when the end of the war in Europe

---

[8] In his memoirs, Churchill chose not to mention Roosevelt's attempts to meet Stalin on his own.

was clearly in sight, and FDR and Stalin made secret deals to which Churchill was not privy.

Lord Moran, Churchill's wartime physician, mentions in his diary that before going to Tehran, Churchill could not accept that Britain and America would not stand united against Stalin. However, once there, Churchill saw that he could not rely on Roosevelt's support and, even more importantly, that the Russians saw this too, which meant that it was pointless for the British Government to try to take a harsh line with Stalin. Churchill, Moran notes, was 'appalled by his own impotence'.

Roosevelt's distancing of himself from Churchill extended to deliberate attempts to humiliate the Prime Minister in front of Stalin. FDR later told Frances Perkins, his Secretary for Labor, that he had managed to break down Stalin's reserve on the third day of the Tehran Conference by making Churchill the butt of a joke. According to Perkins, Roosevelt began to tease Churchill about his Britishness as soon as the 'Big Three' were seated at the conference table. Stalin saw what Roosevelt was doing and began to smile at Churchill's discomfort. Roosevelt kept up this teasing until Stalin was laughing with him at Churchill. At that moment, FDR claimed, he called Stalin 'Uncle Joe' and established a close personal relationship with the dictator. 'The ice was broken and we talked like men and brothers,' Perkins quoted FDR as saying.

This joint teasing of Churchill was not confined to official business. During dinner one night, Stalin, with several toasts under his belt, announced that as the strength of Hitler's armies depended on the General Staff – some 50,000 officers and technicians – the whole lot should be liquidated. Churchill pointed out that the British public would not stand for mass executions, and that he would rather be taken out and shot himself than 'sully my own and my country's honour by such infamy'. Roosevelt intervened with a compromise that only 49,000 and not 50,000 should be shot. Elliott Roosevelt, who had graced the conference with his presence, rose to make a speech agreeing with Stalin's plan, which, he was sure, would be supported by the US Army. Disgusted, Churchill left the dining-room and went to sit in the semi-darkness of an adjoining chamber, where he was presently joined by Stalin who, with a great grin, assured him that they had all been jesting. Mollified, but by no means reassured that 'all was chaff', Churchill returned to the dining-room.

Such treatment should not have come as a surprise to Churchill. That America was out to end the British Empire, the largest the world had ever known, had long been suspected by many British politicians. In fact, Roosevelt made no secret of his intention to dissolve this institution, ostensibly for reasons of humanity, though America, as the world's major industrial power, stood to gain most from the collapse of the Empire's trade barriers.[9] As Chester Wilmot points out, when Churchill made his famous remark in November 1942 that he had not 'become the King's First Minister in order to preside over the liquidation of the British Empire', he was referring, not to a military conquest of British territory by the Axis, but to the economic campaign being waged by Roosevelt against the Empire.

The sale of the American destroyers in return for British bases in the western hemisphere and the Atlantic Charter, which FDR saw as a means not just of freeing those subjugated by Hitler but of separating 'people all over the world from a backward colonial policy', were in fact assaults on British sovereignty, as was Lend-Lease, which, though described by Churchill as a 'most unsordid act', was in reality a scheme which forced Britain to hand over virtually all her assets to the United States (some of which were resold at bargain basement prices), and to open up the 'oyster shell' of the British Empire to America. Indeed, the master Lend-Lease Agreement contained, at Roosevelt's insistence, a clause requiring Britain to agree to 'the elimination of all forms of discriminatory treatment in

---

[9] It has often been claimed that the power behind the 'Free Trade' movement was Secretary of State Cordell Hull. However, in August 1944, Hopkins wrote to Roosevelt urging the President to tell Churchill that this 'is a programme that, from the beginning, has been pushed by you'. (See Sherwood, page 809.) Roosevelt was especially interested in 'liberating' India, whose population, and therefore potential market, was one of the largest in the world. In the same vein, Roosevelt urged Churchill to return the British colony of Hong Kong to China, which was then under the control of FDR's favourite, Chiang Kai-shek, a man whose integrity was not of the highest. After the war, Chiang was forced to flee to the island of Taiwan (Formosa) by the Chinese Communists under Mao Zedong, who wisely decided to allow Hong Kong to continue its fascinating and singular existence.

international commerce and the reduction of tariffs and trade barriers' in the post-war world.[10]

The crushing success of Roosevelt's economic campaign against Britain was poignantly acknowledged by Churchill in a telegram he sent to the President in November 1944, when FDR was once again using Lend-Lease to strong-arm the British Government into making concessions, this time over post-war civil aviation:

> Let me say also, that I have never advocated competitive 'bigness' in any sphere between our two countries in their present state of development. You have the greatest navy in the world. You will have, I hope, the greatest air force. You will have the greatest trade. You have all the gold. But these things do not oppress my mind with fear because I am sure the American people under your re-acclaimed leadership will not give themselves over to vainglorious ambitions, and that justice and fair-play will be the light that guides them.[11]

Given this shift in power, which was so obvious to Hitler that he wrote in his *Testament* on 4 February 1945, 'We can with safety make one prophecy; whatever the outcome of this war, the British Empire is at an end. It has been mortally wounded', it was only to be expected that Roosevelt and Stalin would be prepared to go over Churchill's head and decide between themselves how the remainder of the war would be conducted and what shape the post-war world would take. In short, there was no 'Big Three' at Tehran and Yalta, only a 'Big Two'. Churchill realized this and later described himself as the British

---

[10] Lord Moran, Churchill's wartime physician, noted at the Yalta Conference in February 1945 that Roosevelt 'cannot leave the [British] Empire alone. It seems to upset him, but he never turns a hair when a great chunk of Europe falls into the hands of the Soviet Union.'

[11] After the war, tough negotiations took place between the American and British governments over Britain's Lend-Lease debt. In return for accepting a reduced debt of $650 million, the British Government agreed to make its currency freely convertible on the world's market, a concession which was attacked in Britain as being of sole benefit to American exporters. In a debate in the House of Commons on this matter, Robert Boothby, Churchill's one-time Private Secretary, commented, 'It is not untrue to say that comparable terms have never hitherto been imposed on a nation that has not been defeated in war.'

donkey stuck between the Russian bear and the American buffalo. He knew what should be done, but was powerless to do it.

In his plans for the future, Roosevelt showed an attitude towards Europe and her people which can be called less than sympathetic. He said that he was 'sick and tired' of Europeans arguing over territory, and he apparently once considered a plan to round up European refugees and resettle them in Africa. In a private conversation with Britain's Foreign Secretary, Anthony Eden, Roosevelt spoke of policing Europe in general, not just Germany, and of disarming all European countries, except, of course, Britain and Russia. Eden found Roosevelt's views 'perplexing' and 'alarming in their cheerful fecklessness', and that the President 'seemed to see himself disposing of the fate of many lands, allied no less than enemy'.

With regard to Stalin's takeover of eastern Europe, Roosevelt's main worry seems to have been the effect which the Soviet occupation would have on American voters, many of whom were of eastern-European origin. He told Stalin jokingly that he was not prepared to go to war with him over the Baltic states, which were reabsorbed back into the Soviet Union after the German defeat. As for Poland, the country for which Britain and France went to war in 1939, Roosevelt effectively allowed the country to fall under Stalin's control in return for a firm promise from 'Uncle Joe' to participate in the war against Japan once Germany surrendered – a matter which, it will be recalled, was described in Harry Hopkins's paper quoted earlier as 'the most important factor the United States has to consider in relation to Russia'. George Kennan, the American diplomat who would develop the theory of 'Containment' to prevent the expansion of the Soviet Empire during the Cold War, studied Roosevelt at work with Stalin and formed no impression that the President had 'substantive objections – any real political objections – to seeing those areas go to Russia, or indeed that he cared much about the issue for its own sake.'

Roosevelt's feelings towards western Europe were not much warmer. He seemed to want a strong Britain as some sort of defence against the Soviet Union, but he had a definite animus towards France, a feeling shared by Stalin, who wanted that nation reduced to the level of a third-class power. In the conversation with Anthony Eden

mentioned above, Roosevelt spoke of dismembering France and join-
ing the north of the country, including Alsace-Lorraine, with part of
Belgium and Luxemburg to form a new state called 'Wallonia', a project on which Eden 'poured water'. The President also wanted the
Allied armies, not the French civil authorities, to administer France
following the invasion, an aim which led Eden to conclude that
Roosevelt wanted to ensure that he would determine that country's
fate. In Tehran, Roosevelt agreed with Stalin in saying that France
deserved nothing from the war because she had collaborated with
Hitler, and that she should be deprived of her colonial possessions. It
was largely due to the persistence of Churchill, who argued that Britain
needed a strong France as an ally, that FDR relented at the Yalta
Conference and persuaded Stalin to allow France to take part in the
occupation of Germany.

It was not just over territory that Roosevelt sought to please Stalin.
When the Red Army approached Warsaw in the late summer of 1944,
the Polish Home Army, which had been promised Russian help by
Radio Moscow, came out of hiding and fought the Germans for control
of the capital city. However, Stalin, who had no love for the Polish
force, which owed its allegiance not to him but to the pre-war Polish
Government in exile in London, ordered his soldiers to halt, thus
leaving the betrayed Poles to fight the Germans on their own. Churchill
tried desperately to help the Poles, and considered dropping weapons
and supplies to the insurgents from the air, but he was thwarted by
Stalin's refusal to allow British planes to land on his airfields to refuel.
In late August, Churchill drafted a plea to Stalin and asked Roosevelt to
join him in sending it to the Soviet dictator. FDR declined, on the
grounds that it would not be 'advantageous in the long range general
war prospect' for him to do so. After several weeks of savage fighting,
the Polish Home Army was destroyed. Only then did Stalin order his
soldiers to continue with their advance.

A further example of Roosevelt's desire to please Stalin was his
attempt to give Russia one-third of the Italian fleet, which had surrendered to the Allies in the autumn of 1943. Roosevelt made this
announcement without prior consultation with Churchill, or apparently anyone else, to a press conference in March 1944. The news

pleased no one, except of course Stalin, and Roosevelt, under criticism from Churchill and his own military men, who required the vessels for campaigns of their own, was obliged to 'alter' his public statement. In the end, a compromise was found whereby Stalin received temporary use of a British battleship and an American cruiser.[12]

These instances of 'co-operation' between FDR and Stalin are a reminder that the strategy of the latter part of the European war is often seen as one drawn up by these two rulers in the face of opposition from Churchill, who questioned the wisdom of assaulting Germany through France when the Reich could have been more easily attacked from Italy (where the Allies had a strong foothold from the autumn of 1943) and the Balkans. This was an approach in which Churchill was supported by many strategists, American as well as British. Stalin's reason for opposing the presence of Anglo-Saxon forces in eastern Europe is obvious: he wished to keep that area to himself, and for that reason he pushed not only for the 'Second Front' to be opened in Normandy, but also for the American invasion of southern France, Operation Anvil, which ensured that no appreciable Allied forces were available for what Roosevelt described as an 'adventure' into the Balkans.[13]

That Roosevelt had such an opinion is not surprising in view of the near-certainty that America's broad strategy was spelled out by Douglas Miller in his book *You Can't Do Business with Hitler*, where he advised that America should maintain the military pressure on Germany *from the west*, via first a lengthy campaign of aerial bombing designed to cripple Germany's ability to make war and then an 'attack at the heart of the enemy' in the form of a mechanized invasion of Europe. Indeed, Elliott Roosevelt, in his book *As He Saw It*, quotes his father as saying that 'the way to win as short a war as possible is from the west and from the west alone . . .'

Stalin's opposition to the Anglo-Saxon armies arriving too soon for his liking in central Europe could also explain the dispute over Allied strategy which broke out between the British General, Field Marshal Montgomery, and his American superior, General Eisenhower, after

---

[12] Churchill refers to this dispute in his memoirs, but does not mention Roosevelt's public commitment to hand one-third of the Italian fleet over to Stalin.
[13] See Chester Wilmot, *The Struggle for Europe*, Chapter XXIII.

their crushing victory in Normandy in late August 1944, which effectively destroyed the German army in France and left the way to Germany wide open. Chester Wilmot states in the preface to his *The Struggle for Europe* that this victory had given the western Allies the power to ensure that they and not Stalin would liberate the major capitals of central Europe – Berlin, Prague and Vienna. In the event, all of these cities fell to the Soviet tyrant in the spring of 1945. To understand why this happened, one must consider the strategic argument between Eisenhower and his outspoken British subordinate.

In simple terms, Montgomery argued that the Allied armies should launch an immediate and powerful pursuit of the enemy through Northern France and across the Rhine to seize the Ruhr industrial area, without which Germany could not long survive, and then move rapidly on Berlin. His optimism was grounded not just in what the Allied armies had achieved, but in the fact that deciphered German messages were revealing to the Allies just how weak the *Wehrmacht* in western Europe was. A well-aimed and powerful blow, Montgomery argued, would surely succeed in routing what was left of Hitler's armies in the west, and in breaking through to the heart of Germany. This punch was precisely what the German generals at the time feared. Chester Wilmot quotes General Blumentritt, the Chief of Staff to the German Commander-in-Chief West, Gerd von Rundstedt, as saying, 'Such a breakthrough *en masse*, coupled with air domination, would have torn the weak German front to pieces and ended the war in the winter of 1944.'

Eisenhower, however, disapproved of what he inaccurately termed Montgomery's 'pencil-like thrust', and ruled that the Allied armies should advance more slowly on a 'broad front' in order to ensure that they did not outrun their supply lines. Common sense dictates that a good, well-aimed punch is far more likely to finish off a groggy opponent than a clumsy shove, but Eisenhower, for once apparently more circumspect than his usually cautious British subordinate, did not seem to see things that way.

Chester Wilmot questions Eisenhower's case, pointing out that the Allied supply position was not as bad as Eisenhower maintained, and that the needs of Allied divisions were not as great as the Supreme

Commander asserted. Moreover, as Montgomery says in his memoirs, the Allies after Normandy followed *no clear-cut plan at all;* they moved forward, not on Eisenhower's 'broad front', but 'by disconnected jerks' on several 'un-coordinated' fronts. It is certainly curious that the man who, in a remarkably short period, organized the Normandy landings – probably the most complex military operation in history – did not use those same skills and resourcefulness to administer a speedy *coup de grâce* on a beaten foe. After all, as the old adage has it, 'Where there's a will, there's a way.' Commenting on this strategic dispute, Chester Wilmot writes that what was at stake in this debate was nothing less than ending the war quickly, 'with all that meant for the future of Europe'.

Wilmot was undoubtedly correct. However, the problem was that the future of Europe was then being determined by Roosevelt in co-operation with his main ally, Stalin, *much of it in secret sessions.* These two men had begun their face-to-face discussions at Tehran in November 1943, when the approximate date of the Normandy landings was approved, and would continue them at the Yalta Conference, on Stalin's home patch, in February 1945, where the division of Europe between the two new superpowers was decided. At Yalta, it must be remembered, Stalin made clear his willingness to continue the war, despite the cost to his Red Army, until he had constructed the Poland he desired. Moreover, it was not until after Yalta that Eisenhower finally ordered the full Anglo-Saxon invasion of Germany. Surely therefore, there are grounds for concluding that the real reason for Eisenhower's 'broad front' strategy was that Roosevelt did not want the war to end until he and Stalin had reached a satisfactory agreement about post-war Europe and Russia's role in the war against Japan.

Here it is instructive to note the views of Lord Hankey, a British politician who served in Churchill's Government, and who writes in his book, *Politics – Trials and Errors,* that the policy of Unconditional Surrender made inevitable not just the Normandy landings, but also the 'terribly exhausting and destructive advance' through France, Belgium, Luxemburg and Holland into Germany. This lengthening of the conflict, Hankey claims, allowed Stalin to occupy eastern Europe and to set up the 'Iron Curtain' which divided the continent from the Baltic to the Adriatic.

This is another example of a London-based politician failing to appreciate the perspective of Europe as seen by the Washington Government from across the Atlantic. Hankey is certainly right in regarding all of the above as the consequences of Roosevelt's policy of Unconditional Surrender, which, as a British politician and an inhabitant of a Europe partly occupied by Stalin, he naturally viewed with deep concern. But what Hankey does not appear to have considered is the possibility that all of the above happened because Roosevelt *planned* it – in the light of Douglas Miller's book and General Marshall's Estimate, and in subsequent dealings with Stalin. If it is too much to say that Roosevelt *wanted* eastern Europe to fall under Soviet control, he was certainly prepared to let that happen. That is to say, everything mentioned above by Lord Hankey came to pass because Roosevelt saw these events well in advance as being in the strategic interests of his country.

Roosevelt's plan, as outlined in Douglas Miller's 1941 book, involved not just the overthrow of Hitler, but an invasion of Germany 'from the west' (i.e. Normandy), so that an American peace could be established. That explains why, once in the war, Roosevelt refused to encourage the German resistance to remove Hitler, a development which could have led to a *negotiated* peace with a new government in Berlin without the need for an all-out invasion of the Continent. It is clear from both Miller's book and General Marshall's Estimate that a negotiated peace with Germany was something which Roosevelt had ruled out even before he brought America into the war. Moreover, Roosevelt saw his alliance with the Soviet dictator as the key to achieving his higher aim, which was to ensure that a united Europe under one dominant power did not come into being. As Marshall's Estimate made clear, that aim would be achieved through the establishment of a balance of power in Europe, which is precisely what Roosevelt (and his successor, Truman) achieved with Stalin.

It is with this American *planning* in mind that the role which Eisenhower played in 'the race for Berlin' must now be considered. To say that the symbol of Berlin was originally the main American objective would perhaps be an understatement. After all, even before America entered the war, Wendell Willkie, a leading Republican politician who backed FDR's stance on the war in Europe, claimed that there were only two possible outcomes to the conflict – either Berlin or Washington would become the capital of the world. Now, in late 1944, with the Allies poised to enter Germany, Berlin – or, to be exact, the huge, futuristic *Germania* into which Hitler and his architect friend Albert Speer had intended to transform the Reich's capital – lay at last within the grasp of the US army. How would America deal with this perceived rival to Washington as the capital of the globe?

Eisenhower laid out the official policy on Berlin in a letter to Field Marshal Montgomery, 'Monty', his British Field Commander, on 15 September 1944: 'Clearly Berlin is the main prize, and the prize in defence of which the enemy is likely to concentrate the bulk of his forces. There is no doubt whatsoever, in my mind, that we should concentrate all our energies and resources on a rapid thrust to Berlin.' This aim was confirmed at a meeting between Churchill and Roosevelt held on the Mediterranean island of Malta in late January 1945, when the two men were *en route* to the Summit with Stalin at Yalta.

However, an abrupt change appeared on 31 March (i.e. after Yalta), when Eisenhower sent a message on his future dispositions to 'Monty', whose armies by this time were crossing the Rhine and moving deep into Germany. This message ended: 'You will note that in none of this do I mention Berlin. That place has become, so far as I am concerned, nothing but a geographical location, and I have never been interested in these. My purpose is to destroy the enemy's forces and his powers to resist.' On 28 March, unbeknown to the British Government, or to any of his British subordinates (including his Deputy, Air Chief Marshal Tedder), Eisenhower had sent *direct to Stalin* a telegram on his plans in which, by omission, he made it clear to the Soviet dictator that the Anglo-Saxon armies would not head for Berlin. Instead, Eisenhower would push south of Berlin to Leipzig and Dresden, where his forces would meet up with the Red Army and surround the remaining German units in the area. He would also send a force through Regensburg to Linz in order to prevent the creation in southern Germany of a mountain 'redoubt' where Hitler and his die-hard fanatics were *reported* to be preparing to make a last-ditch stand. In his reply, Stalin declared that Eisenhower's strategy 'entirely coincides' with his own because 'Berlin has lost its former strategic importance.'

'This statement,' Churchill writes in his memoirs, 'was not borne out by events.' Indeed, Churchill's doctor, Lord Moran, quotes Field Marshal Montgomery as telling Churchill in 1953 that the problems being experienced by a divided post-war Europe began at Casablanca. According to Moran, Montgomery told Churchill that as the policy of Unconditional Surrender meant the Russians would enter Germany, the western Allies should have ensured that they were first in Berlin, Prague and Vienna. Montgomery, Moran maintains, was adamant that it 'could have been done'.

Needless to say, Churchill was furious when he found out what Eisenhower had done. Eisenhower's authority to send a telegram straight to Stalin was not in doubt. It had been decided at Yalta that Eisenhower should liaise directly with the Soviet High Command on operational matters. At such a late stage in the war, this was only sensible, if for no other reason than to prevent the nightmare of a violent collision between Anglo-American forces and Red Army units. However, what Eisenhower did on this occasion extended well beyond the area of military operations into the realm of Grand Strategy, which was a matter only for politicians to decide. The capture of Berlin, and the other capitals in eastern Europe, was a political issue which would obviously have considerable bearing on the balance of power in the post-war continent. It was not a subject to be decided by a soldier, no matter how senior.

After conferring with his own senior advisers, Churchill wrote to Eisenhower on 31 March, urging the Supreme Commander to reconsider his strategy. 'Why should we not cross the Elbe and advance as far eastward as possible?' Churchill asked, adding that this move would have important political consequences in view of the fact that the Russians were about to enter Vienna and occupy Austria. Churchill went on: 'If we deliberately leave Berlin to [the Russians], even if it should be in our grasp, the double events may strengthen their conviction, already apparent, that they have done everything.' Churchill

declared that Berlin had lost neither its military nor its political significance, and that as long as that city remained 'under the German
flag it cannot, in my opinion, fail to be the most decisive point in
Germany.'

Churchill repeated this argument in a telegram to Roosevelt on 1
April in which he urged a drive east into Germany and 'should Berlin
be in our grasp we should certainly take it.' It was to no avail. Roosevelt
declined to intervene and General Marshall made it clear that he fully
supported Eisenhower. Convinced that Eisenhower was not going to
change his mind, Churchill wrote to Roosevelt on 5 April, stating, via a
Latin quotation, that the dispute had been a form of lovers' quarrel and
that he now regarded the matter as closed.[14]

To Stalin, though, the matter was very much alive. Regardless of
what he might have said in his reply to Eisenhower, Stalin had every
intention of storming Berlin, the symbol of a system which had done so
much harm to his nation and the place where Hitler himself was likely
to be found. On 1 April, before telling Eisenhower that he was planning to deploy only secondary forces in the area of the German capital,
Stalin summoned to his office General Zhukov and General Koniev,
the commanders of the two Soviet armies which were encamped to the
east of Berlin, and told them to prepare for a gigantic battle. The two
Soviet generals, Stalin made it clear, were to race each other to the
Reichstag.

Eisenhower's decision to inform Stalin that the Anglo-American
armies would not march on Berlin has remained one of the most
controversial episodes of the war. The armies under Montgomery's
command, which included the American Ninth, could probably have
reached the city before Stalin without encountering any major resistance. There were certainly signs that the Germans were willing 'to let
in the West' rather than suffer the fate which would befall them should
the Russians attack the city. That Eisenhower should give up such a
prize and bother instead with a (mythical as it turned out) mountain

---

[14] Lovers or not, Churchill chose not to attend Roosevelt's funeral, which took place on
15 April. On the fate of Berlin, Henry Kissinger points out in *Diplomacy* that, as there
were practically no German forces left at that time, the rejection of Churchill's appeal
was obviously a 'matter of principle' for Eisenhower and Marshall.

redoubt where the Nazi 'werewolves' would fight to the bitter end seems *totally absurd*. What, then, is the truth behind Eisenhower's decision?

On 22 April 1945, Drew Pearson wrote in a column in the *Washington Post* that on 13 April an advance American unit had reached Potsdam on the outskirts of Berlin only to be told to retire the following day to the river Elbe. Pearson explained, 'This withdrawal was ordered largely because of a previous agreement with the Russians (at the Yalta Conference) that they were to occupy Berlin and because of their insistence that the agreement be kept.'

This article prompted Harry Hopkins to record his feelings in a memorandum:

> This story by Drew Pearson is absolutely untrue. There was no agreement made at Yalta whatever that the Russians should enter Berlin first. Indeed, there was no discussion of that whatever. The Chiefs of Staff had agreed with the Russian Chiefs of Staff and Stalin on the general strategy which was that both of us were going to push as hard as we could.
>
> It is equally untrue that General Bradley paused on the Elbe River at the request of the Russians so that the Russians could break through to Berlin first. Bradley did get a division well out towards Potsdam, but it far outreached itself; supplies were totally inadequate and anyone who knows anything about it knows that we would have taken Berlin had we been able to do so. This would have been a great feather in the Army's cap, but for Drew Pearson now to say that the President agreed that the Russians were to take Berlin is utter nonsense.

Hopkins was without doubt speaking in good faith. But even he did not know what went on in Roosevelt's mind at all times. After all, Roosevelt described himself as a 'juggler' and boasted that his left hand did not know what his right hand was doing. In view of the fact that Roosevelt chose to keep Hopkins in the dark about the adoption of 'Unconditional Surrender', it is reasonable to suggest that he adopted similar tactics in respect of Berlin. Hopkins's military estimate was certainly inaccurate, as the generals on the spot have themselves testified. There was, it must be stressed, no *military* reason why the Anglo-Saxon armies could not have advanced on Berlin.

In his book, *Roosevelt and Stalin*, Professor Robert Nisbet considers all the available evidence on this contentious matter (pages 84–90) and argued that Berlin was yet another 'gift' from Roosevelt to Stalin, and that the Soviet dictator had in fact been promised the city during one of his secret discussions with the American President at Yalta. In support of this view, Professor Nisbet quotes an unidentified Lieutenant-General who worked on Eisenhower's staff in the latter part of the war. When questioned about Eisenhower's actions, the general smiled and said, 'George owed the President a good deal and knew it.' The implication here is that General Marshall (George), the American Chief of Staff, who played an increasingly prominent role in the last few months of the war as FDR's health deteriorated, knew that his President wanted to hand Berlin to Stalin and that, at the right moment, he ordered his loyal deputy, Eisenhower, to send an appropriate message to the Soviet dictator.

What makes Professor Nisbet's theory about Berlin so plausible is not just all that has been mentioned above about Roosevelt and his determination to obtain Stalin's friendship, but the similar fate which befell Prague, the capital of Czechoslovakia, and the last major city in central Europe to be liberated from the Nazis.

Towards the end of April 1945, General George Patton's Third US Army approached the Czechoslovakian border from the west, only to be ordered by Eisenhower not to advance on Prague, even though Patton – as his superior, Omar Bradley, concedes in his *A Soldier's Story* – could probably have been in the Czech capital within 24 hours. This would have been welcomed by the Czechs themselves who, expecting imminent liberation, rose in rebellion against the hated German occupiers. Field Marshal Montgomery states in his memoirs that he never understood why Patton was halted. Officially, Eisenhower's decision had its roots, as in the case of Berlin, in his seeming obsession with the national redoubt, the rumoured stronghold which diehard Nazis were said to be building in southern Germany, but which turned out to be completely fictitious. In order to deal with this imaginary fortress, Eisenhower had told Stalin that he would not advance into Czechoslovakia, a promise which Stalin insisted on being kept, even after the Czechs rebelled against the Germans in early May. Consequently, Eisenhower refused to allow Patton to advance on Prague and save the Czechs from the German army. Czechoslovakia, as Omar Bradley states in his memoirs, had been 'earmarked for liberation' by Stalin. Here, so it seems, was yet another 'gift' for the 'Christian gentleman' from Georgia.

Fate decreed that Roosevelt would not live to hear about the Russian assault on Berlin, which started officially on 16 April 1945, four days after FDR's death. He had obviously been in failing health since the autumn of 1944 and, after his return from Yalta, where he shocked people by his gaunt appearance, he was advised by his doctors to spend his time at his home in Warm Springs, Georgia. There, on 12 April, whilst sitting for a portrait painter (and in the presence of his mistress, Lucy Mercer), he collapsed and died. Most magnanimously, the Japanese Government expressed its 'profound sympathy' to the American people and, most accurately, attributed America's 'advantageous position' in the world to the late US President. FDR, the 'Lion and the Fox' who, in keeping with Machiavelli's dictum, employed both force and guile to secure his aims, had indeed achieved 'great things'.

Hitler, by then a very ill man himself in an advanced stage of Parkinson's disease, had been in Berlin since mid-January, forced by the near-constant aerial bombing to live in his underground bunker close to the Chancellery and a few hundred yards from the Reichstag. He heard the news of Roosevelt's death there, via a telephone call from Goebbels, shortly after midnight. Goebbels, who had just returned from the eastern front to a city set in flames by a British air raid, was excited: 'My Führer, I congratulate you. Fate has laid low your greatest enemy. God has not abandoned us. Death, which the enemy aimed at you in 1939 and 1944, has now struck down our most dangerous adversary. A miracle has happened.' Clutching at the slenderest of straws, Hitler and Goebbels drew a parallel here with the death in the Seven Years War of the Tsarina, whose sudden demise brought about the dissolution of the alliance against Frederick the Great and saved him from near certain defeat.[15] However, there was to be no miraculous escape for Hitler: Roosevelt's death did not lead to the collapse of the Grand Alliance against the Third Reich as the Führer, in his land of delusions, believed it would. He, and his capital, would be forced to pay for his actions.

On 25 April, the Red Army broke through the outer defences of Berlin and surrounded the city. The following day, a Russian force half a million strong, and supported by tens of thousands of artillery and mortar pieces, burst into the city centre and, in bitter hand-to-hand fighting, pushed its way towards the Reichstag and Hitler's bunker. On the afternoon of 30 April, Hitler, warned that the Russians would soon overrun his position, committed suicide alongside his newly taken bride, Eva Braun. The battle for Berlin continued until 3.00 p.m. on the afternoon of 2 May, when the Germans finally surrendered and the guns, but for a Red Army victory salute, fell silent over the smoking ruins of the city.

After Roosevelt's death, Hopkins prepared to retire from public service; but such was his prestige that FDR's successor, Harry Truman, asked him to fly to Moscow as his envoy to Stalin. Accompanied by his wife, Hopkins left Washington for the strenuous trip to the Russian capital on 23 May. They stopped first in Paris and then carried on over Germany towards Russia. As he passed over the wreckage of Berlin, he surveyed the scene from his window and said, 'It's another Carthage.'

The capital of the globe was no longer a matter of dispute. A world had been gained.

---

[15] To comfort Hitler, Goebbels had taken to reading him extracts from Thomas Carlyle's *History of Frederick the Great*. Apparently, Hitler's favourite chapter was that which concerned the Tsarina's sudden death and Frederick's change of fortune.

Epilogue

Harry Hopkins, the one-time social worker who rose to become his country's unelected 'Deputy President' during its 'date with destiny', retired from the United States Government on 2 July 1945. The digestive problems which had plagued him for years worsened and he died the following January before he could write his memoirs, a task later undertaken by his old friend, Robert Sherwood, whose book, *The White House Papers of Harry L. Hopkins*, must surely be the most important single published source on America's involvement in the Second World War.

William Donovan's star waned after the demise of Roosevelt. The new President, Harry Truman, a political ally of Donovan's enemy, Senator Burton Wheeler, did not look favourably on the wartime spymaster. Truman abolished Donovan's OSS in September 1945, and when he created its successor, the Central Intelligence Agency, in 1947, he did not appoint 'Wild Bill' as its head. Donovan returned to the private sector, other than for a short period in the early 1950s when he served as US Ambassador to Thailand. He died in 1959.

Following the death of FDR, General George Marshall (1880–1959) was hailed as the 'greatest living American'. He retired from the US Army after the war and, in 1947, took up the post of Secretary of State, in which capacity he gave his name to the 'Marshall Plan', the US Government scheme to reconstruct a Europe devastated and impoverished by war. In this way, the soldier, who in September 1941 advised his President to invade Europe and bring about the 'complete military defeat of Germany', became the statesman responsible for the economic renaissance of the continent. Such is the irony of the Second World War.

And what of Douglas Miller who in his 1941 book, *You Can't Do*

Business with Hitler, foresaw the Marshall Plan when he predicted that, after securing an American peace, the United States would have to rebuild Europe? What became of this diplomat turned author who played a central, if unheralded, role as assistant to William Donovan in winning the war for America and creating the modern world? This author regrets to say that he is unable to answer this question – not for want of trying, but for want of information. Miller seems to have almost vanished from the record for, incredible as this may seem, there are very few references to him in any of the standard works on the war, or indeed in any prime sources perused by this author.

A particularly curious omission is in *The Rise and Fall of the Third Reich* by William L. Shirer, the American newspaper correspondent turned historian, who developed a close friendship with Miller in Berlin during the 1930s, and who came to regard the diplomat as the leading expert in the US Embassy on 'all aspects of life under the Nazis'. Shirer encouraged American businessmen to read Miller's first book, *You Can't Do Business with Hitler*, and actually wrote the foreword to Miller's second book, *Via Diplomatic Pouch*.

It is therefore very strange that Shirer did not find space in his own book, which is over 1,400 pages long, for *any mention of Miller*. This is to say that in a major book on the Second World War, Shirer did not include the fact that his diplomat friend had written a work in early 1941, *prior to America's entry into the war*, which outlined how the United States should attack Germany 'from the West' (i.e. Normandy), secure a total American victory (i.e. Unconditional Surrender) and then rebuild Europe after the war (i.e. the Marshall Plan). In short, here was a blueprint for an international order which promised American businessmen 'a world to gain', and Shirer makes no mention of it in his enormous book – a work which relegates the subject of 'Unconditional Surrender' to a curt, dismissive footnote; does not even mention the Morgenthau plan; and, it will be recalled, contains an incomplete translation of Hitler's declaration of war speech.

It is almost as if Miller has been airbrushed out of history. But surely this cannot be. After all, such things do not happen in a democracy. Do they?

Select Bibliography

Documentary Sources

Public Record Office, Kew
Cabinet Papers 65
Cabinet Papers 66
Cabinet Office Index to Minutes & Memoranda Cabinet Papers 65 & 66
Cabinet Papers 99
Cabinet Papers 120
Premier Papers 3 Series
Premier Papers 4 Series

Printed Primary Sources
Documents of German Foreign Policy 1918–45, Series D, vols. XII & XIII (1949)
Foreign Relations of the United States, vols. I–V (1962)
Max Domarus (ed.), *Hitler, Reden und Proklamationen 1932–45* (1973)
Adolf Hitler, *Hitler's Table Talk 1941–44* (1945)
——, *The Testament of Adolf Hitler* (1961)
Warren Kimball (ed.), *Churchill and Roosevelt: The Complete Correspondence 1939–45* (3 vols., 1984)
Gordon Prange (ed.), *Hitler's Words* (1944)
Count Raoul de Roussy de Sales (ed.), *My New Order* (1941)
Elliott Roosevelt (ed.), *The Roosevelt Letters, vol. 3: 1928–45* (1953)
Rosenmann (ed.), *The Public Papers and Addresses of Roosevelt 1938–45* (1938–50)
Robert E. Sherwood, *The White House Papers of Harry Hopkins, September 1939–May 1945* (2 vols, 1948–9)
H.R. Trevor-Roper (ed.), *Hitler's War Directives, 1939–45* (1964)
Sir Llewellyn Woodward, *British Foreign Policy in the Second World War* (5 vols, 1970–6)

Memoirs and Diaries

Dean Acheson, *Present at the Creation* (1971)

Earl of Avon, *The Eden Memoirs, vol. II: The Reckoning* (1965)

Sir Winston Churchill, *The Second World War*, vols. I–VI (1948–54)

D. Dilks (ed.), *The Diaries of Sir Alexander Cadogan 1938–45* (1971)

Karl Dönitz, *Admiral Dönitz Memoirs* (1959)

Baron Francis-Williams, *A Prime Minister Remembers: The War and Post-war Memoirs of the Rt. Hon. Earl Attlee* (1961)

Heinz Guderian, *Panzer Leader* (1952)

W.A. Harriman, *Special Envoy to Churchill and Stalin, 1941–6* (1975)

Cordell Hull, *The Memoirs of Cordell Hull* (1948)

Harold L. Ickes, *The Secret Diary of Harold L. Ickes* (1954)

George Kennan, *Memoirs* (1967)

Major-General Sir John Kennedy, *The Business of War* (1957)

William Langer, *In and Out of the Ivory Tower* (1977)

William D. Leahy, *I Was There* (1950)

James Leutze (ed.), *The London Observer: The Journal of Raymond E. Lee 1940–41* (1971)

Douglas Miller, *Via Diplomatic Pouch* (1944)

Lord Montgomery of Alamein, *The Memoirs of Field Marshal Montgomery* (1958)

Lord Moran, *Churchill: The Struggle for Survival* (1966)

Joachim von Ribbentrop, *The Ribbentrop Memoirs* (1953)

Elliott Roosevelt, *As He Saw It* (1946)

William Shirer, *Berlin Diary* (1941)

—, *End of a Berlin Diary* (1947)

Henry L. Stimson and M. Bundy, *On Active Service in Peace and War* (1947)

Fred Taylor (ed.), *The Goebbels Diaries 1939–41* (1982)

Ernst von Weizsäcker, *The Memoirs of Ernst von Weizsäcker* (1951)

Burton K. Wheeler, *Yankee from the West* (1962)

Other Sources

Anne Armstrong, *Unconditional Surrender* (1961)

Thomas Bailey and Paul Ryan, *Hitler v. Roosevelt: The Undeclared War* (1979)

Alan Bullock, *Hitler* (1952)

—, *Hitler and Stalin: Parallel Lives* (1992)

James Macgregor Burns, *Roosevelt: The Lion and the Fox* (1956)

—, *Roosevelt: The Soldier of Freedom* (1970)

Peter Calvocoressi, Guy Wint and John Pritchard, *Total War: The Causes and Courses of the Second World War* (1972)

Anthony Cave Brown, *Bodyguard of Lies* (1975)

—, *Donovan: The Last Hero* (1982)

—, *The Secret Servant* (1987)

John Charmley, *Churchill: The End of Glory* (1993)

—, *Churchill's Grand Alliance* (1995)

Peter Collier and David Horowitz, *The Roosevelts* (1990)

Birger Dahlerns, *The Last Attempt* (1947)

Louis de Jong, *The German Fifth Column in the Second World War* (1956)

Herbert Feis, *Churchill, Roosevelt and Stalin* (1957)

Frank Freidel, *Roosevelt: A Rendezvous with Destiny* (1990)

Saul Friedländer, *Prelude to Downfall: Hitler and the United States 1939–41* (1967)

J.F.C. Fuller, *The Decisive Battles of the Western World, vol. 2* (1970)

Martin Gilbert, *Winston S. Churchill, vols. VI & VII* (1983–6)

Sebastian Haffner, *Germany's Self-Destruction* (1989)

Max Hastings, *Overlord* (1984)

Waldo H. Heinrichs, *FDR and American Entry in World War II* (1988)

Sir Nicholas Henderson, 'Hitler's Biggest Blunder', *History Today*, April 1993

Michael Howard, *Grand Strategy, vol. IV* (1972)

David Irving, *Hitler's War* (1971)

David Kahn, *Hitler's Spies* (1978)

John Keegan, *Six Armies in Normandy* (1982)

—, *The Second World War* (1989)

Paul Kennedy, *The Rise and Fall of the Great Powers* (1988)

Warren Kimball, *The Most Unsordid Act* (1969)

W.F. Kimball, *The Juggler: Franklin Roosevelt as Wartime Statesman* (1991)

—, *Forged in War: Churchill, Roosevelt and the Second World War* (1997)

Henry Kissinger, *Diplomacy* (1994)

Richard Lamb, *The Ghosts of Peace* (1987)

—, *Churchill as War Leader* (1991)

Walter Langer, *Hitler's Mind* (1977)

W.L. Langer and S. Gleason, *The Challenge to Isolation* (1952)

—, *The Undeclared War* (1953)

Joseph P. Lash, *Roosevelt and Churchill 1939–41* (1973)

Basil Liddell Hart, *The Other Side of the Hill* (1951)

—, *Memoirs* (1965)

——, 'Churchill: The Military Strategist' in *Four Faces and the Man* (1969)

——, *History of the Second World War* (1970)

T.J. McCormick, *America's Half Century* (1989)

Niccolò Machiavelli, *The Prince* (1970)

Douglas Miller, *You Can't Do Business with Hitler* (1941)

H. Montgomery Hyde, *The Quiet Canadian* (1962)

Ted Morgan, *FDR* (1985)

Edgar Ansel Mowrer, *This American World* (1928)

——, *Germany Puts the Clock Back* (1933)

——, *Triumph and Turmoil – A Personal History of Our Time* (1970)

Robert Nisbet, *Roosevelt and Stalin: The Failed Courtship* (1989)

Raymond O'Connor, *Diplomacy for Victory: FDR and Unconditional Surrender* (1971)

James P. O'Donnell, *The Berlin Bunker* (1979)

Gordon W. Prange, *At Dawn We Slept* (1981)

——, *Pearl Harbor: The Verdict of History* (1986)

Anthony Read and David Fisher, *The Fall of Berlin* (1992)

Bertrand Russell, *Prospects of Industrial Civilization* (1928)

Cornelius Ryan, *The Last Battle* (1966)

William L. Shirer, *The Rise and Fall of the Third Reich* (1959)

William Stephenson, *A Man Called Intrepid* (1976)

John Tebbel, *An American Dynasty: The Story of the McCormicks, Medills and Pattersons* (1968)

John Toland, *Adolf Hitler* (1976)

——, *Infamy: Pearl Harbor and its Aftermath* (1982)

H.R. Trevor-Roper, *The Last Days of Hitler* (1950)

James P. Warburg, *Germany: Bridge or Battleground* (1946)

Gerhard L. Weinberg, *Germany, Hitler and World War II* (1995)

Chester Wilmot, *The Struggle for Europe* (1952)

R. Wohlsetter, *Pearl Harbor – Warning and Decision* (1962)

Newspapers and Other Publications

Chicago Daily Tribune

Current Biography 1941

Hansard (1943 & 1949)

The Times